CW01217667

SPEED

SPEED

The Life of a Test Pilot and Birth of an American Icon

BOB GILLILAND and **KEITH DUNNAVANT**
FOREWORD BY CHESLEY "SULLY" SULLENBERGER

Potomac Books
AN IMPRINT OF THE UNIVERSITY OF NEBRASKA PRESS

© 2021 by Robert J. Gilliland Jr.
Foreword © 2021 by the Board of Regents of the University of Nebraska

All rights reserved. Potomac Books is an imprint of the University of Nebraska Press.
Manufactured in the United States of America.

♾

Library of Congress Cataloging-in-Publication Data
Names: Gilliland, Robert J., 1926–2019. | Dunnavant, Keith, author. | Sullenberger, Chesley, 1951– writer of foreword.
Title: Speed: the life of a test pilot and birth of an American icon / Bob Gilliland and Keith Dunnavant; foreword by Chesley "Sully" Sullenberger.
Description: [Lincoln, Nebraska]: Potomac Books, an imprint of the University of Nebraska Press, [2021] | Includes bibliographical references and index.
Identifiers: LCCN 2020044096
ISBN 9781640122680 (hardback)
ISBN 9781640124677 (epub)
ISBN 9781640124684 (mobi)
ISBN 9781640124691 (pdf)
Subjects: LCSH: Gilliland, Robert J., 1926–2019. | United States. Air Force—Biography. | Test pilots—Biography. | Air pilots, Military—Biography. | SR-71 Blackbird (Jet reconnaissance plane)—History.
Classification: LCC UG626.2.G534 A3 2021 | DDC 358.40092 [B]—dc23
LC record available at https://lccn.loc.gov/2020044096

Set in Minion Pro by Mikala R. Kolander.

For all the test pilots who soared off into the distant skies, looking for the future, and never came home.

CONTENTS

List of Illustrations ix
Foreword by Chesley "Sully" Sullenberger xi

Introduction 1
1. Two Wars 3
2. Anchors Away 31
3. Taking Flight 57
4. Two Worlds 81
5. The Man in the Brooks Brothers Suit 111
6. Kelly's Masterpiece 133
7. Warning Lights 155
8. Out of the Shadows 197

Acknowledgments 233
Notes 237
Index 241

ILLUSTRATIONS

Following page 80

1. Frank Gilliland Sr.
2. Bob with his father, mother, and brother
3. Bob at Webb School
4. Bob at the Naval Academy
5. & 6. Bob during the Korean War
7. Bob in an F-84 during the Korean War
8. The SR-71 on December 22, 1964
9. Skunk Works director Clarence L. "Kelly" Johnson
10. Bob in the "moon suit"
11. & 12. The Blackbird
13. Vice President Hubert Humphrey with the Blackbird
14. Bob with the Blackbird
15. Bob speaking at the National Aviation Hall of Fame
16. Bob with his son, Robert Jr., and daughter, Anne
17. & 18. Bob on the Legends of Aerospace Tour in 2010
19. Bob with Andrew Green, Eric Brown, and Neil Armstrong

FOREWORD

Chesley "Sully" Sullenberger

OVER THE LAST CENTURY, THANKS TO THE WORK OF some very dedicated and gifted professionals who learned to harness the wonders of science, air travel has evolved from risky to routine. Most of the passengers who regularly cruise from city to city at 600 miles per hour, six miles above the earth, do so with a confidence approaching certitude. After all, flying in an airliner is now much safer than other forms of transportation.

Of course, sometimes things go wrong.

On January 15, 2009, when I was sitting in the captain's seat of an Airbus A320 climbing away from New York's LaGuardia Airport, multiple bird strikes caused the loss of both engines. Suddenly U.S. Airways Flight 1549 was crippled. As we glided above Manhattan, the silence of those usually roaring engines was eerie. With only seconds to react to this catastrophic failure, First Officer Jeff Skiles and I quickly worked the problem.

Making the decision to head for the Hudson River, rather than try to return to LaGuardia or plot a course for a New Jersey airport, I knew it was merely the best of several bad options. But thankfully, everything went right, and we saved the lives of all 155 passengers and crew, turning a potential tragedy into a triumph that captured the imagination of the American public.

The so-called Miracle on the Hudson profoundly changed us all, and it was humbling to be hailed as a hero. But that moment of working through pit-of-my-stomach anxiety was merely the culmination of many years of preparation. After forty-two years of making small, regular deposits in a bank of experience, education, and training, fortunately, the balance was sufficient for me to make a very large withdrawal.

This is an idea Bob Gilliland understood very well.

As an elite test pilot working in the shadows during the Cold War, Bob dealt with many emergency situations.

He knew how it felt to lose an engine.

He knew how it felt to have a stick go dead in his hands.

As an Air Force Academy graduate who spent several years flying the F-4 Phantom, one of the greatest fighters of its time, I have always admired the SR-71 Blackbird. What a tremendous technological achievement. In this book you will learn all about Bob's leading role in developing the world's fastest airplane, which played such a vital role in our intelligence gathering for a quarter century.

Especially during his days as the chief test pilot of the SR-71, Bob regularly flew off in an unproven machine to demonstrate the power of the great Kelly Johnson's masterpiece while dealing with a long list of unknowns and potential perils. This was a dangerous business, and it took a skilled and gutsy pilot to ride that cutting edge.

Often things went wrong, but somehow, while negotiating an environment of unprecedented heat, speed, and altitude, Bob always leaned on his accumulated knowledge and experience to find his way home.

This is an important book about a remarkable pilot who helped extend the frontier of American aviation.

SPEED

Introduction

ONE MORNING IN EARLY 1965, A TALL MAN WEARING dark glasses pulled up to the main gate at Edwards Air Force Base. The guard waved him right through. Driving onto the sprawling outpost in California's high desert, into a realm of legends and ghosts, Robert Jordan Gilliland, known to one and all as Bob, could not wait to get back in the air. How he loved going high and fast.

By the time the Lockheed test pilot parked his Mercedes Benz 220 next to the cavernous Skunk Works hangar, Dick Miller was already in his office.

"We still doing this thing?"

Miller nodded and they started looking over the day's flight plan.

When they walked out into the glaring sun beating down on the desert like a blow torch, wearing specially designed silver pressure suits nearly identical to the familiar nylon shells worn by the NASA astronauts racing the Russians to the moon, Gilliland and his reconnaissance systems officer stepped into a sleek black aircraft. It cast a futuristic aura, like something out of a science fiction film.

Within minutes they were streaking through the stratosphere at Mach 2.8—2.8 times the speed of sound. Only a select few aviators had ever gone so fast in an air-breathing jet. They were headed for a majestic view only a select few had ever glimpsed, terrestrial blue melding with heavenly black.

But something happened on the way to the top of the world.

While working through a series of scheduled tests, the stick became unresponsive in Bob's hand. He lost control of the aircraft. Suddenly, he and Miller were trapped inside a titanium bullet, and he knew he had a matter of seconds to avert disaster.

No stranger to emergency situations, Gilliland had negotiated five dead-stick landings in the F-104 Starfighter and once fled North Korea while being chased by a fast-approaching MiG-15.

Now he had hit a wall in the sky and desperately needed to find an open door. Fast.

ONE

Two Wars

WHEN DAWN BEGAN TO BREAK ACROSS THE FRENCH countryside on September 29, 1918, a mist filled the air, casting the nearby no-man's-land in a murky haze. Positioned just west of the village of Bellicourt, the men of the 30th Division of the U.S. Army waited for the order dreaded by all in the age of trench warfare.

Four years into the conflict then known as the Great War, as Russia hurtled into the chaos of the Bolshevik Revolution and brought its troops home, ending hostilities on the eastern front, the western front remained mired in bloody stalemate, especially along a series of fortifications known as the Hindenburg Line. Among the most impenetrable barriers was the St. Quentin Canal, which flowed north to south, through Bellicourt and a large swath of northeastern France, in the shadow of the Belgian border. The Germans had spent four years reinforcing the area surrounding the canal and an accompanying tunnel, which had been built by Napoleon I, with barbed wire, land mines, machine guns, trenches, and stationary barges. Historian Nick Lloyd called it "five miles of the most formidable defensive position in the history of warfare."[1]

America had tried to stay out of the latest European war. During his campaign for reelection in 1916, President Woodrow Wilson vowed to maintain the United States' official neutrality. But a series of provocative acts by the German government—including the 1915 sinking of the British ocean liner *Lusitania*, which killed 1,196 civilians—slowly changed public opinion, and Wilson started pushing the country toward intervention. A nation with deeply rooted isolationist tendencies began to tentatively embrace its future as a world power.

When Wilson asked Congress to declare war on Germany on April 6, 1917, vowing to make the world "safe for democracy," the British and French were fading fast.

By the end of 1917, the two leading allied powers had lost a staggering five million men and were running out of reinforcements. Public support for the continued carnage was waning. Their only hope was for the United States to tip the scales and save the day, but America was completely unprepared. It had one of the smallest standing armies in the Western World, an inconvenient truth that could only be countered with the sort of massive mobilization not seen since the Civil War.

One of the four million men who answered the call to arms was a twenty-seven-year-old lawyer from Memphis.

The son of a high-end dry goods merchant who sold items generally referred to as "queenswear," Frank Marshall Gilliland was intelligent and ambitious. At the age of thirteen, his parents sent him off to the prestigious and academically rigorous Webb School in Bell Buckle, Tennessee, where he became the only student in the history of the institution to complete four years of study in three years. He was, by all accounts, a man in a great big hurry. At Vanderbilt University, Frank continued his record of academic achievement while also serving as president of his fraternity, pitching for the baseball team, and handling various administrative duties as president of the football team. After graduating with honors in 1912, he decided to pursue a law degree at Washington & Lee. But he never finished. First came a bout of typhoid fever, and when his father's business teetered into bankruptcy, he was forced to discontinue his studies and return to Memphis, where, according to his younger brother, John, he "took charge" of the family and "got us all through it."[2]

Undeterred by the setback, he accepted an invitation from E. B. McFarland, a prominent local attorney, to "read law" at his office. Unable to afford law school and burdened with various family obligations, he nevertheless seized the opportunity to soak up as much knowledge as possible about his chosen profession. Two years later, he took the Tennessee bar exam and passed it.

Gilliland was just starting his career when America entered the war. Swept up in the patriotic fervor, he quickly volunteered. After enlisting the assistance of a family friend, he was commissioned a first lieutenant in the U.S. Army and assigned to the newly formed 30th Division, which eventually wound up in Europe as part of the American Expeditionary Forces, under the command of General John J. "Black Jack" Pershing. Pershing had famously chased the bandit Pancho Villa into Mexico, but the AEF would make him a military legend.

Known as the Old Hickory Division, in honor of Tennessee-born president Andrew Jackson, the 30th consisted primarily of young men from the Southeast, including many who had previously served in the National Guard.

After several engagements with the enemy in Belgium, the men of the 30th moved into northern France, where their greatest challenge loomed in the shadow of the St. Quentin Canal.

For four years, German machine guns had proved extremely effective in repelling heroic charges across the no-man's-land. As part of the 120th Infantry Regiment, attached to the British Fourth Army, First Lieutenant Gilliland commanded a battery of 37 mm guns tasked with the critical assignment of silencing the enemy guns, to pave the way for the infantry assault.

In a coordinated attack that included a tremendous artillery barrage and tank offensive by the British and eventually featured a wave of Australian infantry, the Old Hickory Division assaulted the Hindenburg Line at its strongest point. Thousands of doughboys followed their orders to go "over the top," climbing out of trenches and stepping into a hell none of them would ever forget. Those who were lucky enough to survive the tangled barbed wire, the machine-gun barrages, the exploding mines, and the comrades falling at their feet found themselves engaged in hand-to-hand combat with the enemy, when the bayonet thrusting they had learned in basic training at Camp Sevier in Greenville, South Carolina, became the difference between life and death.

Describing the scene in a letter to a friend back home, Gilliland wrote, "It was a bitter dose and he [the Germans] fought like a tiger to hold."[3]

Several times, the German machine guns fell silent as the manning soldiers were mowed down, only to roar back to life under the control of a new contingent of replacements. As chaos engulfed the battlefield, the morning mist melding with smoke and fire, Gilliland led his platoon on a penetration deep into German territory and eliminated "four or five" machine guns, effectively punching a hole in the line.

At one point, the Germans began concentrating their massive firepower on his battery, and as his unit scattered, Gilliland found himself trapped in a forward ditch. "He shelled me and machine gunned me and sniped at me all day. From that you may judge how glad I was when night came. From my hole, I saw a battalion try to come over the same hill I did and I saw it practically wiped out."[4]

Ultimately, the brave men of the 30th seized the canal and the village of Bellicourt, moving the front a few miles closer to Berlin. The breakout marked the beginning of the end for the Hindenburg Line, but the bloodbath would continue for another six weeks. It would take many Bellicourts to win World War I.

When the armistice was signed on November 11, ending a conflict that claimed more than thirty-eight million lives, counting combatants and civilians, and America celebrated the decisive role played by its doughboys at various points along the western front, the surviving men of the Old Hickory Division returned home to a hero's welcome.

In less than five months of combat, the Old Hickory Division became one of the most decorated American units of World War I, producing a total of twelve Medal of Honor winners. The price of victory was high. The 120th alone suffered a total of 1,512 casualties, according to the unit's official history, out of an initial contingent of roughly 1,500 men, before replacements joined the action.

After making it back to Memphis in one piece, Gilliland resumed his law practice and tried to forget.

While Gilliland was pursuing his college degree in Nashville, Memphis businessman Robert Jordan and his family embarked on a trip, the kind of journey most people of the day took on a train. They did something radical. They drove.

At a time when only a tiny percentage of the American public owned an automobile, the Jordans loaded up their new Hupmobile, which could achieve a maximum speed of 35 miles per hour, and headed off to visit relatives in Pulaski, a small town located in south central Tennessee. The two-hundred-mile journey would take three days to negotiate. Traveling on narrow dirt roads intended for wagons and horses, they encountered a series of problems. Once, they were forced to stop and wait out a severe rainstorm, which made the road too muddy to navigate. Another time, the driver lost control of the car while traversing a steep hill and wound up splashing it into a creek, which caused the engine to go dead. He waded out into the water, fortunate that the engine cranked, because it would be many years before auto clubs, tow trucks, and cell phones.

When the Jordans encountered a wagon, they were all struck by the frightened looks on the faces of a young woman, who was holding a baby, and the young boy seated next to her. Evidently, it was the first automobile they had ever seen. The astonishing sight of the horseless carriage spooked their mules, causing the boy to tumble out of the wagon, and Jordan stopped his car long enough to help calm the beasts.

The driver's daughter, Elizabeth, would hold this memory close to her heart for a lifetime. The young girl watched her father struggle through the sort of trip that one day would become a routine four-hour journey. She was headed for many great adventures in a fast-changing world, and this outing always served as a subtle reminder of the remarkable progress she had experienced.

Born into a prominent family in 1898, the year of the Spanish-American War, Elizabeth was a descendant of John Sevier, the first governor of Tennessee and a political rival of Andrew Jackson. A hero of the Revolutionary War, Sevier led a contingent of militia to victory in the Battle of Kings Mountain and later helped tame the wilderness during a series of battles with the Cherokee Nation. His statue occupies a place of honor in the rotunda of the U.S. Capitol.

Elizabeth spent her first six years in Savannah, Tennessee, the place of her birth, located in Hardin County, named for her third great-grandfather Colonel Joseph Hardin, who obtained a large land grant encompassing much of the surrounding territory for his service in the Revolutionary War.

She was also connected to a grand home in Savannah that eventually became listed on the National Register of Historic

Places. In the late 1830s, David Robinson built the large antebellum house on a bluff overlooking the Tennessee River and presented it as a gift to his second daughter, Elizabeth, who married Alexander McAlpin Hardin. Both husband and wife died at a fairly young age, and the house eventually passed into the Cherry family, who became related to the Hardins through marriage.

Elizabeth Jordan's grandmother grew up in the Cherry Mansion, as it became known, and got to know a prominent visitor.

During the second year of the Civil War, after capturing the key Confederate stronghold of Fort Donelson, north of Nashville, General Ulysses S. Grant moved his army south, to a bend in the Tennessee River, and began preparations for a battle he expected to fight in northern Mississippi. It was early 1862 when the future president set up headquarters at the Cherry Mansion.

Many years later, near the end of her life, Mrs. Alexander Hardin, Elizabeth Jordan's grandmother, told a reporter about the moment the bloody Battle of Shiloh started. "We were sitting at breakfast and my sister was handing the general a cup of coffee when we heard the first canon sound," she said. "Grant, taken completely by surprise, jumped up from the table without a bite of breakfast."[5] According to a family history later compiled by Elizabeth Jordan, the general uttered one sentence before bolting through the front door: "The ball is on."[6]

The massive loss of life at Shiloh—twenty-three thousand dead and wounded, the bloodiest single engagement in American history up to that time—shocked the nation, but the resulting Union victory propelled Grant toward his future as a revered military figure.

The son of a medical doctor who had once served with the Confederate general Nathan Bedford Forrest, Robert Jordan moved his family to Memphis in 1905, becoming successful in the tobacco business and eventually owning the city's first automobile dealership. They lived in a big house and employed a staff of servants. Elizabeth was a child of privilege who grew accustomed to the finer things.

Educated at Miss Hutchison's School, reserved for the city's elite girls, she then went off to college, which was exceedingly rare, unless you came from money, attending National Cathedral School in Washington DC before earning her degree at Finch College in New York City. These were known in the parlance of the day as "finishing schools," and when she returned to Memphis, Libby, as her friends called her, exuded refinement and sophistication. She attended society parties and balls and was pursued by a long list of eligible suitors. When her time arrived, she became a debutante and was presented just before Christmas in 1919, dazzling in a white satin dress. In the glow of postwar euphoria, she joined two girlfriends in a monthslong tour of Europe and the Mediterranean.

Elizabeth also saw anguish rip through her family, losing an older sister to diphtheria and watching a younger brother hobbled by polio. Both afflictions remained common in those days, before the miracle of vaccines. Writing many years later about the effects of the devastating blows on their family, she said, "My dear mother seemed always sad to me.... My heart brimmed over for her as I felt she had more sorrow than she could bear."[7]

She grew into a striking young woman. The Jordans commissioned a portrait of her by the famed artist Nicholas R. Brewer, which would become her most prized possession. In later years, she often told family members, "If the house burns, save the painting. It's worth more than everything else."

At the suggestion of her mother, Elizabeth and several of her friends began volunteering at the Crippled Children's Hospital. After all those years of watching her brother struggle with polio, pushing hard against the debilitating disease and its various indignities, and seeing the desperation in her parents' eyes when they took Robert to the best doctors in New York, St. Louis, and Baltimore, in a futile search for a cure, the charity work struck a deeply personal chord. She and the other young ladies spent many hours visiting, reading, playing games, mending clothes, arranging transportation, buying necessities and treats out of their own pockets—providing the sort of tender loving care that made the boys and girls, and their often-beleaguered parents, feel special, without regard to income, class, or color. Memphis was still a segregated city and would be for decades, but this effort transcended Jim Crow. After a while, Libby suggested they name their little club, and since most had been to college and spoke French, they christened it, "Le Bonheur." Precisely translated, this meant "the good hour," but in a broader sense, it was understood as "happy time."

In the years to come, the ladies all married and moved on to other causes, but they were replaced by a steady stream of others who understood the importance of providing a "happy time" for many of the city's neediest and most vulnerable children.

Three decades later, when a group of civic leaders united in the need to start a full-service hospital for children, dealing with the wide variety of diseases afflicting the young, and members of the club helped in the fundraising efforts, the search for a name eventually reached a logical conclusion. The president of Le Bonheur Children's Hospital began referring to the then-middle-aged Elizabeth as one of the "founders" of the facility, recognizing that Le Bonheur was an idea long before it was a place.

In the Roaring Twenties, Memphis could be an electric and intoxicating place. A century after rising on the eastern banks of the Mississippi River, the city hummed with prosperity deeply connected to cotton. The steady march to the future could be seen in various ways, as the population exploded from 162,351 to 253,143 during the decade. The impact of the musical sound known as the Memphis blues was starting to filter through American culture. Piggly Wiggly, founded by Memphis entrepreneur Clarence Saunders, was fast altering consumer habits as the country's first self-service supermarket chain. In 1923, the year WMC became the city's first radio station, the Peabody Hotel opened in the heart of downtown, bringing Memphis a touch of elegance and drawing comparisons to Paris's legendary Ritz.

Veterans of the war began to assert themselves on the local scene, including Frank Gilliland. As his law practice flourished, he was elected president of two important civic institutions: the local American Legion post, which solidified his status as a leader among West Tennessee veterans, and the University Club, which demonstrated the sort of respect he engendered among the business elite who gathered at the stately institution for lunch, cocktails, cigars, and cards.

Shortly after taking over the University Club, Frank led an initiative by younger members to move to a new building across town, a decision that turned on a close vote and caused resentment among some of the old guard. Gilliland was not the sort of man to cower in the face of opposition, and the stand he took would be widely admired by many members in the years ahead.

Around this time, the handsome lawyer met Elizabeth Jordan, the beautiful former debutante who soon became his wife.

"People considered him brilliant, amusing and quick-witted," Elizabeth recalled of the prized bachelor, who was nine years older. "And always good company."[8]

With prohibition the law of the land, the newlyweds took a honeymoon cruise to Havana, then a playground for rich Americans. The trip was even more eventful than they had hoped. After leaving Cuba, the ship encountered an unexpected hurricane, and the captain struggled to steer it safely through the storm without capsizing. Salt water leaked into the cabins, unnerving the passengers, including many who struggled with seasickness, and damaging Elizabeth's prized trousseau. Frank later told friends the experience was "more terrifying than the war."

On May 1, 1926, when Robert Jordan Gilliland was born, his parents could not imagine how the event would reverberate through the future of American aviation.

After living briefly in two different homes—moving once because the telephone company refused to string lines to the edge of the city—the couple built a large house on a secluded lot shaded by tall oak trees. The land was a gift from Elizabeth's father, who had added real estate development to his various business interests. The new Mrs. Gilliland was blessed with an artistic sensibility, and her imprint was visible on various aspects of the Galloway Drive house, which struck a sophisticated but comfortable tone, from the big bay window in the living room to the mahogany furniture in the dining room. The architect's design was inspired by England's Sulgrave Manor, the ancestral home of George Washington. It cost $27,000 to build, an incredible sum for the day. They employed a live-in cook and nanny, another servant who resided in the garage, and a woman who came in to do the wash once a week. Life was good.

Nothing symbolized Memphis ambition and optimism in those days quite like the Sterick Building. In 1928 a group headed by Ross Sterling, soon to become governor of Texas, and his son-in-law, the architect Wayne Hedrick, broke ground on a majestic twenty-nine-story office tower stretching 365 feet above North Third Street. (Sterick was a combination of their last names.) Building the tallest skyscraper in the South made a statement. It said Memphis was on the move, and since Sterling was one of his clients, Gilliland handled the legal work and secured a minority interest in this prime piece of real estate. It opened in 1930, and the timing could not have been worse.

The stock market had crashed the previous October, and the country was spiraling into the Great Depression. As unemployment soared, eventually reaching 24.9 percent, and millions of Americans struggled for their next meal, the largely empty Sterick Building was forced into bankruptcy, becoming yet another symbol of the good times that suddenly seemed like a distant memory.

Like many others, Robert Jordan lost virtually his entire fortune, killing his spirit. Young Bob Gilliland grew up understanding the effects of the downturn in the context of his grandfather's deflated sense of self. "He was one of those who was devastated by the Depression," Bob recalled. "I don't think he was ever the same."

Watching her father fall so far profoundly affected Elizabeth, who felt his pain and would be forever shaped by Depression-era values. While Frank occupied himself with his law practice and other business pursuits, she had her hands full raising three boys. Frank Jr. was born in 1927, eighteen months after Bob, and Jim arrived in 1933.

Before marrying Libby, Frank had bought a farm in Arkansas, where he raised cotton. Many Sundays during the growing season, he drove off in the wee hours of the morning and headed west, across the big river, to keep an eye on his investment. As they became old enough, all three boys spent time working in the fields, alongside the farmhands, for meager wages. This was one of the ways their father reinforced the value of hard work.

Many years later, while leafing through some of his father's papers, Jim learned that when the Depression hit and the price of cotton collapsed, his dad had been unable to pay the mortgage on the farm. It was a startling find. At a time when many people were losing their homes and abandoning properties, Frank wrote a letter to the man who owned the note, pledging to pay when he could. At that moment, the most valuable thing he owned was his good name, and Frank Gilliland's word meant something. When times improved, he made good on his promise, saving a property that would remain in his family for decades.

"Even though we had all these advantages, those years were very tough on our parents," Jim said. "We never knew how tough."

Sometimes a memory can be a clue.

Around the age of five, little Bobby Gilliland pulled a book down from an upstairs shelf. The cover, which featured two pistols, caught his eye. The Zane Gray western novel was the first book he would remember reading, and it captured his imagination, introducing him to the wonders of learning about faraway places and different kinds of people. Soon he was methodically devouring the nine volumes of encyclopedias his father kept in his downstairs study, demonstrating the first flashes of the intellectual curiosity that would empower him in the years ahead. Like father, like son.

In various ways, his path to the stratosphere began on Galloway Drive, while being nurtured by parents who set high standards, encouraged learning, demanded achievement, and fostered the sort of self-reliance that can only result from a certain level of independence.

"The bar was set pretty high for Bob at home," said lifelong friend Toof Brown, whose family once owned the Memphis landmark Graceland, which was named for his great-aunt. "He always had a sharp, quick mind, and he was always very competitive."

The defining relationship of Bob's life was with his father, whom he remembered as "a take-charge guy" who "marched everywhere he went." He admired his dad, who showed love like most men of his generation, by being tough on his sons, shaping them in a manner that prepared them for the harsh realities of life. Bob never wanted to disappoint him. From an early age, he displayed an independent streak but was never disobedient.

"Self-confidence was sort of wired into the family," Jim said. "Bob was driven to be successful in large measure because of our dad."

Frank was not the sort to open his gut to his sons or his wife, who once wrote, in her family history, "I could not understand why a man who made his living so successfully by using words would use them so little to convey his thoughts to those around him. He replied that his profession trained him not to talk about anybody's business."[9]

While Frank could be distant, Elizabeth, whom Bob adored, was more demonstrative in her affections. She was the epitome of a gentile southern lady who exuded an unmistakable warmth, forever reflecting those finishing-school manners and a widely admired zest for life. She was a good and loving mother who often went to great lengths to help her boys enjoy childhood.

Libby kept a diary, recording many of the large and small moments of their lives, including the details of an outbreak of appendicitis that struck the family. Over a five-month period in 1936–37, Frank Jr., Grandmother Carolyn, and Bob all required appendectomies. "Three appendectomies in five months! Can any family beat our record?"[10] One of the surgeries required the family doctor to be called off the golf course.

In the evenings, when the weather was nice and the sun began to sink in the distance, Libby often walked with Bob, and eventually Frank Jr. and Jim, to the municipal golf course near their house. The players had finished their rounds, and Elizabeth would let Bob throw a few balls onto a green and putt, watching him take careful aim, in the gathering darkness, and cheering for him when he sank one. The man of the house never accompanied them on this ritual. "Dad thought golf was a complete waste of time," said the eldest son.

The sibling rivalry that developed among Bob, Frank Jr., and Jim pushed all three toward high achievement. Because they were so close in age, Bob and Frank Jr. cemented a lifelong bond. While Bob was more overtly competitive with his younger brothers and friends, Frank was more calculating and patient in pursuit of the goals they shared—on the playing field, in the classroom, or in the perpetual pursuit of their parents' approval. Coming along six years later, Jim would be forced to chase two extremely successful older brothers.

"There was a significant amount of pressure from Mr. Frank on those boys," said Tandy Gilliland, who married Frank Jr. and saw how the father's ambition filtered through the family. "He was a very driven man, and he expected his sons to excel."

The big oaks overlooking the Galloway Drive house provided a certain amount of welcome shade, but in those days before air-conditioning, the heat of the Memphis summer could be oppressive. Like many other southerners of means, the Gillilands routinely escaped the steamy city, spending several weeks in an idyllic retreat destined to become an oasis for three generations of the family.

Many years before Frank and Elizabeth married, Robert Jordan had purchased a rustic little cabin in the Smoky Mountains, located a few miles above the village of Gatlinburg in the Upper River Valley of East Tennessee. Elkmont was a world away from Memphis. Elizabeth often told stories of the early days around the onetime logging community, when she rode the train to the top of the mountain and the locomotive would strain to climb the steep grade, filling the air with billowing black smoke. Sometimes, the young men jumped out and raced the locomotive to the top.

Bob was no more than two months old when he made his first trip east by northeast with his mother. The place profoundly shaped his development. With Jake's Creek running directly behind the cabin—"So close you could hear the water running at night, when you were in bed," he said—and

Mount Leconte and various breathtaking vistas nearby, he spent most of his waking hours outside. Fishing. Swimming. Hiking. Exploring.

It was a place where he bonded with his mother, and it was a place where he learned about himself. It was a place where he began to understand there was life beyond paved streets and perfectly manicured lawns, where the unspoiled landscape was populated with bears, rattlesnakes, mountain men selling moonshine, a country store where bologna and cheese were considered delicacies, a restaurant where all the men showed up wearing bib overalls, and a feeling of peace he could never quite describe. It was a place where he got to be a boy, and it was a place where he started to become a man.

The demands of his practice usually kept Frank in Memphis for most of the season, leaving Elizabeth and the boys—and sometimes their friends—at the cabin for extended periods. The summer before Bob started first grade, Elizabeth decided to delay their return home for a week or two, which made the eldest Gilliland boy late for the beginning of his formal education. For Libby, this was no cause for concern. Her little boy was smart. He could make up the ground in no time.

When they finally showed up at the school, she led him to his new classroom and presented him to his new teacher, Miss Favreau. "Well, we're a little late, but here we are!"

Seeing a familiar child, she took charge of the situation. "Oh, there's Giles!" Giles Coors was a son of family friends. "Why don't you let Bobby sit by Giles? He can do what Giles is doing, and we can take it from there."

Elizabeth was never one to let an arbitrary rule stand in her way, and this moment and others like it shaped Bob's development. "I guess you could say I learned from my mother that not all rules carried the same weight," he said.

By this time, Bob had started to develop an interest in aviation. Three decades after the Wright brothers took flight on a windy day at Kitty Hawk and just a few years after Charles

Lindbergh became the first man to fly solo and nonstop across the Atlantic—landing to a hero's welcome in Paris on May 21, 1927, his *Spirit of St. Louis* surrounded by an ecstatic throng of 150,000—commercial air travel was still in its infancy. It was the age of the barnstormer, when daredevil pilots brought the romance of flight to wide-eyed patrons who gathered at county fairs and in random pastures and vacant lots across the land, often utilizing biplanes left over from World War I. Most Americans had never seen an airplane close-up.

According to the careful markings left behind by his mother, Bob built a little wooden biplane at age seven. Elizabeth packed it away, unaware of its significance until many years later. Featuring a fuselage painted red and carefully carved wings and rudder, it suggested the evidence not just of a budding aspiration that would eventually take flight but also of a rather meticulous nature.

Prior to entering the second grade, Bob told his mother, "I don't see any reason why I shouldn't be number one in my class, except for maybe one guy."

By this time, Elizabeth had begun to see flashes of her husband in her eldest son: the way he spoke and the way he pushed himself. She recognized this rather bold pronouncement for what it was: the pounding life force of great expectations.

"Oh really?" she replied. "Who is he?"

"Jack Wilson."

"Oh. Thank goodness for Jack Wilson."

Libby understood that even her very bright and driven son needed to be challenged.

He rarely disappointed his parents or himself. Certainly a big part of the equation was his innate intelligence, but he also worked very hard. He ranked at or near the top of every class, because his parents expected him to and because he expected it of himself.

"Doing well in school was always important to me," Bob

said. "I felt a responsibility, to my family and to myself. I wanted to get the most out of the ability I had, and I learned very early on that studying and working hard paid off."

It was important for him to feel the satisfaction produced by achievement.

As long as they took care of their household chores, especially feeding their father's beloved bird dogs, who lived in a pen behind the house, Bob and the other boys were free to explore the world around Galloway Drive with precious few rules or restrictions. Like most boys of the day, Bob made his own fun without parental supervision. His only obligation was to be home in time for supper. No key was required, because the front door remained unlocked at all times of the day and night. It was a more innocent age, before a certain kind of insecurity and caution descended on the world. This freedom often led him to the vacant lot down the street, where, depending on the season, the large contingent of neighborhood kids could be seen playing football, basketball, or baseball.

Bob developed into a good athlete. Headed for a lanky six feet three, he was always one of the tallest of the group, and he could shoot a basketball and throw a baseball better than most. He was also a good tennis player. Regardless of what they were playing, he competed vigorously, because he hated to lose.

Frank was not the sort of father to spend time playing with his children or attending their sporting events. He had his world, and they had theirs.

"If our father had shown up at one of our games," Jim remarked, "we would've wondered what was wrong."

In the summer of 1940, Bob enjoyed the greatest adventure of his young life, riding a train with Troop 42 of the Boy Scouts to the New York World's Fair. It was an exciting time and place. He experienced various marvels of the fast-approaching future, including television, and soaked up the sights of a city that overwhelmed his senses. The boys slept in Indian-style tepees and ate some strange food. Most memorably, he went aloft for the first time. The big balloon was tethered to the ground the whole time, but from the vantage point of a few hundred feet above the Queens fairgrounds, he could see the skyline of Manhattan, dominated by the Empire State Building. "It was a great thrill, to be up so high and to be able to see so far into the distance," said Bob, who attained his Eagle Scout rank on July 14, 1941.

After returning to the ground, he came across a machine that pressed a name into a commemorative coin. This he had to have, so he pulled out his wallet and set it on top of the contraption while he started feeding it with the required amount of change and pushing the buttons to spell out his name. Several minutes later, he walked away with a personalized keepsake but forgot to retrieve his wallet. It was an embarrassing mistake that would stay with him for a lifetime. By the time he returned, the wallet was gone, requiring him to place a long-distance telephone call to his father, who wired him more money.

Not long after this trip, his parents sent him away.

Frank understood that Webb School had been central in his development, and he wanted his sons to be forged in the same crucible.

"Bob always told the story that when it came time for him to go to Webb School, Miss Libby looked at him and said, 'I'm sorry, I can't help you,'" recalled Tandy Gilliland. "Those boys were going to Webb School and there was nothing she could do about it."

Asked many years later if he had wanted to go off to boarding school at age fourteen, Gilliland laughed and said, "It wouldn't have mattered whether I wanted to go or not. I was going. End of story."

Founded in 1870 by Sawny Webb, the academy in rural Middle Tennessee was one of the South's most prestigious prep schools. At one point, Webb produced more Rhodes Scholars than any other secondary school in America. Over the course of its long history, the school has routinely sent graduates to the nation's most prominent colleges and universities, graduating future governors, congressmen, state supreme court justices, diplomats, university presidents, and high achievers in various fields.

By the time Frank drove Bob to Bell Buckle in September 1940, in the shadow of the Nazi blitzkrieg through Poland, France, and the low countries, the Germans occupied much of Europe. A dark cloud was gathering, but the United States remained at peace, slowly recovering from the lingering effects of the Great Depression. The freshman from Memphis had his hands full, adjusting to life away from his parents and to the challenging academic experience conducted in an old building heated by potbellied stoves.

"Bob was a very good student," recalled his friend Carroll Johnson, who roomed with him during part of their time at Webb. "Of course, we broke every rule we could think of."

The school operated on an honor system. If you broke a rule—such as being outside your room after curfew, smoking, drinking, or cursing—you were obligated to report yourself. Even as he distinguished himself in the classroom, Bob developed a disdain for what he considered "silly" rules.

His report card from March 1942:[11]

Deportment	C
English III	A
History, Ancient	A
Latin II	A
Mathematics II	A
Physical Education	A

Two letters from school officials opened a window into his tendency to get in trouble outside the classroom:

Webb School
Bell Buckle, Tenn.

April 7th, 1942

Mr. Frank M. Gilliland
Sterick Building
Memphis, Tennessee

Dear Frank:

I am very sorry that it was necessary to cut Bob's deportment on this report. The three boys involved in this are very much ashamed and it will not happen again.

    These boys began to play jokes on one another and on other companions, and as often happens in these cases, they became excited and went too far. They placed a vessel of water over the door of the cook's toilet so that when the cook opened the door she received a wetting. We simply had to put a stop to this. I am sorry to make you this report.

                                      With kindest regards
                                      Very truly,
                                      Wm. R. Webb[12]

Webb School
Bell Buckle, Tenn.

April 8th, 1942

Mr. Frank M. Gilliland
Sterick Building
Memphis, Tennessee

Dear Frank:

Mr. Webb has written to you about Bob's deportment grade. None of us consider it as otherwise than a boyish prank. Had the boys put the water over a student's door, it probably would have been overlooked but cooks are getting to be as scarce as hen's teeth and the cook in the dormitory is somewhat of a touchy person. We had to be sure that this prank would not be repeated either by this group or any other and so it was necessary to make an impression. I am sure that it will not be repeated by Bob.

I could hardly keep a straight face, however, when I saw his father in this whole affair. How many buckets of water his father threw out of the windows of Kissam Hall only the Lord knows! I didn't tell Bob about that and I won't.

While Bob is getting his deportment cut, old Frank, Jr. is barging along with a set of mighty fine grades. You better watch that boy. He has poise, is self-contained, punctual, and conscientious to the last degree. He isn't tense like Bob and therefore may have better health and a longer life. I am telling you, you better watch him, because he is going places!

Cordially yours,
Webb Follin[13]

During their sophomore year, when Johnson was rooming with another student, the teacher who managed the dormitory caught him in Bob's room after the appointed hour. This represented a major rule violation, and the teacher grabbed Johnson and started beating on him. "The guy had a mean streak, and he was going to beat me up," Johnson said. Somehow, while striking the student, the teacher accidentally yanked a wire dangling from the ceiling—the single wire that controlled all the lights in the room. "When it went dark and we had to straighten that out, he sort of cooled off . . . and I guess the darkness saved me."

The same teacher once forced Johnson to go to the bathroom and start chomping on a bar of soap, because he had heard him say a word on the forbidden list.

Isolated in a small community with no girls and nothing

much to do, the students made their own fun, playing football, hiking into the countryside, sneaking beer and cigarettes, and playing cards. A student could own a radio but was allowed to listen to it only on the weekends. He was required to check it into the office at the beginning of the week, because the teachers didn't want their students distracted on school nights by *The Shadow* or *Fibber McGee and Molly*. Some of the more mischievous boys—including Bob—would walk down to the Bell Buckle station and throw rocks at passing trains. Sometimes the engineers responded by tossing little pieces of coal, which the students sold for spending money.

William Webb, son of the founder, ran the institution with a firm hand and also taught a Latin class while employing a rather unusual method of instruction and grading. The boys sat in long pews, the type usually seen in churches. Son Will, as Mr. Webb was known, stood before the row, asking questions about that day's lesson. A correct answer allowed a student to move up the line, which was known as "trapping," but a wrong answer pushed him to the opposite end of the pew. In time, the boys understood that they were studying more than a foreign language. They were learning the power of preparation and recall. They were learning to compete. This process continued until someone emerged victorious, creating enormous pressure for a bunch of students already conditioned to pursue academic achievement.

"There was so much tension in that," Bob said. "I loved it. I think it taught me how to operate under heavy tension."

Well into his fourth decade of teaching, Son Will was a stickler for what he considered correct behavior. If a student said or did something he didn't like, the teacher would pull him across the stage at the end of the classroom and into a small room. "You'd hear him whack the boy two or three times," Bob recalled, "and then they'd come back and we'd continue the lesson."

The rigorous academics and the strict code of conduct tested Bob in various ways, forcing him to grow up much quicker than many of his peers back in Memphis who lived at home and attended public schools. He was allowed to take the train home for several days around Christmas but otherwise was confined to campus for the duration of the school year.

"All of a sudden you're gone from your mama's skirt tales. You're on your own. That was the way my dad thought was right," Bob said. "Was it tough? Sure, it was. But you learn a lot of independence that way. I'm sure glad I went through that experience, because it prepared me for many things."

Frank never talked about his war. Elizabeth tried to get him to open up about it, but this was not a subject he wanted to discuss, at least around civilians. His boys knew very little about his service, except that people around town thought of him as a hero. Eventually, their curiosity would lead them to a trunk in the attic. One by one, they unfurled his old maps, marveled at the collection of captured German helmets, including one with a bullet hole, slipped on his gas mask, and tried to learn more about his past, even as a new war consumed the globe.

By the fall of Bob's sophomore year, the students frequently found themselves caught up in heated discussions, mirroring the debate then dividing the country. Some believed the United States should join the fight against Hitler. Others thought the country should stay out of Europe's problem. "The debate ended when the Japanese bombed Pearl Harbor," Johnson said.

Years later, Bob's perspective on the turning point in U.S. history would be framed by a personal memory. A future college classmate was then a teenager living in Hawaii, the son of a marine officer. He was in his yard that Sunday morning, when the lady who lived next door raised her window and yelled out to him, "Young man, go inside and awaken your daddy immediately!"

Back at Webb, several teachers started volunteering or being drafted, and as the country mobilized to fight a global conflict against Germany and Japan, Bob knew his time was approaching. A patriotic young man who was prepared to do his duty, he was starting to understand the way his father must have felt before he boarded that troopship to France.

With graduation looming in the spring of 1944, Bob took a train to Atlanta and volunteered for the V5 program, which trained naval aviators. To his astonishment, he flunked the physical because his blood pressure was too low.

He quickly found a pay phone and started filling it with quarters. When his father came on the line, Bob explained what had happened, including the news that he could take the physical again in three days. However, if he failed again, he was out for good.

The lawyer listened carefully and seized control of the situation. "Hang up and stay by the phone."

He said he would call back within thirty minutes. Fifteen or twenty minutes later, the phone rang, but this time it was an unfamiliar voice, a friend of Frank's from their Vanderbilt days who lived in Atlanta, a doctor who was now on the case. Acting quickly, the man sent his wife to retrieve Bob and move him into their guest room. He had a plan to get the young man's blood pressure up.

On the morning of the third day, at breakfast before sending his patient to take another physical, the doctor gave him an unusual prescription: a small steak, eggs, and a glass of beer.

The unorthodox prescription worked.

Gilliland passed the physical, breathed a sigh of relief, thanked the doctor and his wife, and caught the train back to Bell Buckle, where a big envelope was waiting for him.

Puzzled, he placed another long-distance telephone call to his father. "Dad, I've got a big sheaf of papers here from the U.S. Naval Academy," he began to explain. "Do you know anything about this?"

"No. Put it in the mail to me, and I'll investigate."

At that point in his life, Bob was not aware of the existence of the Naval Academy, but soon he learned that, apparently out of an attempt to curry favor with Frank, Senator Kenneth McKellar had given Bob a prized secondary appointment for the next class in Annapolis. In this case, having a secondary appointment meant he was the first alternate for the next class and would be admitted to the Naval Academy and potentially be able to pursue a career as a naval aviator, if the primary selection passed on the opportunity or could not qualify, which frequently happened.

When Frank got to the bottom of the situation, he called Bell Buckle and told his son, "This may be a better deal than the one down there in Atlanta."

The academy required him to pass a test to be admitted, which meant he needed to take the train to Columbia, the nearest major town, to have the examination proctored at the post office. When he arrived, the man in charge said, "You can take one of two tests. Which one do you want to take?"

"What do you mean?"

The postman explained that the academy offered one test (which lasted one day) for those who made good grades and another (which took three days) for those who didn't have stellar academic records.

"What kind of grades do you get?"

"I make excellent grades. Straight As."

"Sounds like you want to take the one-day deal."

Bob took the one-day test and scored well, but several weeks later, he learned that the academy rejected him because he had not taken a chemistry course.

Now he faced a dilemma. Aware that he might have to wait months for the call to come from the v5 program, he signed up to go into the fleet as an enlisted man, determined to do his duty and not about to wait to be drafted.

On the day he left for basic training, as a graduate of the class of 1944 bound for an uncertain future in the weeks after the Normandy invasion, he drove with his mother and father to meet the train.

When the *Panama Limited*, which ran between New Orleans and Chicago, pulled up to the station, it was packed, mostly with servicemen. Bob was lucky to get a seat next to a pretty girl, while his mother and father stood on the platform, waving goodbye. As the train pulled away, he stared at his father's face, not quite believing what he was seeing.

"I could see emotion in my dad's eyes," he said. "That was the first time I had ever seen that look, the first time in my entire life."

TWO

Anchors Away

AS AMERICAN FORCES LIBERATED PARIS AND GUAM and many other cities and islands in the summer and fall of 1944, seizing the momentum in both theaters, Bob Gilliland followed the action closely in newspapers and newsreels. He was busy learning how to be a good sailor at Great Lakes Naval Station, a massive training facility overlooking Lake Michigan, north of Chicago. Of the four million men who served in the U.S. Navy during World War II, more than a quarter started their journey at Great Lakes. Bob thought it was just a matter of time before he shipped out as an apprentice seaman.

Mastering the art of folding his clothes, making his bed, and snapping a proper salute, Gilliland found himself under the watchful eye of a hard-charging drill instructor who was not much older than the men he was leading but demanded perfection and berated the subordinates who came up short. "There's two ways to do things," he liked to say. "The right way to do it and the navy way to do it. And around here we use the navy way to do everything!"

Hoping to be assigned to submarines, Bob completed his training and wound up instead at Bainbridge Naval Center in Maryland. He discovered that his 1944 secondary appointment to the Naval Academy would be upgraded to a primary appointment in the autumn of 1945. But he could not seem to make any of the brass understand that the navy had made a mistake.

While trying to straighten this mess out, he saw some very good football. During the war, many of the best former—and future—college players competed for service teams, such as El Toro Marines and North Carolina Pre-Flight. Gilliland would always remember seeing Charlie "Choo Choo" Justice, destined for stardom at the University of North Carolina, score on a long touchdown run and then run around shaking the hands of his blockers. "We all thought that was impressive."

Gilliland knew he was in the wrong place, so he took the initiative and went straight to the top.

Somehow, Frank Gilliland's son got Senator McKellar on the phone and began explaining his predicament. "Sir, they sent me to Bainbridge, and I shouldn't even be here," Bob told him. "I need to go somewhere where I can get chemistry."

Soon McKellar handed the phone over to an aide, who saw the error in the navy's ways and started pulling some pretty powerful strings. (McKellar's clout reached its zenith several months later when he served the first of two terms as president pro tempore of the Senate. After President Roosevelt's death in 1945, he was among the leaders to push for the Presidential Succession Act, which placed the speaker of the House and the president pro tempore of the Senate in the line of leaders who would be elevated in the case of a future president's death or incapacity.)

Next thing he knew, Bob was no longer a sailor. He was a student at Vanderbilt University, taking two levels of chemistry simultaneously—which required personal approval from the dean—as well as calculus and Shakespearean literature.

"All of a sudden, I'm a civilian," Gilliland recalled. "At Vanderbilt at that time, we had 4Fs who were disqualified for military service for some reason and a few shot-up GIs [back from the war]. Well, I'm not in either category. It was very unusual, and it was the power of Kenneth McKellar that made it happen."

Passing chemistry made him eligible for his Naval Academy appointment, but he still had to overcome one more obstacle on the road to Annapolis: the U.S. Postal Service.

After finishing his semester in Nashville, Gilliland returned to Memphis and awaited his orders. He spent a rather lazy afternoon at the Memphis Country Club, much of it diving into the swimming pool. Late in the afternoon, he called home.

The war in Europe was over and Hitler was dead, but the bloody island-hopping march toward Tokyo continued. The military was busy planning a massive invasion of the Japanese home islands, and no one knew how long it would take or how many American lives would be lost bringing the Japanese war machine to its knees.

Half a world away from this sober reality, some friends had extended a dinner invitation, and Bob wanted to make sure his mother didn't have anything special planned.

She got right to the point. "You come home at once, young man!"

"What is it, Mother?"

"You've got a sheaf of papers here from the navy."

After rushing home, Gilliland ripped open the envelope and discovered that someone in the senator's office had neglected one detail of their plan. The orders had been sent to Bainbridge by mistake, before being rerouted, and because of the delay, he had already missed his report date by two weeks.

"I was very worried," Bob recalled. "Even though I was the principal appointment, I thought they would assume that since I hadn't shown up on time, I didn't want it . . . and they'd give it the next guy on the list."

Taking no chances, he bypassed the train the next morning and instead bought a plane ticket.

Commercial air travel remained rare and expensive, but the industry was poised for dramatic growth in the coming postwar boom. The heated competition between Juan Trippe's Pan American Airways and Howard Hughes's Trans World Airlines filled the skies with Lockheed Constellations, Douglas DC-4s, and Boeing 307 Stratoliners, as the safety and convenience of the modern airliner slowly started to win over the public. The fastest propeller-driven planes could fly from New York to Los Angeles in about nine hours. It was only a matter of time before the airliner brought an end to the primacy of the passenger train, consigning it to a much more specialized future.

When he arrived in Annapolis, Bob quickly smoothed over the situation and embarked on what the Naval Academy called Plebe Summer. With the upperclassmen away until fall classes began in September, the first-year men eased into academy life by learning various nautical basics, including sailing techniques honed in tiny crafts on Chesapeake Bay, as well as the proper way to march.

When Japan surrendered on August 15, in the shadow of the two atomic bombs that ushered in a new age of warfare, Gilliland and all of his new friends felt enormous relief. "It was such a shock, after such a long war," Bob said. "We didn't quite know how to act. It was the greatest news. We were all so happy."

The official celebration on campus included a Naval Academy band and several high-ranking officers offering heartfelt words about the heroic sacrifices made by so many fine navy men, but the most telling response to the gathering euphoria may have taken place in a second-floor room of the campus hospital. That's where Jim Matheney, soon to become one of Gilliland's friends, was confined to a bed with an ear infection. When the news flash came on the radio, sending a shockwave of pandemonium across the country, a nurse and her boyfriend smuggled a fifth of whiskey to the ward, hid-ing it in a shoebox and lifting it on a carefully tethered string through a second-floor window. About that time, an enterprising corpsman showed up with a pint of pure grain alcohol, which they mixed with grapefruit juice. They all drank themselves silly. Soon the corpsman passed out on the floor. For some reason, Matheney took a pin from his dresser and jabbed it into his own hand, just to test the effectiveness of his poison. The war was over and he was still alive, but he couldn't feel a thing.

Several weeks later, with Plebe Summer over, the upperclassmen back, and the first school term of the postwar era about to commence, Jim McVoy took a walk across campus, soaking it all in. He happened upon his friend Hamilton Perkins, known as Ham, standing on the edge of the athletic field.

"Jimmy! Jimmy, guess how many upperclassmen I've got to see tonight?"

McVoy shook his head as his buddy answered his own question.

"Four! On the first day!"

Neither one of the plebes quite understood the full measure of an upperclassmen ordering a first-year man to "come see me tonight," but they knew enough to realize it wasn't good.

"Ham had a way of getting into trouble," McVoy recalled.

Some weeks earlier, McVoy stopped by the Bancroft Hall room where Perkins and Mel Davis were moving in with a third man. Perkins, Davis, and McVoy had grown up together in Birmingham, Alabama, and McVoy and Davis had attended the same prep school, Episcopal High School, in Virginia. "Mel and I were like brothers," McVoy said. They spent much of their free time back in Birmingham playing tennis, often until the last rays of light faded in the evening sky.

When he walked into the room for the first time, McVoy saw a tall guy with a rather prominent nose and a firm jaw. (Some of his new friends started calling him Beak, which he did not like.) His feet were propped up on a desk, and he was smoking a cigarette. Jim would always remember his introduction to Bob Gilliland.

"I liked Bob from the start," McVoy said. "He was a very engaging guy who projected a certain confidence that you noticed right away."

Like Gilliland, McVoy understood the pressures of legacy. He, too, had gone away to the same boarding school as his father, although his family's money was more new than old. His dad was a manufacturer's representative for a steel-products company, in the days when Birmingham was known as the Pittsburgh of the South, and he had made a small fortune after landing the contract to provide the roofing for the new National Gallery of Art in Washington DC, which enabled him to build a big house in the tony suburb of Mountain Brook. The demands of his booming career eventually led the family to New York City, but he died suddenly at the age of forty, from complications caused by a botched appendicitis.

"Going to the Naval Academy had been a goal of mine for a long time, and Mel's father and mother knew that, which is how I got to Annapolis," McVoy said.

Davis was the scion of an Alabama political dynasty. His great-uncle had been speaker of the U.S. House of Representatives. His grandfather Senator John H. Bankhead II, a prominent New Deal Democrat then serving his third term, provided him with a principal appointment to Annapolis. When the family learned that McVoy wanted to go as well, they set the wheels in motion, arranging a secondary bid that got him in after two others bowed out. The good news arrived in a telegram, filling McVoy with such excitement that he showed up two weeks earlier than everybody else and was there to show Mel and Ham around when they finally arrived.

Gilliland and Davis had roomed together at Vanderbilt, living in a tiny apartment over Miss Polly's beauty salon. Bob quickly hit it off with the blond-haired, affable Davis, who had spent a year at Marion Military Institute.

"Mel was a muscle guy," Bob said. "He could do more push-ups and do 'em faster than just about anybody."

At Annapolis, three students shared a room, and the pairing of Gilliland, Davis, and Perkins cemented a lifelong bond. "We sort of thought of the three of them as a unit," said Robert Finnigan, who was in the same company and became another of Gilliland's lifelong friends.

Gilliland's unusual path to Annapolis infused him with a certain stature among the plebes, who were mostly straight out of high school. "I had been part of the fleet, and a lot of those guys thought that was a pretty big deal," he said.

Bob developed a reputation as a good student, especially in the subjects that fascinated him. He excelled in classes dealing with electronics and engineering, not fully appreciating how this knowledge would provide part of the intellectual foundation crucial to his career. He enjoyed taking a test given frequently to judge each midshipman's understanding of current events, because, as someone who read the *Baltimore Sun* and the *Washington Post* regularly, he was always well informed.

Gilliland's classmates recognized many of the qualities that would drive his success, including his intelligence and his calm demeanor. He was perceptive and keenly attuned to the subtlety of language and liked to ask probing questions of friends, family members, and random strangers. This was not just his way of seeking knowledge; it was a big part of the way he interacted with people and sized them up.

He wanted to know how things worked. He struck all who knew him as rather fearless and mentally tough. He was empowered by a prodigious memory.

"Bob was very articulate, and he had strong opinions," Finnigan said. "He spoke his mind without holding anything back, and I liked that about him."

During the two or three times Frank Sr. visited his son in Annapolis, Bob's friends could recognize similarities as well as differences.

Frank Sr.'s bluntness was legendary, exemplified by the time several midshipmen tried to probe into his World War I experiences. "Mr. Gilliland," one of Bob's friends asked, "I understand you were attached to the British Army. Were you attached to one of their staffs or something?"

"Staff hell! I was attached to their frontline trenches!"

The boys exploded in laughter, and the onetime first lieutenant took a measure of delight in busting the chops of a young man silly enough to ask such an uninformed question.

"Dad was not the kind of guy who suffered fools easily," Bob explained.

As an adult trying to gain a bit more perspective on his father's life, Bob asked him, "How come the governor of Texas chose you to be his representative in Memphis?"

"Because I was a damn good lawyer! That's why!"

Anyone who spent any time around Bob could see he had the makings of a leader, but he chafed at the restrictive nature of academy life. Over four years, he amassed a mountain of demerits, so many that the cumulative weight of all that disobedience very nearly prevented his graduation.

"I was always very independent and was confronted with a lot of these silly rules that really had nothing to do with being a good naval officer," Gilliland said. "I wanted to do things the way I wanted to do 'em. If that meant I got a bunch of demerits, so be it. I would rather accept the extra duty than conform."

Conformity was not Gilliland's style.

"Bob often chose to ignore the rules he didn't agree with," Finnigan said.

"He was something of a rebel, and at the Naval Academy it could be a little dangerous to be a rebel," McVoy said.

In a culture driven by the acronym RHIP (Rank Has Its Privileges), the lowly plebes were placed at the mercy of the upperclassmen, especially at mealtime, when they could harass them in a variety of ways, such as forcing one to eat his entire meal standing up.

One night during dinner, Gilliland and a friend were ordered under the table. Rather than meekly submit to this humiliation, they sneaked some butter from the table and started rubbing it onto several of the upperclassmen's perfectly shined shoes. "They were furious, but I didn't care," Bob said. This brazen act of defiance led to a series of reprisals, burnishing his reputation as a troublemaker.

"So much of it was really childish stuff," Gilliland said. "What made it even harder to take was that some of these guys making me do this stuff might be a year younger than me or my same age."

By the time he arrived in Annapolis, Bob's tolerance for ritualistic hazing had already been tested. After joining a fraternity as a teenager, he was forced to submit to a severe paddling at the hands of a boy he didn't like. Some months later, Bob went looking for the boy, who was much smaller than him, and intended to exact a measure of revenge. His anger very nearly got the better of his judgment. But when confronted, face-to-face, with the fear in the boy's eyes, Gilliland resisted the urge to brutalize him. "Without that paddle and without [the authority of] the fraternity, he wasn't so tough," Gilliland said.

At the academy, the hazing was encouraged, or at least tolerated, by the school's hierarchy as part of a time-honored system intended not just to train competent officers but also to push them to their physical and mental limits. "A lot of it was psychological warfare," recalled Finnigan. "It really tested you." The sense of brotherhood this process fostered was unmistakable, but so was a certain amount of resentment.

"I thought hazing was for the birds," Gilliland said, noting that even after he became an upperclassmen, "I never hazed anybody. I treated everybody with respect."

In this, Gilliland was influenced by the example of All-American football player and brigade boxing champ Leon Bramlett, a native of Mississippi whom he knew through a cousin. "He treated the lowliest plebe the same way he did the highest-ranking admiral," Bob recalled. "I always admired the way he operated; he was a guy I wanted to learn from and emulate."

Most dreaded of all was when an upperclassman ordered someone junior to him to "come see me tonight," as Ham Perkins learned on day one. This was an invitation to some private torment, away from the prying eyes of the active-duty officers, and it could not be refused. "Some of those guys were just bullies," Finnigan said. "They were the ones who made it difficult for all of us, because they enjoyed being bullies."

After being summoned to one room, Gilliland and Davis were instructed to hit the deck and do forty-nine push-ups each (since they were members of the class of 1949). Several minutes later, Bob was still moving up and down, counting to the magic number, when Mel popped up and stood at attention before his superior.

"Goddamn it!" the upperclassmen screamed. "I told you forty-nine push-ups, and I meant it!"

"I did, sir!"

"Don't lie about it!"

Recalling the scene, Gilliland said, "The guy wasn't paying attention, and he didn't understand how strong and fast Mel was."

The third man in the room, Ham Perkins, was not from a rich family, but he glided with ease into their world. He walked with a swagger that approached a strut—"like a top caddie," in the words of McVoy—and was able to work his way up the ranks to become part of the company staff. Ham always referred to Bob, admiringly, as "fiercely independent."

Perkins was equally rebellious. "Ham was defiant," Gilliland said. "He would turn the tables on upperclassmen and get into fights. He didn't give a damn about demerits, either."

Compelled to march from class to class, forbidden from owning or riding in a private car during the school year, and restricted to a five-mile radius of the campus, unless they obtained liberty, the midshipmen could be written up for a variety of minor offenses, such as keeping an unapproved photograph in their room or wearing shoes that failed to meet certain standards. "They wanted you to shine your shoes so well that you could count your teeth in the shine," recalled Jim Matheney.

Two midshipmen during the period became the central figures in a cautionary tale and part of Naval Academy lore. After renting a car and driving off to Baltimore with two girls—violating two major rules—the two Annapolis men started toward home and were involved in a minor traffic accident. Soon they were caught trying to sneak back onto campus after hours, and when the commandant found out about the whole sordid affair, the leadership prepared to deal with the situation. One of the young men had a fairly clean record and was allowed to escape with some extra duty. But his friend had a history of rule breaking, and this class A violation pushed his case over the line.

The commandant was planning to kick him out of the academy, just before graduation. However, his father was politically connected, and just before the ax fell, the commandant was shocked to pick up his telephone and hear the familiar voice of President Harry Truman, who was calling to ask a personal favor. Couldn't they work out something that allowed the boy to graduate?

This put the Naval Academy in a very difficult situation. Faced with a dilemma, a clever member of the staff devised a way of punishing the young man that fell just short of expulsion, saddling him with a rank that had not been utilized since the nineteenth century: passed midshipman. The good time in Baltimore cost the young man his commission, but at least he was allowed to graduate. Many others who violated the rules were not so lucky.

"I've always admired the guy's verve for getting a certain governor on the phone and pressing his case . . . which is how it got to Truman," Gilliland said. "Otherwise he would have been gone."

The risk of violating such a major rule was understood by all, but all that psychological pressure could make the place feel like a prison, especially during the bleak winter months. "When you were dealing with this very demanding situation on several levels, it could be pretty depressing," Matheney said. Many could not handle the academic workload, the harassment, or the requirement that they cede so much control of their daily lives. Many were quietly called in to the commandant's office and asked to leave. Others simply slipped out in the middle of the night, without a word. One by one, rooms emptied.

When they became upperclassmen, Gilliland and several of his friends appropriated a vacant room down the hall, bought some barbells, and turned it into a miniature gym, lifting for a few minutes between classes. Always considered one of the most athletic of his group, Bob also competed as a pole-vaulter for the Navy track-and-field team.

Gilliland and his friends often tried to devise ways to escape their confinement for a few precious hours. They were usually allowed out on Saturday afternoons but quickly learned that the only way a plebe could leave campus on Sunday was if he was invited out by an officer. Several times, he and Matheney wrote letters to themselves, pretending to be officers who were extending dinner invitations. Liberated by their own handwriting, they took the opportunity to walk several miles through Annapolis' cobblestone streets to a place that served cheap T-bone steaks and beer. The momentary taste of freedom was especially sweet. Sometimes, they took a bus to a nearby town on the bay, where they walked another couple of miles to a little dive where they ate their fill of crabs and drank a few beers before negotiating the long journey back to campus.

Once, they made this trip in a driving rainstorm on a brutally cold day and hit the jackpot, opening the door to see the place filled with students from a girls' school who were visiting the area on their senior trip. "We were all wet, but suddenly we didn't care," Matheney said. "That turned out to be one of our all-time best liberties."

The various, mostly minor offenses that frequently landed Gilliland in the penalty box typically resulted in extra duty. He often was joined by Perkins and Davis; the trio's combined demerits made their room one of the most frequently punished in Bancroft Hall. "I remember several times walking through the rotunda about six o'clock in the evening and seeing the extra-duty squad falling in, and there would be Bob, Ham, and Mel," McVoy recalled. At the end of an already grueling day, they were forced to march several miles across the parade ground, with full leggings, row a boat across the bay, or perform some other taxing chore. Bob resented the punishment, but it was the price of the limited freedom he was able to achieve by bucking the system.

Many of the demerits were recorded during spot inspections of the rooms, when the officer of the day arrived in full-dress uniform, including a draped saber, trailed by an aide carrying a notebook. The slightest infraction was noted and turned over to the authorities, who assigned punishment. Some students were better than others at concealing contraband, including Davis, who regularly kept several bottles of mouthwash on his dresser, which he filled with bourbon. "They never caught on," Matheney said. "I remember him telling me how one of the inspectors one time said to him, 'You must have awful bad breath.'"

Like alcohol, having food in your room was strictly forbidden. During their plebe year, several weeks after Mel received a cake from his mother in the mail, the vast majority of it lingered in a box, uneaten and molding. It was starting to omit a foul odor.

With an inspection looming, Ham and Bob started tidying up the room.

"What do we do with this?" Bob asked, pointing to the cake.

"I don't give a damn."

Gilliland grabbed the box and flung it out the fifth-floor window.

Bill the Goat, the Navy mascot, was being kept in the courtyard, where he was free to eat his fill of grass as football season approached. But did he eat more than grass? No one could say with any certainty whether the goat ate the rotting cake, but the circumstantial evidence was extremely compelling. The very next day, he mysteriously died.

"They tried to get people to come forward and tell who dumped the cake out there, but nobody ever told," Finnigan said.

The boys closed ranks and kept a lid on their little secret.

Poisoning the school mascot was not a ticket to Bancroft popularity.

According to contemporary news reports, a "temporary" mascot was acquired from a local farmer before the Texas governor Coke Stevenson provided an Angora goat from the Hill Country. Bill X, also known as Chester, in honor of Admiral Chester Nimitz, was escorted to the academy by a Texas Ranger.[1]

As Bill X embraced his new prominence in the goat community, Navy enjoyed one of its greatest football seasons. The year built to a dramatic climax as number-one-ranked Army and number-two-ranked Navy collided in Philadelphia, with the national championship on the line and President Truman in attendance. The game was notable because it was beamed to a small universe of television viewers in the pioneering cities of New York; Philadelphia; and Schenectady, New York, making it the first network telecast of a college football game. Coach Earl "Red" Blaik's Army powerhouse, led by the explosive running tandem of Glenn Davis and Doc Blanchard, won the game, 32–13, to clinch a second straight national title.

The perpetrators of the Molded Cake Caper of 1945 maintained their anonymity until the class convened for its sixtieth reunion in 2009, when Ham entertained the aging Annapolis boys with an elaborate confession.

The story became a defining moment in the academy tenure of Gilliland and his roommates.

"Ham loved to tell that story," Bob said. "I used to tell him, 'Hell, it's better that goat dying from that cake than us.'"

"Any gum chum?"

Seven decades later, the sentence could take Gilliland all the way back to the postwar years, to the day he made his first trip to Scotland. He was stepping off a liberty launch, a small craft that ferried the sailors from their carrier to the shoreline, the first time he heard the question waft through the salty air.

The young boys and girls who saw the Americans in uniform coming ashore near Edinburgh in the summer of 1947 ran to meet them, because they had grown accustomed to their generosity, and the Americans liked to oblige, often buying gum specifically for the purpose of tossing it into tiny outstretched hands. Great Britain and continental Europe were still trying to rebuild from the massive destruction caused by the war. Rationing was still a fact of life.

"You have to remember what it was like in those days," Finnigan said. "The war was just over, and if you were an American serviceman visiting Europe, you were treated like a conquering hero. We inherited the aura of the men who really fought the war."

Like other midshipmen, Gilliland spent three summers cruising on U.S. Navy ships, holding jobs that allowed him to learn what it was like out on the high seas.

Soon after boarding the battleship USS *North Carolina* in the summer of 1946, he and Finnigan were assigned to the bridge, where their first-day job was rather surprising: steering the massive vessel. "We had never been aboard any ship, and here we were controlling the big stick," Gilliland said, recalling the wonder that filled his twenty-one-year-old self. "It was pure happenstance. Both of us thought that was pretty amazing."

He would always remember his first night in a battleship bunk, slipping into a space so tight that he could not turn his shoulder until the guy above him moved out of his.

After dropping the hook and going ashore at Guantanamo Bay in Cuba, they soon moved into the Caribbean for a live-fire exercise. Gilliland was assigned five decks down, manning the magazine section supplying the *North Carolina*'s 16-inch guns. Taking the cue from one of the regular sailors, he learned the routine—lifting three massive shells into a conveyance and pushing a button so the ammo moved up to the rammer man at just the right moment, all while being bombarded by the sound and feeling the jolt of the big guns firing their deadly payload as far as twenty-nine miles into the distance.

"I thought that was a lot of fun," he said. "I liked the action of it, and the pressure of having to keep up [with the demand of the guns]."

Liberties in several different European ports broadened his perspective.

When the USS *Randolph*, one of the new Essex-class carriers, docked in Copenhagen, the sailors started lining up on the pier to change their dollars into krones. Hearing that hotel rooms were in short supply and wanting to get a jump on their shipmates, Bob, Ham, and Mel skipped the conversion cue and sped off to the Hotel d'Angleterre. They had all the currency they needed. On the cruise to Europe, the guys had methodically accumulated a large bankroll—of cigarettes.

One of them carried a little satchel, and when they arrived at one of Europe's finest hotels in a city that had until recently been occupied by the Nazis, a case of cigarettes slipped over the front desk was greeted like a bar of gold. Soon they had a suite.

Later that evening, after meeting some girls, the Naval Academy guys returned to their suite, only to find all of their belongings lined up in the hall. Forced to scramble for a new room, they discovered that they had been evicted because the clerk had given them some VIP's suite, a situation that had been rectified.

The next day, a large group of midshipmen were having lunch at a nice restaurant, when one of the executive officers from the academy stormed through the front door. He did not look happy. As the crowd rose in unison to salute, the officer yelled out, "Which three of you are Gilliland, Davis, and Perkins?"

The boys knew they were in trouble. "Here, sir!"

"You think you are pretty smart, don't you?"

Some problems could not be solved with a carton of smokes.

On September 18, 1947, as Gilliland started his third year at the Naval Academy, President Truman signed a law establishing the U.S. Air Force, previously a division of the U.S. Army, as a separate and distinct branch of the U.S. Armed Forces.

The sibling rivalry among the services quickly intensified, especially with regard to the training of the officer corps. Eventually, the Pentagon, united under a new secretary of defense, decided on a transitional strategy. Until the air force could establish an academy of its own, a small percentage of the graduates from West Point and Annapolis would be given the opportunity to transfer to the air force, helping solve the next-generation officer problem but fueling a certain amount of resentment among the old guard.

At the Naval Academy, the two major gathering places inside Bancroft Hall, the massive dormitory building that housed more than three thousand midshipmen, struck very different tones. Memorial Hall was a holy place. It featured various artifacts commemorating the navy's history of service and sacrifice. It was the sort of room where you felt compelled to whisper. On the opposite end of the rotunda, Smoke Hall was a place where the students could go to relax and even take dates. It featured several pool tables, and midshipmen were allowed to smoke cigars.

On Sunday nights, Smoke Hall often hosted speakers on a variety of subjects. In the spring of 1949, as Gilliland and his friends approached graduation, an officer showed up to explain the option that had been the subject of swirling rumors. The air force would accept a maximum of 6 percent of that year's Naval Academy graduating class, and only about 2 percent would be allowed to go into pilot training. With a graduating class of slightly more than eight hundred, the demand to switch was more than double the supply of available slots, which caused the air force to conduct a lottery.

Not long after the meeting, a midshipman named Tom Nemzek approached Gilliland with a proposition. He was eager to go into the air force and wanted to increase his odds.

"If we go in together and you draw it and I don't, I'll give you a thousand dollars for your envelope," Nemzek said.

Gilliland wasn't sure Nemzek could put his hands on a thousand bucks, which was a ton of money in 1949. But it didn't matter. He told Nemzek he would give him the envelope for free. "That was a very stupid thing for me to do," he said. "I should have been smarter than that."

While ambivalent about the choice, Bob knew he wanted to become a pilot. The navy's tradition of sending all Naval Academy graduates to sea for a year before they were allowed to become aviators frustrated him, and there was no guarantee he would ever wind up in flight training in Pensacola, especially with all the services downsizing to meet a postwar footing. He decided he was willing to take his chances with the new air force. Except that he had promised his envelope to the other man if . . .

When the appointed time arrived, the long line of contenders for those few precious slots walked into stately Memorial Hall. Each midshipman carefully retrieved an unmarked envelope from a table, as if they were contestants on a high-stakes game show. To Bob's astonishment, both he and Nemzek drew air force invitations.

Thus, Gilliland's life veered off into the wild blue yonder, toward a series of adventures shaped quite literally by the luck of the draw.

In the years between the wars, Frank Gilliland's work with the American Legion and other military support groups often took him to Millington Naval Base, located north of Memphis. Among the officers he met was Felix Stump, a gregarious West Virginian who would eventually become a highly decorated admiral and one of the most powerful figures in the U.S. Navy.

One point of connection between the two veterans of World War I was their shared disdain for golf. "They both agreed that they liked each other right away because they both believed anybody who would go out and waste his time playing golf was a moron," Bob said.

Whenever an admiral visited Annapolis, the sound of a ceremonial canon burst rumbled throughout the academy. This was a Naval Academy tradition, and in the late 1940s, the sound often signified the arrival of Admiral Stump, who commanded the Atlantic fleet, based out of Norfolk, Virginia.

Stump was a good friend to have.

The spring of 1949 was a happy time around the Gilliland family. Not only was Bob graduating from the Naval Academy, but his younger brother Frank Jr. was earning his bachelor's degree from Vanderbilt. Jim was at the top of his class at Webb School, fully invested in the family tradition of high achievement.

Because the two graduation ceremonies were scheduled at nearly the same time, it was decided that Elizabeth would head to Nashville to celebrate with Frank Jr. and Frank would drive to Annapolis to watch Bob throw his cap into the air. But the plan hit a snag. Frank had recently bought a new Cadillac, and several days before he was scheduled to depart from Memphis, he encountered a slick patch on the road near Nashville and skidded into a ditch. He was lucky, but the accident resulted in an injury that temporarily confined him to a wheelchair. Frank was planning to join Admiral Stump in Annapolis, but after the crash, he reluctantly called his friend to tell him that under the circumstances, he would not be able to make the ceremony.

Stump then stepped in to save the day, arranging to fly Frank to Annapolis in his plane. Problem solved.

Neither man knew Bob was in danger of not graduating.

Just beyond the wall of the Naval Academy stood Carvel Hall, a sprawling two-story hotel with roots that stretched back before the American Revolution. It was popular with parents and dignitaries, and midshipmen were allowed to visit, as long as they did not go upstairs. "It was understood by all of us that the second floor was off limits," McVoy said.

In defiance of this rule, a group of midshipman surreptitiously booked a suite in the spring of 1949, invited some girls, and had a party. Gilliland was not in on the planning, but he was well liked among the organizers, who asked him to stop by their little shindig, urging him to tell no one. Bob didn't like to miss a good party, especially if there were going to be some pretty girls in attendance.

Not long after he arrived, Gilliland heard a knock on the door. Wearing a T-shirt and drinking a beer, he casually walked over to open the door and was confronted by the stern face of the officer of the day, who was trailed by his messenger holding the dreaded notebook. Bob was caught, and when he looked around the room, he suddenly realized he was all alone. The other partiers had scattered, apparently tipped off by a lookout.

Called into the office of the commandant, Captain Frank Ward, Gilliland was fortunate that the second-ranking official at the Naval Academy was an old friend of Admiral Stump's. This fact may have influenced his survival.

After being cited with a class A offense, which resulted in a large number of demerits, Gilliland was skating on very thin ice. In time, he would speculate, with a measure of pride, that he may have graduated with more demerits than anyone in the history of the Naval Academy. He was certainly in the running for this dubious distinction, along with future U.S. senator John McCain.

"Bob was in serious jeopardy of getting thrown out if anything else happened," McVoy said.

Several days before graduation, McVoy was passing through the rotunda when he saw Bob holding a regulation book, which meant he was going on watch. He was muttering to himself and seemed agitated.

"What's wrong, Bob?"

"That damn Cathode Law!"

Jim knew his friend was referring to a particularly despised officer, R. R. Law, who was so gloomy many called him Cathode behind his back, like a negatively charged electrode.

"What did he do?"

"He put me on report."

"For what?"

"For wearing an officer's cap color for inspection."

"Well, were you wearing the wrong color?"

"Yeah, but that was no reason to put me on report."

McVoy's mind raced. The two friends had big plans, and he was afraid Bob's latest brush with the authorities might just ruin everything.

As he walked off to assume his post, McVoy told his buddy, "For God's sake, stay out of trouble."

After passing his exams and somehow making it to graduation without committing another serious offense, Gilliland graduated with his class, without Frank finding out about the Carvel Hall incident. With his father watching from his wheelchair, understandably proud of his boy, Bob was commissioned a second lieutenant in the U.S. Air Force.

Soon Bob would be heading off to flight training in Texas. But for the next thirty days, he was on leave, and he and McVoy were headed for Europe for some much-needed rest and relaxation.

Their trip was delayed by three days when Frank insisted the new graduates join him at Admiral Stump's house in Norfolk. Neither man knew quite how to say no to the admiral. So they ate some steaks and drank some whiskey and generally had a good time listening to the admiral's stories.

"Admiral Stump was really a great guy," Gilliland said. "He was very gracious."

At one point, Bob pulled Jim aside. "The admiral likes you," he said. "Since you're staying in the navy, he could be a great help in your career."

When Stump discovered that he had scrambled their plans, he seemed genuinely sorry and said he wanted to help get them on their way. Since they needed to somehow make it to an air base in Chicopee, Massachusetts, where they could get a seat on a military plane headed to Europe, the admiral made arrangements to inspect a base in Rhode Island. Then

Bob and Jim could take a bus the rest of the way. It was all scheduled to commence the following morning.

However, through some sort of miscommunication, the admiral's aide failed to pick up McVoy at the agreed time. He kept looking at his watch. Eventually, Jim realized he needed to give up on the ride and start walking. Soon the walk turned into a spirited run, all the way from the bachelor officers' quarters to the airstrip.

The DC-3's big propellers were turning by the time he dropped his bag, snapped a salute, and started apologizing, while sweating through his uniform.

Stump flashed an irritated look. "If you're going to be in naval aviation, you can't carry on like this!"

On the plane ride, Bob smoothed things over with the admiral, and when they landed in Rhode Island and said their goodbyes, Stump understood that McVoy's tardiness was the fault of his lieutenant.

After checking in at Westover Field and putting their names on a list, it took two days for Bob and Jim to get a seat on a flight to Europe on the Military Air Transport System, which operated a regular schedule for members of the U.S. Armed Forces and dependents. (More than a half century later, in April 2000, Bob happened to be back in the area and sent his old friend, then a retired navy captain, a postcard celebrating the base. "While browsing I saw this card; you are the only one in the world for whom this is appropriate as coming from me!")[2] Their trip happened to coincide with a goodwill tour featuring several prominent actors and actresses, and in the crush of VIPs waiting for seats, the men from Annapolis were separated.

When his name was finally called, Gilliland was waved onto the tarmac and onto a waiting C-54 Skymaster, the military version of the DC-4.

Stepping into the crowded cabin, Gilliland looked around

and told an enlisted man holding a clipboard, "It looks like you've miscounted."

"No, sir. I didn't miscount."

As the pilots prepared for takeoff, he led Bob to the only empty seat in the plane, next to a pretty young lady who turned out to be the actress June Lockhart, who was well on her way to a long career in movies and television. They were the same age. She was traveling with her father, the actor Gene Lockhart.

"I thought you would be sitting with your father," Bob said.

"Oh no. He's the last one I want to sit by."

They shared a knowing laugh.

It was the middle of the night when the plane landed in the Azores. They all disembarked and walked into a terminal building, where the big attraction was a bank of slot machines.

When Bob finally made it to Copenhagen the next day, he was two days ahead of Jim, who wound up crossing the Atlantic surrounded by screaming children. They spent some time getting better acquainted with a couple of young ladies they had met on a previous trip to the continent, eventually rendezvoused at a predetermined hotel (because they had no way of contacting each other), soaked up the sights, ate some tasty food, drank some good wine, danced in some swanky nightclubs, and took the opportunity to truly relax after four grueling years in Annapolis.

"Bob really wanted to see Berlin," McVoy said. "He kept talking about it, even as our time started running low. I kept saying, 'How in the world are you going to get to Berlin?'"

When Jim was forced to start heading back to the United States, because he had been given a shorter period of leave, Bob was determined to make the most of his vacation. He traveled from Denmark to Germany, working the military transport system, and started trying to maneuver his way to the divided city.

World War II had been over for four years, but a different

sort of conflict was gathering steam. Since the Soviet Union blocked highway and rail access to West Berlin in the summer of 1948, the United States, Great Britain, and other allied countries had been engaged in a massive effort to resupply the free side of the city by air. It was one of the greatest logistical challenges in the history of the world. Over a fifteen-month period, more than 2.3 million tons of cargo would be transported by crews operating around the clock while dealing with Soviet fighters that sometimes pursued and harassed them. No one knew what might happen if the Russians ever shot one of the planes out of the sky.

Attracted to the glamour of air travel, even amid a mission fraught with such tension, many West Germany families entertained themselves by lining up in their cars to watch the planes take off and land.

The need for pilots was so severe that the U.S. Air Force started calling World War II veterans back into service, including Norman Gaddis, who interrupted his premed studies at the University of Tennessee. Gaddis flew several escort missions and eventually wound up as the copilot of a c-47 that took off from Tempelhof Air Base loaded with supplies, including potato sacks filled with coal.

"It was quite an operation," Gaddis recalled. "I don't think there's any doubt, an awful lot of people in Berlin would have starved to death or frozen to death if it had not been for that massive response to Soviet aggression."

This was something Gilliland wanted to see for himself.

After making his way to a British air base, Bob talked his way into a room where several pilots were playing cards. He waited for them to reach a stopping point before asking, "Could anybody here tell me how I can get a ride into Berlin?"

One of the British officers turned to him, shoved his low-hanging cap back over the top of his head, and said, "Why do you want to know?"

"I'd just like to go."

The man sized up the young American and finally said, "I guess you could see me."

"That's great. When are you going to go?"

"I'm going in about an hour and a half."

About an hour and a half later, Gilliland stepped into a Douglas C-47, better known as a Gooney Bird, becoming a passenger on a flight in the Berlin Airlift. The plane was loaded with coal, and the soot got all over his uniform and stung his eyes and throat.

Looking out over the onetime Nazi capital gave him a surreal feeling, especially knowing that the West was now engaged in a struggle with a new enemy, with Berlin as a dividing line and a symbol.

This was his first exposure to the Cold War. It would not be his last.

THREE

Taking Flight

GILLILAND DID NOT FULLY APPRECIATE IT AT THE TIME, but the same system that had tried to mash his "fiercely independent" streak into submission was now prepared to exploit and reward this defining characteristic. Certainly, he was seduced by the mystique of the fighter pilot, the thrill of competition, the rush of speed, the danger. But perhaps more than anything else, he was attracted to the job because "everything was all on your shoulders, the pressure to perform, the pressure to make all these decisions very quickly."

As General Norman Gaddis, who was to become his lifelong friend, explained, "Those of us who wanted to become fighter pilots wanted all that control and responsibility and were not bothered by the hazards."

After returning from Europe in the summer of 1949, Gilliland reported to flight school at Randolph Field near San Antonio, Texas. Because the newest West Point graduates had been granted sixty days' leave, twice that of their Annapolis colleagues, the program would not officially start for another month, when the service academy graduates would be joined by other volunteers who needed to earn their wings to be commissioned.

"During those first thirty days, they were looking for stuff to keep us busy," he said.

Several of the Naval Academy boys were shipped off to Dallas and given a ride in a B-36, the largest piston-driven bomber ever mass-produced. The plane's tremendous wingspan (which stretched 230 feet) and range (10,000 miles) made it one of the most potent weapons in the U.S. Air Force arsenal at the start of the Cold War, when it was prepared to deliver nuclear payloads.

Carefully studying the plane, Bob took note of its enormous wheels. "When the thing got airborne," he recalled, "it shifted as it accelerated, and it took almost an hour before the wheels finally stopped spinning."

As the B-36 roared into the clear blue skies above North Texas, the pilot demonstrated several simple techniques and eventually motioned for Gilliland. "Here," he said. "You make that turn."

Bob took the yoke and tried to do exactly what the pilot had just shown him, banking the craft slowly to the right.

"That was the first time I ever had the controls," he said.

Gilliland was not the type of man to make a big deal about such things, and he would recall his first opportunity to take the yoke and guide the massive machine through the air as rather unmemorable. He did not feel anything special stir inside him. It was just a piece of metal attached to another piece of metal, and he followed the man's instruction to complete a routine mechanical task. "I wanted to be a fighter pilot, and this thing was so big and ponderous," he said. It was just a first step, the first of many on the way to a future he could not yet imagine.

Around this time, the air force asked for volunteers from the onetime midshipmen to go up as passengers in a C-47. They were trying to develop a new airsickness pill and needed some warm bodies to help with the experiment.

"I never get carsick, seasick, or airsick," Bob assured his superiors, as he signed up alongside his Annapolis buddy Pat Murphy.

The ride was bumpy as the pilot of the Gooney Bird went looking for rough air, but Gilliland and Murphy managed to keep their lunch down, even as many of the Naval Academy men started filling the cabin with the acrid smell of vomit.

Soon after the official program started at Randolph, Gilliland began training in a T-6 Texan, a two-seater built by North American Aviation, the same company behind the P-51 Mustang, one of the fighters that helped win World War II. His instructor was the same officer who had previously tutored Doc Blanchard, the 1945 Heisman Trophy winner from West Point, on his path to air force fighter pilot. The instructor emphasized three-point landings, in which the main landing gear and the tail gear touched down at the same time, which could only be accomplished from approaching in a "three-point attitude," but Gilliland resisted this level of micromanagement.

He quickly discovered that the biggest challenge in learning to fly the T-6 was avoiding what the pilots called "ground looping," or losing control so that it swirled around, causing one wing to drag. "I knew they would never wash anybody out that had never ground looped one, so I was awful careful not to let that happen," he said. "I didn't care so much about the three-point landings."

At first, his instructor sat in the back seat, showing him how to take off, level, turn, ascend, descend, and land. So much of it was a matter of touch, and from the start, Bob displayed a deft hand on the controls. He was precise and smooth, and most of it seemed very natural. One day, after landing, the instructor climbed out of the back seat and told his student it was time to solo. Soon he was back in the air, all alone, one man among the many who filled the skies above Randolph with aspiration and audacity.

Not long after this, his dream started slipping away.

Bob was disheartened to learn that the air force had instituted a rule: no fighter pilots over six feet tall. The cockpits in the one-man crafts were especially tight, and someone at the Pentagon had determined that no aviator above this height could comfortably fly in such cramped conditions. The six-foot-three Gilliland was disqualified for fighters and assigned to the multiengine program at Enid, Oklahoma, where he would learn to fly B-25 bombers.

He admired heroic figures like Jimmy Doolittle, who led the B-25s that bombed Tokyo four months after Pearl Harbor, and he understood the vital role played by the B-17 and B-24 squadrons in winning the war against Hitler. But for a hard-charging young man looking for adventure and independence, the thought of commanding a crew of six in a large plane that thundered along at such a plodding speed, with the sort of maneuverability that more closely resembled a big battleship, seemed rather dull. He wanted to fly a high-performance aircraft, something that zoomed, and besides, he knew himself well enough to understand that he was better suited to single-engine airplanes, where he could turn his need for control and self-reliance into an asset.

Most second lieutenants straight out of Annapolis would have accepted the disappointment and the assignment, but Gilliland was not the type to concede defeat without a struggle. There was a fighter pilot inside him trying to get out, and he had no doubt he could fit his lanky body into the allotted space. The same man who once got a U.S. senator on the telephone and sold his way out of the fleet was now determined to work the system to overcome an arbitrary standard.

"I was always wrangling to try to do different things," he explained. "I did that all my life."

After paying a visit to the flight surgeon, who was unable to help, he changed out of the flight suit he wore every day, put on his dress uniform, and headed for the commanding officer's house on a Saturday night. When he knocked on the door, Colonel Strickland answered, shook his hand, and said, "Come on in, Lieutenant." He could see a crowd of people in the house and suddenly realized the colonel thought he was just another junior officer who had been asked to his home.

"Sir, I'm not invited to the party, and I hope I'm not disturbing you," Gilliland said. "But I wish I could have your attention for about two minutes."

The welcoming smile on the colonel's face faded, and he told the lieutenant to wait on the darkened porch. A few minutes later, he returned. "What's this all about?"

Gilliland got right to the point, explaining that he was a graduate of the Naval Academy, that he had been assigned to bombers, that he had a colleague from Annapolis who had been assigned to fighters, and that the two of them wanted to trade orders.

"Sir, I was hoping you might consider letting us switch."

The colonel asked a few more questions and finally said, "Come by my office Monday morning at eight o'clock. I'll look into it."

When the appointed time arrived, Bob was already waiting in the office, and when he was finally ushered in to see the boss, Strickland was talking over the situation with a lieutenant colonel. After some pleasantries, he said, "I think we'll be able to oblige your request."

A feeling of relief swept over Gilliland, who would always believe his Naval Academy pedigree played a significant role in the colonel's willingness to bend the rules. "There was a real prestige to [graduating from Annapolis], especially at that time when the air force was just starting out on its own."

The full impact of this turn of events would not be understood for many years, but like the phone call with Senator McKellar and the lucky envelope, Gilliland's decision to petition the colonel and Strickland's willingness to approve the exception pushed his life toward a very different reality. It was another critical perquisite in a career repeatedly blessed by fortune and timing. It was another pivotal step toward his shadowy future.

The paperwork required to cut through the bureaucracy needed to be typed, and after Strickland issued the order, Gilliland eventually wound up in front of a female clerk.

"How many orders do you need?"

Bob thought for a moment and finally said, "Fifty."

The clerk flashed an incredulous look. "Fifty! I never heard of anybody wanting that many."

Bob didn't flinch. "I want fifty."

In this age before copy machines, Gilliland knew enough about military protocol to understand that he and his friend would be required to provide their new orders at various stops along the way. He wanted to be certain they did not run out, so he waited impatiently while the young lady methodically typed fifty copies of the same document on a manual typewriter, filling the room with the rhythmic sound of pounding keys and margin bells.

The young pilot trainee owned a used Ford convertible, which he had purchased after returning from Europe. His affluent father was not the type to give him a new automobile as a graduation present. "He believed I should earn the money and buy my own damn car, which is what I did," he said. With no time to waste, he loaded up the Ford and headed for Williams Air Base in Chandler, Arizona, where he arrived just in time for the birth of the jet age.

The evolution toward jet-propelled planes stretched back to the 1930s and involved manufacturers in several countries—including Bell Aircraft's twin-engine P-59 Airacomet, which never advanced beyond the experimental stage—but the German Luftwaffe changed the game forever by introducing the Messerschmitt ME 262, the first operational jet fighter, toward the end of World War II. The ME 262 was a technological marvel but arrived too late to affect the outcome of the war.

Hustling to catch up, the United States countered with the P-80 Shooting Star in 1945, even as the military dealt with the vagaries of budget cuts, personnel reductions, and a political establishment that proved slow to recognize the hardware that would be required to compete against the various strategic threats posed by the Soviet Union.

For several months in 1950, Gilliland trained on a T-33, a two-seat version of the P-80. The combat-ready P-80 could achieve a maximum speed of 558 miles per hour, nearly 50 percent faster than the best propeller-driven fighters of the day. But the transition from propellers to jets was turbulent, and Gilliland was on the leading wave of an aviation revolution that would sustain hundreds of casualties before the technology could be perfected.

"The engines were so weak we couldn't fly past noon [when the hot weather arrived], because you lost so much thrust," he recalled.

But his closest call while stationed at Williams happened when he was on a weekend liberty, on a dark desert highway headed for Las Vegas.

Behind the wheel of his Ford, with his buddy Bob Wischerd, formerly a star wrestler in Annapolis, sleeping in the back seat, Gilliland saw a pair of bright lights heading his way. It was late, approaching 2:00 a.m., and while traversing the desolate two-lane road, he hadn't encountered another car for many miles.

He clicked the button with his left foot, cutting his high beams.

They were passing through open-range country, and while speeding along at about 70 miles per hour, Gilliland knew he needed to keep a sharp eye out for cows.

When the other car failed to reciprocate, he clicked the high beams back on and suddenly could see a cow standing on his side of the road, dead ahead.

"I had to make a really quick decision: slam on the brakes

and hit the cow at 45 to 50 miles per hour or try to avoid him and then maybe risk losing control," Gilliland recalled.

Like many of the choices that would confront him in the skies in the years to come, he calculated the odds in the blink of an eye and acted decisively, swerving to the left, grazing the cow, and dodging the oncoming car. Wischerd woke up in midair, as the Ford took flight and careened off the side of the road.

After making sure his friend was unharmed, Gilliland looked down to see gasoline leaking onto the ground. "We better jump out of here before it catches fire!"

In the distance, the academy men could see a pair of lights piercing the darkness. It was the car they had just passed, turning around and heading their way.

The convertible approached slowly. Standing in the middle of the road, they could make out the shadowy figures of a man and a woman.

"Anybody get hurt?" the man asked.

Gilliland shook his head. "No. We were lucky."

The man noticed a nasty gash on Gilliland's right elbow. "Hey, you're bleeding!"

"Ah, that's nothing," said Bob, who was starting to understand how close he and Wischerd had come to being seriously injured.

The couple wanted to help. They drove the stranded aviators to the next town as Gilliland held his wound aloft, wrapped in a bloody handkerchief, which flapped in the breeze. The Good Samaritans dropped Wischerd off at a hotel and took Gilliland farther into the night to find medical treatment. A nurse bandaged the wound, advised him to get stitches the next day, and directed him to an old hotel down the street.

"I was really exhausted and needed some sleep," Gilliland said.

It was after 3:00 a.m. when he checked into the hotel. But he found out that the next bus for Las Vegas left at 6:00, and he was determined to be on it. He didn't want a little gash in his arm to mess up his weekend with the guys.

"I'd like to get a wake-up call," he told the desk clerk, who had stumbled out of his own bed to rent the room.

"Sorry, we don't do that."

Gilliland took the room anyway. But as he headed down the hall, he wondered, How am I going to wake up in time to make that bus?

On the way to his room, he noticed a partially open door. He peaked in and saw a man sleeping. More importantly, he noticed an alarm clock on the nightstand. Quietly, he tiptoed into the room, snatched the clock, took it to his room, and set it for 5:45. Then he drifted off to sleep.

"When that alarm woke me up and I started out, I just slipped the clock inside that man's door," Gilliland said. "He never knew I had borrowed it."

After a short bus ride, Gilliland arrived in Las Vegas, which was still a sleepy little gambling oasis, not quite the Sin City of the fast-approaching Rat Pack age.

Bob rendezvoused with his friends at the Nellis Air Force Base, checked in to a room at the bachelor officers' quarters, and made his way over to the base hospital, where a doctor tended to his bloody elbow. For some reason, they were temporarily out of anesthesia, so the nurse gave him a towel, which he stuck between his gritted teeth as the doctor sewed up the wound. Then he went off to have a fun weekend.

"I guess you could say my first trip to Las Vegas was pretty eventful," he said.

Several weeks later, near the end of his training at Williams, Gilliland sprained his ankle, causing him to miss the last requirement for his graduation: night flying. He graduated anyway, as part of class 50D.

When he was not flying off into the morning sun, Gilliland often could be found on the golf course with his friend Jimmy Hartinger, who would one day become a highly decorated four-star general. (Among other assignments, Hartinger ran the North American Aerospace Defense Command during the Reagan era.)

When their orders were posted, Hartinger rushed to break the news. Both were being shipped off to Germany, as they requested, but while Hartinger was assigned to the 36th Fighter-Bomber Wing at Fürstenfeldbruck Air Base, Gilliland was attached to the 86th Fighter-Bomber Wing at Neubiberg Air Base.

Bob knew what this meant.

At Fürstenfeldbruck, the pilots were flying the new F-84 Thunderjets, the cutting edge of U.S. aircraft technology.

At Neubiberg, they were still flying P-47s, relics from the fast-fading propeller age.

"The P-47? That's ancient history," he grumbled.

Several weeks later, Gilliland and the recently married Hartinger lined up on a ramp to board a troopship in New York Harbor, surrounded by soldiers in full combat gear carrying rifles. Hartinger leaned over to his much-taller friend and said, "This is a little embarrassing." The pilots were carrying golf bags.

This scene played to the stereotype of the glamorous flyboys in their perfectly tailored blue suits who were able to maintain a certain distance from the blood and guts of war.

But they were all headed to a dangerous place, where the only thing deterring Communist aggression was the power of U.S. might and will. By the time Gilliland arrived in West Germany in the summer of 1950, the Soviet Union had consolidated its domination over Eastern Europe and exploded its first atomic bombs, casting an ominous shadow over the free nations west of the Iron Curtain.

"There was a real uneasy feeling in the air," recalled fighter pilot Joe Kittinger. "We lived with the knowledge that, at any time, the Russians might decide to cross the [West German] border and start World War III."

The 86th Fighter-Bomber Wing had been flying P-47s for several years, but the Thunderbolt was fast becoming obsolete. It posed various challenges, including producing a tremendous amount of torque on takeoff, which required just the right touch on the rudder to keep it from veering off the runway.

Not long after he arrived in Neubiberg, a onetime Luftwaffe base located near Munich, fighter pilot Ken Solomon saw a tall man jogging around the base.

"Who's that?" he asked one of his colleagues.

The response was telling. "That's the guy from Annapolis."

Gilliland's Naval Academy background quickly emerged as a big part of his identity in a crowd where it represented a mark of distinction.

About three months after Bob was assigned to Neubiberg, the wing upgraded to a fleet of F-84Es. To accommodate the jets, the military expanded the runway to six thousand feet, which required convincing the West German government to reroute a stretch of the nearby autobahn.

Manufactured by Republic Aviation, the F-84 was a significant improvement over the P-80 (known in USAF nomenclature as the F-80) in several critical areas, including speed (600 miles per hour) and service ceiling (45,000 feet). But the Thunderjet experienced a long list of problems and was very nearly canceled before it became operational. Most of the issues were solved by the time the E models reached Neubiberg, but the J35 Allison engines were often defective.

"We had an awful record with those first jets," said pilot Solomon, assigned to the 527th, one of three squadrons working out of Neubiberg. "We had all of these mechanical problems we had to contend with. It was a wicked first two or three years, just trying to stay alive and learn how to fly those planes."

The turbine blades from that particular generation of Allison engines had a tendency to fly off, causing a sudden power failure, often right after takeoff, when the pilots were most vulnerable. Sometimes the blades fell away from the front of the plane harmlessly, and sometimes they punctured the adjacent forward fuselage tank, which threw massive amounts of raw fuel onto the compressor section.

"If that happened, you had a flying torch," Solomon said.

The frequent crashes related to the engine malfunction, which the aviators cynically called the "Allison time bomb," led to a steady and somber procession of funerals. Whenever a pilot perished, the U.S. Air Force renamed one of the surrounding streets in his honor. They eventually ran out of streets.

"We lost some good pilots," said Norman Gaddis, a member of the 525th. "We would have an incident, and they would stop the flying for a few days, trying to get to the bottom of the situation."

The plane also developed a canopy issue. In the frigid air above 40,000 feet, many shattered, wiping out the attached radio antenna. Some pilots reached the end of the line forced to choose between freezing to death or descending to a lower altitude and running out of gas.

Several F-84s vanished over the Mediterranean. Several others crashed while dealing with inclement weather over Germany.

Beyond the love of flying and patriotism that united them all, the pilots who worked out of Neubiberg and similar bases across the globe in those days were putting their lives on the line even before they ventured into combat.

"We were too busy doing our jobs to think about the risks," Gilliland said. "If you started thinking about [the possibility of death] there was no way you could operate effectively. That kind of guy couldn't make it in that world."

It took a special breed of man to become a fighter pilot, especially at a time when the technology remained unproven.

The same swagger that pushed them into the air fortified them with a feeling of invincibility, even when something went wrong. It was more than the sense of calm all the good ones were able to summon when faced with a potential disaster. It was also the raging self-confidence, which was such a defining strength that it sometimes flipped to weakness.

"Too much ego got a lot of guys killed," Gilliland said. "There were guys who had so much faith in themselves that they refused to bail out, until it was too late."

Any pilot worth his pay believed he could always find a way out of trouble.

Many years before he circumnavigated the moon in *Apollo 8* and commanded a team that averted disaster in *Apollo 13*, Jim Lovell was a young naval aviator flying Banshee fighters. The navy was just starting to experiment with carrier-based night flying, and on his first mission into the darkness, the weather turned bad. His radio frequency beacon system had been set incorrectly, which left him lost and running low on fuel over the Sea of Japan. To make matters worse, he suddenly blew a fuse and lost all the lights in the cabin, including those illuminating his instrument panel.

"Suddenly I was completely in the dark," Lovell recalled.

Working the problem, he fumbled around for a penlight, which was stuffed into a pocket of his flight suit. He placed it between his teeth and started manipulating it to read his instruments. Ultimately, however, the darkness saved him.

When he turned off the light to see if he could discern any signs of the carrier in the distance, he looked down and saw a green glow shimmering across the water.

"There was this long trail of algae . . . which I knew was churned up by the screws of a large ship . . . and it led me home."

Some of the men in Neubiberg had already been tested by emergency situations, including Lou Schalk, who would one day become an important figure in Gilliland's story.

During a live-fire exercise through a range with rocky terrain, the oil line in Schalk's P-47 was severed by a ricocheting bullet from his own gun. The plane caught fire, and the pilot knew he needed to bail out. After ascending to a sufficient altitude, he pulled back the canopy and began his escape but lost his footing because of all the spewing oil and slammed into the tail. The collision knocked him out cold but also activated his parachute, pulling him out of danger. He woke up in the hospital with a back injury and a broken arm, very lucky to have survived.

Remarking on the scare many years later, he said matter-of-factly, "I shot myself down."[1]

Thirty days later, he was back in the air.

All too aware of these sorts of close calls, which infused their bull sessions at the officers' club or in the squad room with a certain dramatic texture, Gilliland never suffered a catastrophic failure at Neubiberg. The air force eventually solved the engine and canopy problems as he dedicated himself to learning every aspect of the F-84—what it could do and what it could not do. He was starting to understand the power of gravity forces and how they impacted the tolerances of his craft. "If you tried to dive with it and got it going too fast, it could suddenly snap on you and break off the tail or the wing. Everybody was conscious of that." Such a condition was often fatal, at least until they perfected the ejection system.

Gilliland demonstrated his skills in the combat exercises known as "rat races" and developed a reputation for professionalism, unflappability, and ingenuity.

"Bob was one of the most brilliant guys I've ever known," Kittinger said. "He had a tremendous intellect, and he was also the sort of pilot who was very focused on being really good."

Several months into his European tour, the squadron deployed to a tent base in the Libyan Desert for gunnery training. Over the Mediterranean, pilots took turns firing at a canvas banner, called a rag, towed by a B-25.

Each F-84 featured six .50-caliber machine guns, but for the gunnery competitions, only two were active, one on each side. Each pilot's ammunition was dipped in a different color of dye so the judges could differentiate among the competitors, who took turns lining up and firing.

"You only had a limited amount of ammo in there, so you needed to use those bullets wisely," Gilliland said.

At the end of the final competition, the commanders sprawled the massive canvass rag across the ground and pronounced Gilliland the big winner, with the highest score in the entire wing, which significantly enhanced his reputation among the relatively small fighter pilot community.

The intense rivalry among the pilots and the squadrons fueled an atmosphere that pushed every man to push himself. They all were thrill junkies who embraced the adventure of flying off into the winds and competing with each other, performing the sort of maneuvers that had been impossible with conventional planes.

"We all loved what we were doing," Kittinger said. "We were young guys getting to live out our dreams."

They also understood they were living in perilous times, especially after the North Koreans began pouring south across the thirty-eighth parallel, launching the first shooting conflict of the Cold War age.

Just before he caught his troopship to Germany, Gilliland had stopped by to see Admiral Stump. He would always remember watching a newsreel about the invasion at the admiral's house. Those flickering images from a movie projector were his first glimpses of the Korean War.

When President Truman decided to intervene on the Korean peninsula, the Pentagon was determined to keep many of its best pilots in Europe, realizing that any meaningful transfer of forces would be interpreted as a sign of weakness by Moscow. While units, including the 86th, continued to train, vast numbers of relatively inexperienced pilots fresh from the service academies and the National Guard died over the skies of Korea. In the rush to prevent the fall of the U.S.-backed South Korean government, especially after the Chinese Communists joined the war, many F-84 pilots were sent into action with as few as thirty hours in a jet. To the guys at Neubiberg, this sounded like a suicide mission. "I wouldn't have liked those kind of odds," Bob said.

Like Gilliland, most of the cocky young pilots at Neubiberg were eager to be shipped off to Korea, reflecting a raging intensity and desire for action that often spilled over into their off-hours. The competitive tone was set by one wing commander of the era, a veteran of World War II, who insisted that all his pilots show up at the officers' club every Friday afternoon at 4:00 p.m., where they were expected to drink heavily and challenge each other to bar fights. The sessions usually lasted until the wee hours of the morning, often punctuated by the sight of the drunk colonel climbing onto the bar and declaring himself "the world's greatest fighter pilot" and daring anyone to argue with his proclamation.

"It was a pretty wild scene, but you knew you'd better have your butt there or you would hear about it," recalled the mild-mannered Gaddis. "And I resented that very much."

One night, a new pilot from Texas walked up to the bar and ordered a drink. He stood at least six feet four and was well built, with especially large hands.

The colonel, already deep into his nightly poison, walked up to the young captain, began asking him questions about his background and qualifications, and soon learned that he didn't have a fighter pilot background. "This is a man's bar!" he thundered. "Get your ass out of this bar!"

The new man looked the colonel square in the eye and said, "I paid my dues like everybody else. Nobody is going to order me out of this club, including you."

The much shorter commander walked away and never challenged him again.

The colonel was eventually reassigned stateside, and Gaddis was not surprised to hear that a much bigger pilot had "beaten the hell out of him" during an officers' club brawl.

Gilliland was the sort of man who would come in for a drink or two and enjoyed the camaraderie with the guys, but he took great pains to avoid what Solomon called "the craziness." He was as driven as the next man but in a restrained sort of way, dripping with impeccable manners and a southern charm, striking all who knew him as likable and always interested in learning about people, places, and things.

"I admired Bob," Gaddis said. "He had a very warm personality. He would talk to anybody and treated the crew the same way he did the commanding officer. He was very serious about his work but didn't take himself too seriously."

One of the wing commanders during his tenure, Colonel John S. Chennault, son of Claire Chennault of the famed World War II Flying Tigers squadron, was not the sort to start bar fights.

One day, Chennault, who was hard of hearing, called the 526th squadron office, looking for a copilot on a Gooney Bird. When the assistant operations officer checked around and learned that none of his pilots had ever flown a C-47, the commander insisted, "I don't give a damn who it is, whether he's qualified or not." He just wanted to make sure he had another pilot with him, in case he needed to step away from the controls to "take a leak." This is how the second lieutenant from Tennessee, who had never piloted a Gooney Bird, wound up spending the day in the cockpit with Chennault, flying first to Rhein-Main Air Base near Frankfort and then on to Templehof Air Base in Berlin, where they dined at the home of the commander.

"The thing I remember most about that day was how Colonel Chennault was complaining that [the U.S. Air Force] was getting ready to cut back on the flight pay," Gilliland said.

During this period, Gilliland became friendly with his

brother, fellow pilot Claire Patrick Chennault. Bob could not help noticing his significant limp and wondering how he had ever made it into the service with such an infirmity.

"Pat, I guess your dad helped you pass the physical?" he once asked.

Captain Chennault flashed an irritated look. "No. He didn't have a damn thing to do with it!"

Not all handicaps were so clearly visible.

The transition to jets was a major inflection point in the history of the U.S. military. Faster planes, able to achieve higher altitudes, sustain better performance, and carry more potent and sophisticated weapons, represented a generational leap forward, forcing the Pentagon to rethink strategies and alter tactics to fit the capabilities of the modern hardware.

"When the jets came along, you had to think faster and react faster," said Gaddis, one of the pilots who successfully negotiated the bridge between two eras, progressing from a P-51 to an F-84 in three years. "Things were moving very quickly, and you had much less time to make a decision."

Some aviators who had compiled stellar combat records during World War II proved incapable of making the transition. They were good men who had done their duty, but they represented the past. Like the propeller-driven fighters, they were soon discarded, paving the way for a new generation of pilots who could handle the various requirements of the new technology.

Gilliland was a man of the jet age. He thought fast, and he made quick decisions. He took the time to learn every little detail about the machine he was flying. He was able to leverage the same sort of resourcefulness that once saved Jim Lovell. He was as fearless as Lou Schalk. These were not just qualities that made him good. These attributes and various others kept him alive.

Before he shipped out to Germany, Gilliland told his mother he would be stationed overseas for two years. When he volunteered for a tour of duty in Korea, he sat down and carefully crafted a letter to her, attributing the delay in his return to the states on "the exigencies of the service." She was not happy, especially when she learned that her boy soon would be heading off to war. Without his knowledge, she started writing letters up the chain of command.

Some weeks later, Bob was called into the office of the new wing commander, Colonel George B. Simler, a onetime football player at Maryland who would enjoy a distinguished career in the U.S. Air Force, eventually rising to the rank of lieutenant general.

Not knowing why he had been called in front of the commanding officer, Bob stood at attention and happened to look down on his desk, where he saw a letter with a familiar handwriting. He could not read it, but he would have recognized that distinctive script anywhere.

As Simler smiled at him, clearly relishing the moment, Gilliland launched a preemptive strike. After all, he was a man who thought fast and made quick decisions, so before the colonel could get into the matter, he said, "Sir, I don't care what's in that letter. I'll take care of it."

It was a rather comical scene. All those years after Elizabeth realized she did not have the power to stop her husband from shipping her oldest son off to prep school at fourteen, she apparently thought she could wield some clout with the U.S. Air Force in the middle of a war.

"Pretty embarrassing," Bob recalled.

His mother never wrote another letter to the brass, and soon he was on his way to Korea, where the jet age was kicking into high gear.

A significant part of the tension that made the Cold War so unnerving in the West was the lack of knowledge about

Soviet capabilities. The fear of the unknown drove Washington policy as much as the fear of the known, but when the Soviets unveiled the MiG-15, which featured a revolutionary sweptwing design, every pilot in the U.S. military quickly learned that their enemy had jumped ahead in jet fighter technology. This became abundantly clear in the autumn of 1950, when the first squadrons of MiG-15s, including many covertly piloted by Russians, joined the Korean War, where their superiority to the F-80s and F-84s was undeniable.

By the time Gilliland arrived at Taegu Air Base, known as K-2, in 1952, he was an expert on the F-84. "I knew that plane cold," he said.

Like the other F-84 pilots, he knew he wanted to avoid combat with a MiG-15. After suffering a massive number of losses with the first- and second-generation fighters, the U.S. military leveled the playing field by introducing the F-86 Sabre, a sweptwing plane produced by North American Aviation that eventually seized the advantage from the MiG-15.

Gilliland would always remember the first time he heard a sonic boom. It was caused by a Royal Canadian Air Force F-86 passing in the distant sky above his head. He knew immediately what it was, because by this time, the sonic boom had entered the military lexicon as the clarion call of the supersonic age.

The fierce dogfights between the MiG-15 and the F-86, the two great technological achievements of the superpowers, in the area near the Yalu River known as MiG Alley, represented a microcosmic proxy for the larger Cold War.

After shooting down sixteen MiGs to become the leading American ace of the war, F-86 pilot Joe McConnell emerged as such a hero that Hollywood produced a motion picture about his life, starring Alan Ladd.

About two years later, after both had returned to the United States, Gilliland met McConnell and discovered they shared a mutual appreciation for Ping-Pong. "I liked the quickness of it," Bob said. "You had to think and act in a flash, just like you do in a plane."

"I can walk into any fighter squadron and play the best Ping-Pong players, to determine the best fighter pilots," McConnell told him.

The two Korean War veterans wound up playing about seven games over the space of several days. They pushed each other, point for point.

Less than a year later, McConnell was killed while testing the latest version of the F-86 at Edwards.

In at least one instance, the Sabre was utilized for an entirely different purpose.

The concept of aerial reconnaissance was still rudimentary and rather haphazard, but U.S. Air Force first lieutenant Mele Vojvodich made a daring raid into Manchuria—350 miles deep into Communist China—with a modified F-86. It had the ring of a suicide mission, especially when the enemy reacted quickly to repel what it no doubt saw as the prelude to an invasion. Several MIGs chased Vojvodich to the Yalu and beyond, but he made it home alive with valuable photographic evidence showing a wing of Soviet-made bombers capable of delivering nuclear warheads.

Gilliland flew twenty-five combat missions in the F-84, including many involving napalm. A typical assignment called for him to arrive above an enemy camp around dawn, when the Chinese or North Korean troops were starting to move around, and descend to an altitude of about 50 feet before simultaneously dropping two canisters of the highly flammable jellied gasoline. "Sometimes one wouldn't ignite," he explained, "but if you did two at a time, at least one would always ignite." The resulting inferno proved very effective in killing the enemy.

The duty could be extremely hazardous, because the low altitude left him vulnerable to small arms fire and because the darkness and the close proximity of several planes delivering a coordinating attack needed to be tightly managed. One morning, he was part of a raid that went bad; two other planes collided while coming out of a drop, killing both pilots.

Another time, his squadron took off from K-2, assembled in formation, and headed north, crossing the thirty-eighth parallel into North Korea. They leveled at 30,000 feet, maintaining radio silence.

When it was time to descend out of the clouds, the leader gave a hand gesture, and they started to move. At 15,000 feet, he wagged his tail, which the pilots understood as the signal to line up in a trail formation and commence the attack.

"They were having a graduation ceremony for their young officers at this military academy, and we decided to show up with some presents," Gilliland said.

At least some of the bombs found their target, and as the area exploded in flames, the American F-84s started heading for home. But Gilliland had company.

"The first MIG I ever saw was lining up on me."

By this point, he had spent nearly two years preparing for just such a moment. He knew what his jet could do. He knew the range of the MIG's guns. He knew the power of causing the MIG to choose between two potential targets. And he knew what the Soviet pilots feared more than anything else.

No longer in radio silence, he signaled to one of the other pilots, and they executed a scissor maneuver, which divided the lone MIG's attention. "Anybody bouncing one of us would have to worry about the other," he said. "That's why it's safer."

Heading at maximum speed toward the western coast at a low altitude, Gilliland briefly had a shot. He didn't take it. In this instance, in this plane, he knew better. "Since they had a better airplane, you don't necessarily want to hang around to try to get a better shot at 'em," he said. "Plus, you learned that if you tried to screw around with one, you might have another one coming down on you, and then you're dead."

Especially since he had already accomplished his mission,

the sensible decision was to retreat to fight another day, so he decided to exploit his enemy's biggest weakness: fear of capture.

"We all knew that they weren't supposed to go out over the water, because America controlled the water on both sides of the peninsula," he said. "And they didn't want a Russian pilot picked up."

Gilliland's instinct proved correct. Once he reached the Yellow Sea, the MiG disappeared. He immediately zoomed to about 45,000 feet, to preserve fuel. When he finally was able to make his way through a long line to land at the K-4 airport near Seoul, he was running on fumes.

"That was a good feeling to get on the ground," he said.

Serving in combat reinforced Bob's love of flying. He found enormous satisfaction in the intensity and the pressure. He discovered that he was very adept at applying all that knowledge and skill when the adrenaline was pumping and he needed to act quickly and calmly. He felt alive up there.

By the time his tour ended, a few months before the armistice was signed, Gilliland was one of the most experienced F-84 pilots in the U.S. Air Force. The plane was living on borrowed time, but an aviator with his skill and experience was a valuable commodity who would have his choice of assignments in the years ahead.

When he was stationed in Neubiberg, Elizabeth asked him to buy her a fur coat. She had very specific tastes. He never got around to shopping for her in Germany, but on the way back to the United States, he took a friend's advice and stopped in Tokyo, where he found a nice coat for a good price at a bazaar in the basement of the Imperial Hotel, the landmark partially designed by Frank Lloyd Wright.

Several days later, he arrived in Memphis and was greeted warmly by his mother as he threw his bag full of dirty laundry on the floor.

"Mother, how about taking care of this?" he asked.

"Why sure!" she said sweetly.

As Elizabeth started pulling the clothes out of the bag, she discovered something that didn't belong, buried deep in the pile: a luxurious fur coat.

Bob just stood there with a big grin on his face.

1. Frank Gilliland Sr. was a hero in World War I but rarely talked about his service. Courtesy of Gilliland family.

2. Headed to church, circa 1932, with his father, mother, and brother, Frank Jr., Bob's budding interest in aviation could be seen in his aviation cap and goggles. Courtesy of Gilliland family.

3. At the all-boys Webb School in rural Middle Tennessee, playing football was one of the few approved distractions. Courtesy of Gilliland family.

4. Bob wound up at the Naval Academy after a brief stint as an enlisted man. Courtesy of Gilliland family.

5. & 6. Bob volunteered for combat during the Korean War.
Courtesy of Gilliland family.

7. Bob flew twenty-five combat missions in the F-84 during the Korean War. Courtesy of Gilliland family.

8. With Gilliland at the controls, the SR-71 made its maiden flight on December 22, 1964. An F-104 gives chase. Courtesy of Gilliland family.

9. Skunk Works director Clarence L. "Kelly" Johnson considered the SR-71 the crowning achievement of his remarkable career. Courtesy of Gilliland family.

10. Bob needed the "moon suit" while piloting the world's fastest, highest-flying airplane. Courtesy of Gilliland family.

11. & 12. (*opposite*) The sleek design of the Blackbird contributed to its unmistakable mystique. Courtesy of Gilliland family.

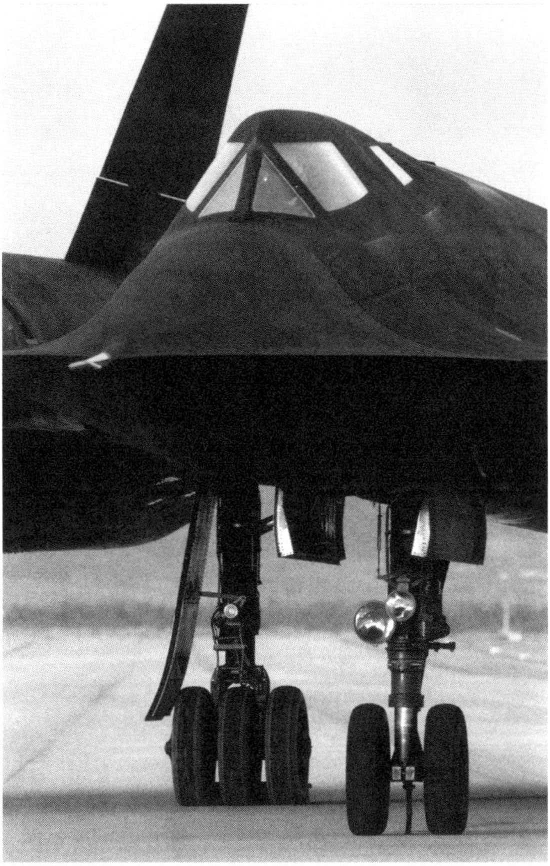

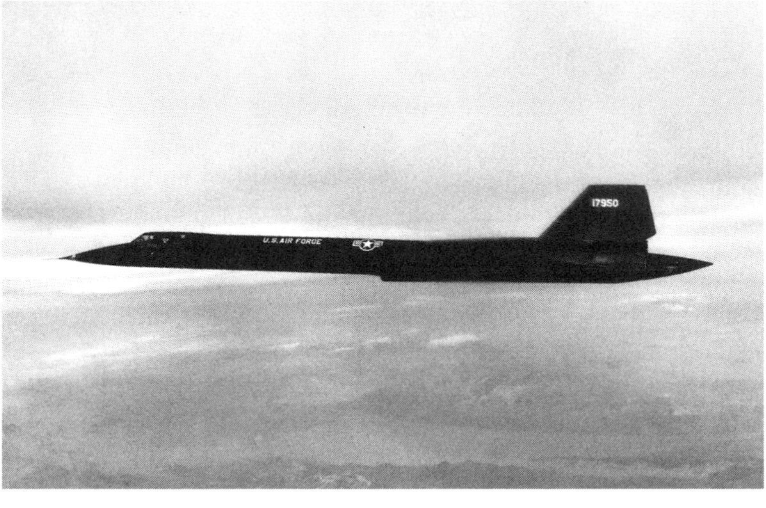
17950
U.S. AIR FORCE

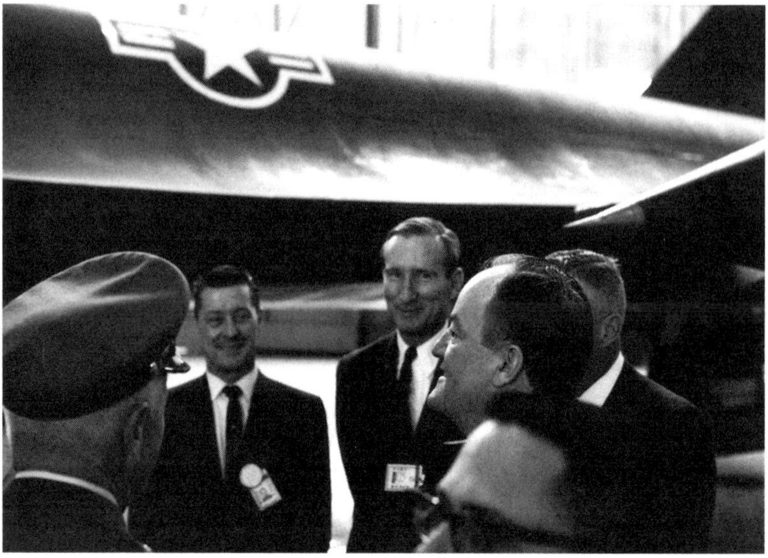

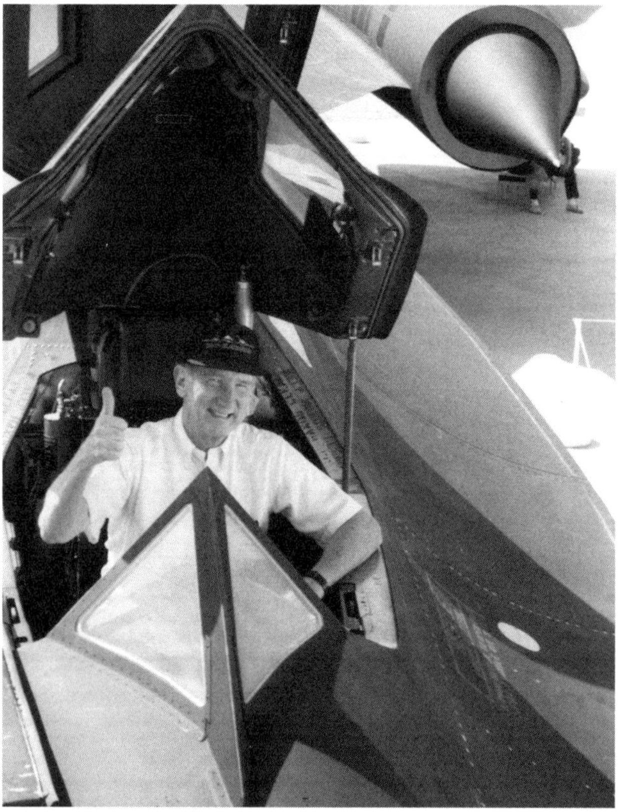

13. (*opposite top*) The buzz around the Blackbird program often attracted dignitaries, including Vice President Hubert Humphrey. Courtesy of Gilliland family.

14. (*opposite bottom*) After the Cold War ended, Bob became synonymous with the Blackbird. Courtesy of Gilliland family.

15. (*above*) Gilliland emerged as a highly sought speaker, including making the induction speech at the National Aviation Hall of Fame for Voyager pilot Dick Rutan. Courtesy of National Aviation Hall of Fame.

16. Son Robert Jr. and daughter Anne were shaped by their father's high expectations. Courtesy of Gilliland family.

17. & 18. (*opposite*) On the Legends of Aerospace Tour in 2010, Bob joined fellow aviators Steve Ritchie, Jim Lovell, Neil Armstrong, and Gene Cernan. Courtesy of Thomas M. Lee.

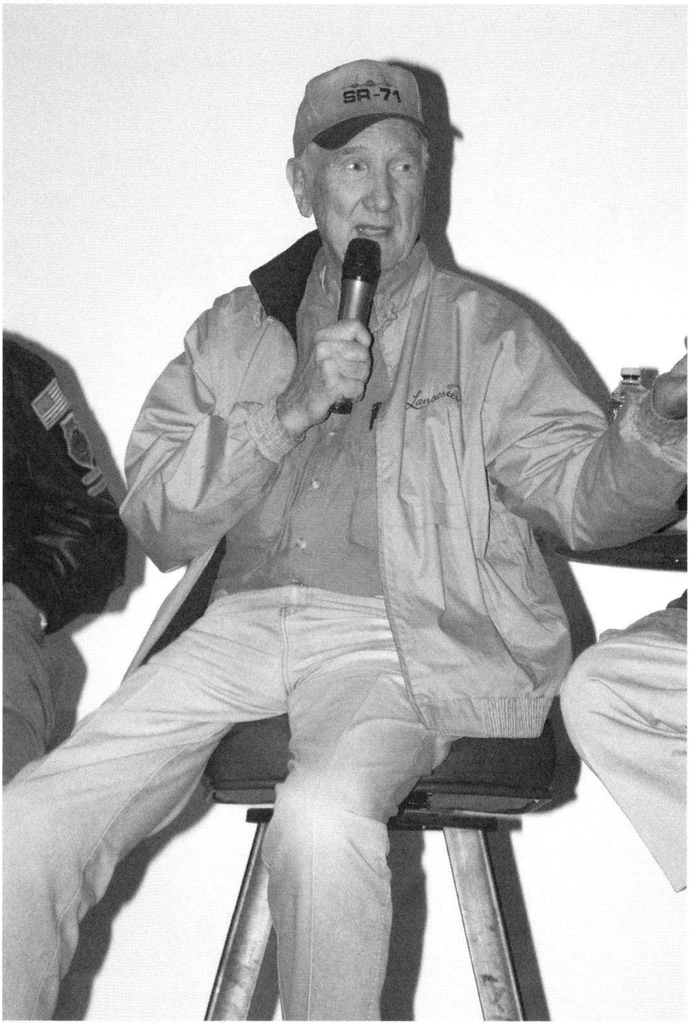
SR-71

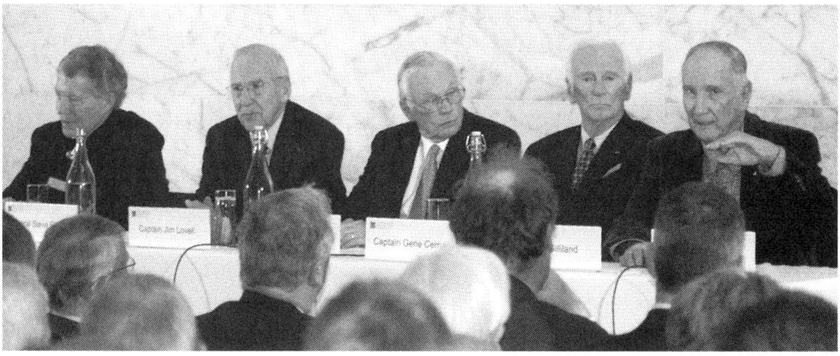
Captain Jim Lovell

19. During a memorable dinner in London, Gilliland (*second from left*) chatted with speed-record holder Andrew Green, legendary test pilot Eric Brown, and Neil Armstrong. Courtesy of Thomas M. Lee.

FOUR

Two Worlds

SOON AFTER BEING REASSIGNED TO A FIGHTER WING at West Germany's Ramstein Air Base, Gilliland took his first F-86 out for a spin. The flight was uneventful. After landing and stopping temporarily on the runway, because the new airstrip did not have taxiways, he took a few moments to carefully study the cockpit and the instrument panel, while still strapped into the seat. Among the latest features of the Sabre was a metal compartment that allowed the pilot to provide information about the flight and feedback about the plane. Somehow, during his jostling, the metallic piece hit something, triggering the ejection seat, fortunately without launching. The canopy violently snapped open, grazing the top of his helmet. He was unharmed, except for his bruised ego.

During routine missions over Western Europe, Bob often kept a sharp eye out for the abundant lakes and streams dotting the picturesque landscape. "I was always looking for a good place to go trout fishing."

The peaceful outings with a fishing rod, often accompanied by his friend Lou Schalk, scratched an itch, tapping into a quest for a certain serenity that contrasted sharply with the adrenaline-pumping existence of the fighter pilot. But Gilliland was also a man who yearned for adventure. He wanted to go fast. He wanted to feel a rush.

During his first winter in Germany, Gilliland bought a pair of oversize wooden snow skis and joined a pilot friend on a trip to Zugspitze, Germany's highest mountain, which stretches 9,718 feet above sea level, in southern Bavaria near the border with Austria. To reach the snow-covered Alpine summit, the Americans rode an elevator up through the massive mountain, their ears popping as it approached the distant summit. "Most of it was unable to be skied unless you were an expert skier," Gilliland recalled. "But they had this one little area where I could learn." After taking careful note of several pointers from his friend, an expert skier from Utah, Bob set off on his own, slowly learning the power of bended knees, precise movements, and unforgiving gravity. "I found it very exciting," he said. He liked the athleticism it required. He liked the feeling of controlled danger. Soon he was hooked.

After rotating back to the United States, Gilliland began maneuvering for a different sort of adventure.

In the unlikely chain of events that led him into the history books, he would always acknowledge the help of George Simler, his onetime wing commander back in Germany, who explained to him the way assignments were handed out at the Pentagon. Simler's bureaucratic knowledge was a pivotal bridge in the Bob Gilliland story. This intelligence, when combined with Gilliland's willingness to push the boundaries in a world governed by a strict adherence to rules, led him to the Pentagon on a fateful day in 1953.

"I thought, 'Well, what do I have to lose?' I'll take a day and go up to Washington and see what I can do."

Somehow, he talked his way past aides and secretaries and into the office of just the right colonel, the man who had the power to determine his next assignment with the stroke of a pen and a form filed in triplicate.

Intrigued with the idea of learning to fly different sorts of planes, Gilliland wanted to wrangle an assignment to Eglin Air Force Base in Northwest Florida, the vast installation along the Gulf Coast, which also happened to be a few hours' drive from Memphis.

After listening to the first lieutenant's request, the colonel chided him for flouting the rules. "This is totally improper, you coming in here to see me!"

A different sort of officer might have recoiled and slinked away, but Gilliland could be as fearless in the face of military protocol as he was in the choppy clouds at 30,000 feet. He was imbued with a certain charm and earnestness that allowed him to approach the line and even step over it without igniting the wrath of his superiors. This was a matter requiring a delicate touch, much like the light fingering he wielded so expertly on the stick of every aircraft he ever flew.

"I know, sir, but is it accurate that you are the one who can do this sort of thing?"

He flashed an irritated look. "Yes. That's accurate."

Instead of tossing Gilliland out of his office, the colonel spent a few minutes talking with the pilot. For some reason, perhaps out of some appreciation for the lieutenant's initiative in the matter, the colonel agreed to see what he could do. No promises. But he would see what he could do, if and when an opening occurred.

Several weeks later, his orders arrived. Bob was thrilled—and a bit surprised—that the colonel had exercised his discretion to reassign him to Eglin as a day fighter pilot attached to the Air Force Armament Center.

"Wish I could thank that guy now," he remarked more than sixty years later.

On the morning of October 14, 1947, when Gilliland was still matriculating at Annapolis, Major Bob Cardenas faced a history-shaping dilemma. He was running out of time, and he had a big problem.

Several months earlier, Cardenas and his small team had arrived at Muroc Army Air Base, an isolated outpost in the Antelope Valley, deep in California's Mojave Desert, facing one of the foremost technological challenges of the twentieth century—how to shatter the sound barrier and live through the experience.

"The truth is, none of us knew what would happen at that speed," Cardenas recalled. "One scientist believed . . . when you passed through the sound barrier, the gravity that would be imposed on the plane would be so great that the force would basically crumple it into a ball of steel."

It took a special sort of man to volunteer for what many believed was a suicide mission. Aware of the extreme hazards, Bell test pilot Chalmers "Slick" Goodlin demanded a $150,000 bonus for conquering the barrier in his company's rocket-powered x-1. Bell balked at such an enormous fee. It was customary for first flights to be flown by contractor pilots, but in this case, the assignment was passed on to the newly independent air force, where even the best pilots earned only a few hundred dollars per month.

Cardenas, a onetime b-24 pilot, flew twenty bombing missions over occupied Europe before being shot down by the Germans, swimming to safety, and eventually escaping from a Swiss internment camp. It was a tale filled with drama and intrigue. He was the sort of man who got things done without making excuses.

After spending the first couple of years after the war testing various planes at Muroc and Wright-Patterson Air Force Base in Dayton, Ohio—including one of the first captured me-262s—Cardenas was placed in charge of the effort to attack the sound barrier by Colonel Albert Boyd, the head of flight-testing, once a renowned test pilot himself and a stickler for rules and regulations. His mandate was clear, and the time allotted was limited.

The man they selected to step into the unknown started his

military career as an aircraft mechanic, a buck private at the bottom of the food chain. He quickly rose through the ranks during World War II, becoming a decorated fighter pilot with eleven and a half official victories and once shooting down five planes in a single day. Chuck Yeager had something special, and he volunteered for the secret mission, understanding that he would likely make history or die trying.

The team also included backup pilot Bob Hoover, who flew fifty-nine combat missions in the European theater and spent sixteen months as a German prisoner of war before escaping to freedom. It was a harrowing five-day ordeal involving a stolen FW-190 fighter. Hoover was well on his way to a legendary career in which he set several speed records. Jackie Ridley, a trained engineer, served as Cardenas's copilot of the B-29, which dropped the X-1. Yeager dubbed the bullet-shaped beast *Glamorous Glennis*, in honor of his wife.

In each of the first seven flights, Cardenas's B-29 took off from Muroc and launched the X-1 into the clear blue sky, through a specially retrofitted bomb bay. Each time, Yeager ignited the rocket and guided the craft into the thin air above 40,000 feet, inching closer and closer to the magic number, hitting a predetermined subsonic speed, and culminating with a three-g turn. On the eighth flight, however, Yeager encountered turbulence above Mach .9 that caused the team significant pause, especially Ridley, who knew the most about the forces threatening the craft as it moved into uncharted territory. "Jackie thought we had a problem with the shock wave from the front, how it was being distributed," Cardenas recalled. "He thought, 'If we go a bit further all hell might break loose.'"

No one could say whether the sound barrier was a brick wall or just another number wrapped in a blanket of air.

Muroc was a place where such questions could be answered, and the high price of acquiring such knowledge was paid by brave men who willingly strapped into unproven machines and soared off into the distant skies.

Since the early 1930s, when General Henry "Hap" Arnold began buying up the land, allowing for a sprawling base stretching over 470 square miles, Muroc had evolved into an important proving ground for the U.S. military, initially as an adjunct of Riverside County's March Field. The first military inhabitants pitched tents, and when Cardenas and his team arrived a decade later, the accommodations remained spartan, even by air force standards. Cardenas and his new bride started their life together living in a desert shack with adobe walls and no electricity or running water.

Located about one hundred miles north of Los Angeles, Muroc offered relative isolation; Rogers Dry Lake, a forty-four-square-mile hard surface, flat enough for use by a variety of planes; and a fifteen-thousand-foot concrete runway, which made it ideal for testing cutting-edge aircraft.

Every pilot who worked out of Muroc eventually found his way over to the Happy Bottom Riding Club, a dive bar owned by Pancho Barnes, a colorful character and enterprising businesswoman who had once been among the country's most accomplished female pilots, shattering a speed record previously held by Amelia Earhart. As a middle-aged tavern owner, Barnes befriended an entire generation of test pilots and presided over a free-wheeling party atmosphere, replete with a bevy of pretty young women, allowing aviators to blow off steam between life-threatening flights.

When a new pilot was escorted to the joint by a veteran for the first time, the foul-mouthed Pancho was known to greet the unsuspecting rookie at the front door wearing nothing but her bra and panties, with her hair all askew. Recalled Cardenas, "If you in any way blanched, she'd send you packing: 'Get your ass out of here!' But if you stuck out your hand and greeted her warmly, she'd welcome you in and buy you a drink. It was like a test. She could tell a lot about you by that moment."

Yeager was one of her favorites. "I probably spent more time at Pancho's than I did in the cockpit," he once said of the place he described as the "clubhouse and playroom" of the test pilots.[1]

Like its owner, like the skies above the desert, Pancho's was untamed and proudly so.

Two days before the ninth and final flight of the x-1 program, Yeager was thrown from a horse, breaking two ribs. He was in significant pain but did what any pilot angling to make history would have done: He hid the injury from Cardenas, well aware that it could cause him to be benched in favor of Hoover.

When Yeager realized he could not muster enough strength with his right arm to close the canopy, which could have caused the scrubbing of the mission at the worst possible time, Ridley came up with a rather inventive way to mitigate the problem—sawing off the top half of a broom handle, which his buddy was able to manipulate successfully to seal the hatch.

When he saw Ridley with the broom handle, Cardenas put two and two together and realized he faced a dilemma. What if Yeager's injury prevented him from handling other duties during the flight?

Hoover, who ordinarily chased the x-1 in a p-80, was on hand for just such a situation, but as Cardenas thought through the possibilities, he realized that turning to the backup pilot was fraught with a different sort of peril. Given the complexities of the machine and the mission, he would feel obligated to give Hoover at least two flights in the x-1, so he could get up to speed. But he didn't have two flights left. If he made the decision to sideline Yeager, he would be unable to live up to his orders. This was a conversation with Colonel Boyd he wanted to avoid at all costs.

When the B-29 dropped the X-1 for the ninth time and Yeager punched a hole in the sky, proving that the sound barrier was just a number, the world thundered into the supersonic age, and the dusty place where he achieved one of the milestones of aviation history became a magnet for hotshot pilots who wanted to prove they had what Tom Wolfe would one day call "the right stuff."

In the fever to push the technology forward, some aircraft were rushed into development with significant flaws that could not be solved, no matter how talented the pilot. The YB-49 bomber, which featured a revolutionary flying wing design that resembled a bat, was a perfect example. Despite various problems, including a debilitating tendency to fall into what the pilots called a negative stall, the air force, the Northrup Corporation, and President Harry Truman continued to push the YB-49—even after one of the prototypes broke into several pieces and tumbled to a fiery crash over the desert on June 5, 1948, killing Major Daniel Forbes, Captain Glen Edwards, and three other crew members. In several diary entries prior to his death, Edwards had expressed his doubts about the aircraft, writing that its "stability is poor" and that the plane was "quite uncontrollable at times."[2] Despite voicing his serious concerns to his superiors, Major Cardenas was ordered to continue the testing using the remaining plane. He took it on a record-setting speed run to Andrews Air Force Base, where Truman gleefully climbed into the cockpit and instructed him to fly the plane at treetop level down Pennsylvania Avenue so the people could get a good look at the future. Cardenas followed orders, flying so low that he nearly hit the U.S. Capitol. Some months later, the only remaining YB-49 crashed into a lake bed near Muroc. "It had too many deficiencies and was never going to be a safe, operational aircraft, not with the technology available at that time," Cardenas said.

By the time Muroc was rechristened Edwards Air Force Base several months later, the place had already begun to gather a mystique, in the shadow of Yeager and all he represented. The new name, which turned Glen Edwards into a symbol straddling the delicate tightrope between aspiration and tragedy, was a powerful reminder for all who cared to notice. The men who converged on Edwards in those heady days, determined to shatter previously sacrosanct barriers and extend the envelope on craft reflecting the most advanced technology of the day, were engaged in a dangerous business, where a measure of immortality could only be achieved by tempting mortality itself.

In time, the man from Memphis would take his place in the line that started with Yeager. One day he would discover for himself that a number was just a number. But only after he wrestled with a choice that rippled through the history of American aviation.

One day in 1953, Jim Matheney stopped by to see his old buddy at Eglin. He was on liberty from his carrier, the USS *Cabot*. Bob insisted on driving to dinner, and when he stepped on the gas, pushing his convertible past 90 miles per hour while heading down a two-lane highway, weaving around slower cars and talking about the good old days as their high-and-tight hair flopped in the breeze, Matheney started to sweat.

"About scared me to death in that thing," Matheney said. "That's when I learned how much Bob liked speed, even when he was on the ground."

Gilliland's appreciation for fast cars connected him to every test pilot who ever drew a breath. Like some fifties version of Maverick, the Tom Cruise character in *Top Gun*, he was young and full of life and liked to the push the edge, on the ground and in the air.

While on vacation with Libby, Bob's brother Jim and a friend watched as Bob buzzed a nearby beach at maximum speed in his F-84—so close that he could see the shadows from the sharks. Fortunately, no one reported his tail number.

"I liked to go buzzing illegally wherever I was stationed," he recalled, noting that he never got caught.

Hardened by combat and the various challenges required to stay alive while harnessing the rapidly evolving technology, he arrived at Eglin infused with an unmistakable confidence in his abilities, which enabled him to push the margins without losing control. But he was not the sort to take stupid chances.

"Bob was a very mature guy who took what he was doing very seriously," said his longtime friend Harry Andonian, a fellow Eglin test pilot who would eventually fly more than 350 different aircraft and still be flying his own small plane into his nineties. "He was very methodical in everything he did."

As the jets became more powerful and sophisticated, one of the biggest challenges facing pilots was their ability to withstand heightened gravity forces, especially when accelerating, banking, or climbing. To alleviate the problem of blood pooling in the extremities, which could cause a pilot to lose consciousness, most wore a G suit around their midsection and legs. It featured an inflated bladder, triggered during periods when a craft's maneuvers accentuated the gravitational pull. In those days, the G suit would fail at a certain point, when the pressure became too great, and every test pilot worth his pay wanted to push that edge, just to see what would happen.

When Jim Stewart learned his new colleague had not been initiated into their elite club, he told Gilliland, "Come up with me, and I'll pop your suit!"

Bob accepted the challenge, went up as a back-seater in a T-33, and said not a word as Stewart pushed the craft to its operational limits, banking hard and going vertical while challenging immutable gravity to a duel in the Florida sun. Somewhere around 6 g's, or six times earth's gravity, the suit popped, and as Gilliland felt enormous pressure assaulting his body, he took a measure of satisfaction from his ability to sustain the punishment without passing out.

In the years after Yeager's historic flight, the government-financed mission to go faster and higher accelerated, especially at Edwards. The x-1 was just the beginning of a hardware race that fueled intense competition among several leading defense contractors, including Bell, Douglas, and Lockheed. When Scott Crossfield became the first man to fly twice the speed of sound (1,291 miles per hour) while piloting the Douglas D-558-11 Skyrocket on November 20, 1953, it was a remarkable feat, one that would have seemed unimaginable just a few years earlier. But progress was swift, and in time Mach 2 became just another milestone on an ever-expanding chart, a record soon vulnerable to the development of more sophisticated aircraft and the imperatives of the Cold War.

The need to control the skies pushed the air force and the little-known National Advisory Committee for Aeronautics (NACA) toward the edge of space. On September 7, 1956, while piloting an x-2 rocket plane, Korean War ace Iven C. Kincheloe Jr. climbed to a record altitude of 126,200 feet. Above him he could see the black void of space. The constant struggle between such stunning achievements and the high price required to push the outside of the envelope was forcefully demonstrated three weeks later, when, after becoming the first man to exceed Mach 3, Milburn "Mel" Apt lost control of his x-2, which began spinning wildly. After struggling for several harrowing minutes to overcome a catastrophic problem known as inertia coupling, he finally tried to bail out. It was too late. Apt died on impact in what would turn out to be the final flight of the x-2.

The first attempt to teach the requirements of measuring

an unproven aircraft came during World War II, when, after watching many of their best aviators go down in flames, the Royal Air Force formed the Empire Test Pilots' School. In time it became the place to go to learn how to become a test pilot, or at least those parts of the job that could be taught.

After distinguishing himself as a bomber pilot in both World War II and Korea, Jesse Jacobs graduated from Empire and would always remember the pivotal moment when the theory of the classroom yielded to the practicality of the open sky. Jacobs recalled, "One of the instructors said, 'See that airplane out there?' And I said, 'Yeah.' 'Well, go out and sort it out for yourself.'"

Although he was never formally trained as a test pilot, Gilliland began his education during those difficult early years in West Germany, when the early models of the F-84 killed so many of his colleagues. He was already well acquainted with the concept of sorting it out for himself.

At Eglin the testing was largely confined to operational aircraft in the air force fleet. Gilliland spent most of his time flying fighters, especially the F-84, the F-86, and a sweptwing version of the F-84 known as the Thunderstreak. The designers at Republic Aviation envisioned the modification as a way to achieve relative parity with the F-86, but it suffered from poor performance, as Bob repeatedly experienced while piloting the aircraft in all sorts of conditions. "It was underpowered to beat hell," he said.

The F-86 remained the leading U.S. fighter, reflecting the widespread belief that the future belonged to the sweptwing design pioneered by the Soviets.

Every aircraft was a work in progress, with thousands of moving parts that needed to be flown hundreds of hours before all the problems could be identified and solved. One of the dilemmas confronting the Eglin center in those days concerned the way the F-86 sometimes flamed out when a pilot fired his machine guns, especially above 35,000 feet.

Gilliland and his colleagues were part of a team assigned to work this problem.

"The only way out of that situation was to descend to about 20,000 feet and restart the engine, but that was not real efficient, especially when you were in combat," Gilliland said.

He tested a new fuel control system that alleviated the problem by temporarily changing the fuel-to-air ratio, which throttled down the engine but prevented it from stopping.

Bolstered by such mechanical experimentation, Gilliland became a dedicated student of how the various systems of an aircraft interacted, learning that most problems could be solved with the right amount of applied knowledge and trial and error. "There was a science to it, and I enjoyed that," he said.

With a wide range of aircraft on base at any given time, Gilliland seized the opportunity to hitch rides on as many planes as he could. He studied their cockpits and their operational characteristics.

"Bob was one of the most curious people I've ever known," Andonian said. "He wanted to know how everything worked."

After surviving the Great Depression, the Sterick Building slowly grew into the most prestigious business address in Memphis. For the owners, however, including minority partner Frank Gilliland, it remained a troubled asset, especially in the years when it was controlled by the mercurial businessman Jim Hammond, whose holdings included the *Memphis Commercial Appeal*. Near the end of 1949, Frank faced a situation quickly spiraling out of control. With the banks no longer willing to deal with Hammond, and no other buyers interested, he was forced to either purchase the building outright or risk losing his 30 percent.

"Dad was in a difficult position, but ultimately, he decided the best thing to do was to protect his investment," Bob said.

The $1.5 million loan required mortgaging their beloved home, which was especially tough on Libby, given what had happened to her father in the Depression. But it turned out to be a very shrewd move.

Several years later, as Frank moved into his midsixties and their financial position stabilized, he began lobbying his eldest son to return to Memphis and help him manage the skyscraper.

"I think Dad's position was, Bob had done his duty [with the air force] but it was time to get on with the rest of his life," Jim said.

Bob was conflicted. He loved his father, valued his advice, and felt a duty to help him. But he didn't want to stop flying, and besides, he owed a commitment to the air force that could not easily be curtailed.

After verifying that it was possible for him to stay in the air by signing up with the Tennessee Air National Guard while taking a job with his father, he started working the system in the sort of full-frontal assault that was quickly becoming his trademark. But for this he needed the cooperation of the air force.

When he learned that his application to resign his active-duty commission and transfer to the reserves had been tossed in the trash by his commanding officer, Gilliland made an appointment to see Major General Edward P. Mechling the following morning.

The details of the meeting were forever imprinted in his memory, especially the way the general rocked back and forth in his chair.

After the usual protocol and pleasantries between a junior officer and his commanding general, Gilliland got right to the point.

"Sir, I've learned from your six-striper that you didn't forward my request for transfer out."

"That's correct," he said firmly. "And I'll tell you why."

"Why, sir?"

"Because I take a dim view of somebody who gets a free education at the hands of the public and then wants to resign."

Gilliland did not know what to say. He thanked the general for his time, saluted, and walked out the door.

Soon he was on the phone with his father, which led to a call to one of his dad's acquaintances, World War I ace Everett Cook, who said he would try to help. At some point, the problem wound up on the desk of General Emmett "Rosie" O'Donnell, one of the most powerful figures in the Pentagon. The man already owned three stars on his collar, and soon he would have four, so his word was respected and feared. According to the story that was related to Gilliland, O'Donnell placed a call to Eglin and demanded that the pilot "be off that base by nightfall."

Laughing at the thought many years later, Gilliland said, "I wasn't ready to go anywhere that fast! Next thing I know, they started moving my belongings out of the BOQ!"

In a July 30, 1954, letter to Jim, Frank's viewpoint about Bob's aviation fascination was clear: "Bobby showed up last Tuesday afternoon as chipper and nonchalant as usual, and the first thing he had on his mind was to get lined up with some National Guard squadron that flies jets. I am hoping to be able to persuade him that time has come for him to be thinking about his life pursuits instead of flying jets, but I feel sure it is going to be a slow process."[3]

Once in Memphis, Bob quickly adjusted to civilian life, dedicating himself to learning everything there was to know about the Sterick Building and Memphis real estate. Determined to reduce the load on his aging father, he spent much of his time dealing with tenants, which allowed him to expand his understanding about the various businesses. He negotiated leases and dealt with vendors and even obtained his real estate license.

"I think Bob enjoyed it, but I never got the feeling that he saw [that position] as his life's work," said his friend Toof

Brown, who managed his family's printing business from an office building across the street. They met for lunch several times each week, and he could see the glint in Bob's eyes when the subject turned to matters of aviation.

Flying B-25s for the Air Guard allowed him to keep his skills sharp, though the twin-engine Mitchell bomber felt like a lumbering relic to a man who had been piloting jet fighters.

Not long after returning to his hometown, he met a striking former model from North Carolina. Sandra Wright was tall, graceful, and gracious. They soon married and moved into the guesthouse on Galloway Drive, which was full of life and laughter.

But in time a pall fell over the entire family.

In 1957 Frank Sr. was diagnosed with terminal cardiovascular disease.

Determined to clean up his balance sheet to make things easier on Elizabeth, the family patriarch sold the Sterick Building to the company that owned New York's Empire State Building. The debt was mostly gone, and the skyscraper brought a tidy profit, securing Libby's future. The budding friendship between Frank and Lawrence A. Wien, one of the principal owners of the Manhattan landmark made world-famous by lovestruck King Kong, launched a business relationship that would eventually pay dividends for the next generation of Gillilands.

Those two years were especially tough on Bob, who spent much of his time at his father's side, talking in great detail about every aspect of his life. He watched his once-vibrant dad become an invalid before finally passing away on September 25, 1959.

"Mr. Gilliland's death hit Bob pretty hard," Brown said.

By this time, his once happy marriage was over.

Soon he was going through a divorce and facing a professional crossroads, caught between two very different worlds.

Although the sale of the Sterick Building eliminated his job, he was a smart young man with options. With a Naval Academy pedigree and the skills he had developed in the air force and at his father's side, he could glide with ease into some other area of the Memphis business community. He did not have to take a job where he faced the possibility of death every day.

While his youngest brother, Jim, was still in the navy's JAG corps and stationed in Japan, Frank Jr., after serving a tour in the navy, was well on his way to becoming a prominent Memphis lawyer. Their bond was especially tight, despite very different personalities. Frank was a workaholic lawyer who spent most of his time at his desk, but he also was very family oriented, dependable, and steady. "My mother used to say Frank had the best disposition of anyone she ever met, male or female," Bob said.

The eldest son was always seeking adventure, never more so than in those conflicted days after his father's death.

"I was unsure of what I wanted to do, but I knew I wanted to keep flying," he said.

Then he heard some news that sent him off to Knoxville, and his life pivoted toward that other world.

In 1932 a small consortium placed a bet on the future. The group, led by brothers Robert and Courtland Gross and Walter Varney, invested $40,000 to purchase the struggling Detroit Aircraft Corporation out of bankruptcy, at a time when the economy was in a tailspin and no one was buying airplanes. Rising from those humble, uncertain days, Lockheed Aircraft Corporation grew into an industrial powerhouse, profoundly shaping the future of aviation.

In contrast to the wooden monoplanes that had brought the company some success in the 1920s, the new Lockheed began developing a twin-engine, all-metal aircraft large enough to carry ten passengers, hoping to attract a market with the still-nascent commercial airlines. During wind tunnel testing at the University of Michigan, the company enlisted the services of an engineering student who displayed a remarkable grasp of aerodynamics. When he graduated, at a time when any job was a good job, Lockheed hired the serious-minded young man, the seventh of nine children born to Swedish immigrants, as an entry-level tool designer earning $83 per month.

His first order of business after arriving at the company headquarters in Burbank, California, was to tell his bosses that the Electra was unstable. This was a stunning pronouncement—offering a glimpse into the unrestrained candor that would mark his career—because nothing was riding on the plane except the future of the entire company. To the engineers and executives who had pinned their hopes on the craft, the suggestion that their masterpiece was flawed and potentially dangerous seemed ludicrous. In time, however, they realized that twenty-three-year-old Clarence "Kelly" Johnson was right.

After conducting more tests and reaching the same conclusion, the team led by Hall Hibbard incorporated Johnson's design suggestions, including the addition of what was known as an H tail, and the Lockheed Electra hit the skies, soon to emerge as one of the signature airliners of the day. The first transport to offer a cruising speed of more than 200 miles per hour, it achieved worldwide fame as the plane Amelia Earhart used on her celebrated but ultimately doomed attempt to circumnavigate the globe in 1937, mysteriously vanishing somewhere over the South Pacific.

The Electra put Lockheed on the map, and Johnson rose quickly through the ranks, designing the P-38 Lightning, one of the most durable fighters of World War II, and the Constellation family of airliners, in partnership with Howard Hughes's TWA. By early in World War II, the man from

Michigan emerged as a powerful force in the company, well on his way to becoming one of the most influential aeronautical engineers of all time.

When he negotiated a deal with the Pentagon to build America's first jet fighter, Johnson convinced Robert Gross, the Lockheed chairman, to allow him a greater level of independence. "I wanted a direct relationship between design engineer and mechanic and manufacturing . . . without the delays and complications of intermediate departments," he said.[4] Located in a new hangar on Hollywood Way, adjacent to an existing wind tunnel, it was initially covered with a circus tent and featured walls constructed from discarded engine boxes. Johnson's Advanced Development Projects division featured its own purchasing department and operated completely independent of the main plant. The clandestine nature of their operations led one of the employees to make a joking comparison to the rickety moonshine still in the popular Li'l Abner comic strip, and the name stuck. The barn-like Skunk Works, officially known as Building 82, became a center of aerospace innovation shrouded in absolute secrecy, animated from early in the morning until late at night by the sight of engineers, mechanics, and other specialists wielding slide rules, pencils, and wrenches in a frenzy of activity, forever wary of the intense man with the jet-black hair and the slight paunch who filled every inch of the place with the power of his enormous expectations. Blackout drapes covered the windows, and the plant was protected like a military installation.

While the independence enabled the workaholic Johnson's need for absolute control, he proved autonomy could yield results. Without a bureaucracy to get in the way, he created a culture emphasizing quick decision-making and problem-solving, which translated into projects that were completed on time and on budget (and sometimes early and with money to spare). Driven, intolerant of mistakes, and consumed with an urgency that reflected the times, he insisted that all who worked for him "be quick, be quiet, and be on time." His fourteen rules of management explained his guidelines on everything from blueprints to funding, and around the Skunk Works, they were treated like the Ten Commandments.

"Kelly was very demanding," said longtime instrumentations expert Hal Weber. "You either did what he expected of you or you were out the door."

In assessing the Johnson-era Skunk Works' secret sauce, author Walter J. Boyne said, "The code of silence ... may have been the only thing that prevented such a critical mass of intellectual brilliance—and often larger-than-average human egos—from exploding under the pressure of working for Johnson."[5]

Beyond his overbearing management style—which former Central Intelligence Agency official John Parangosky once called "ruling by his bad temper"[6]—and his deftness in protecting his power base, particularly from those among the Washington brass who thought he was too powerful, Johnson was a brilliant engineer and designer who consistently exploited a combination of knowledge, creativity, and instinct to solve some of the most complex technical problems of the time. Hall Hibbard once said admiringly, "That damned Swede can actually see air!"[7]

The first test of the Skunk Works' effectiveness was the immense challenge of putting the first operational American jet fighter in the air, in the shadow of Germany's revolutionary ME-262. After receiving the go-ahead from the Army Air Corps in June 1943, it took Johnson and his team just 143 days to make the first flight of the XP-80, which would eventually be known as the P-80 Shooting Star. That was thirty-seven days ahead of schedule.

"In the twenty-first century, that seems almost unbelievable," remarked National Aviation Hall of Famer Clay Lacy.

"Today we would spend more time talking about the possibility of building that plane than Kelly spent actually building it."

It took a test pilot to prove those planes in the unforgiving skies, and one of the greatest of all was Tony LeVier, who would make a total of twelve first flights for Lockheed and Kelly Johnson.

LeVier's fascination with flight began on Armistice Day in 1918, when, as a five-year-old boy in Minnesota, he was walking across the street with his mother. He heard a sound that caused him to look up to the sky, casting his eyes on a Curtiss JN-4, a biplane known as the Jenny, one of the most iconic craft of the day. "That was the first airplane I ever saw . . . [and] the first time I remember hearing the word 'airplane,'" he said.[8]

After his mother remarried and the family moved to the beach town of Venice, California, not far from Santa Monica's Clover Field, where Douglas Aircraft started, fourteen-year-old Tony walked into the kitchen one morning, aglow with the news about Lucky Lindy. "I'm going to become a pilot," he breathlessly told his mother.

"Great, Tony," she responded. "Be a good one."[9]

LeVier soloed at seventeen and quit school to concentrate on flying, carving out a career as a racer and instructor, which eventually led to opportunities as a test pilot. By the time the war broke out, unable to pass an army physical, he wound up at Lockheed, where his skill and nerve in the cockpit quickly earned Johnson's trust. "I like LeVier to fly my aircraft first," Kelly once said, "because he always brings back the answers."

Shortly after takeoff in one of the early test flights of the XP-80, the engine exploded and blew the tail off. "I thought I had bought the farm,"[10] recalled LeVier, who managed to put the plane on the ground but wound up with a broken back.

The company rushed him to a hospital, where the massive trauma required extensive treatment and convalescence.

His young wife looked at his mangled body in disbelief. "She must've thought, 'What in the world have I gotten myself into, married to a man like this? But she stayed with me."[11] Within a few months he was back in the air, leading the way as Lockheed tested and perfected many of the systems that would be necessary to make the next generation of planes practical, including hydraulic-boosted controls, dive flaps, guidance radar, trim switches, warning indicators, afterburner ignitions, and the operational know-how to survive catastrophic engine failure.

In the air and on the ground, Johnson tried to stay one step ahead. As war engulfed the Korean peninsula, he traveled to the combat zone to meet with commanders and pilots.

"What do you want in a new fighter?" he asked again and again.

The answers were nearly universal: speed and altitude.

Determined that Lockheed would lead the way with the next generation of fighters, Johnson returned to Burbank and began making sketches and working the numbers. Three hundred sixty-six days after the Pentagon awarded Lockheed the contract, LeVier made the first flight in the F-104 Starfighter, the world's first Mach 2 jet, on February 28, 1954.

As the development moved forward under a cloak of secrecy, Gilliland heard some interesting scuttlebutt from his friend Lieutenant Colonel Jimmy Hartinger. "I don't know anything else about it," he said, "but this latest fighter isn't going to be sweptwing." Like Hartinger, he found this very intriguing, because the conventional wisdom at the time was that the sweptwing design exemplified by the MIG-15 and the F-86 allowed the greatest supersonic performance.

After intense testing that involved retrofitting small rockets with model wings and firing them off into the desert at Edwards, Johnson took the resulting intelligence and designed a plane featuring short, straight, thin wings. The sleek design achieved the desired performance. In separate flights in May

1958, the F-104 set new world records for speed (1,404.009 miles per hour) and altitude (91,249 feet) in a jet aircraft. The Starfighter represented a remarkable leap forward but would have a checkered history.

Two months later, on July 26, 1958, after a routine day of flying his B-25 as part of his Tennessee Air National Guard duty, Gilliland landed at a base in Mississippi, where someone told him the news: Iven C. Kincheloe Jr., a onetime Korean War fighter ace who had been the first pilot to climb to more than 100,000 feet, was dead. Bob had known him during flight training at Williams.

Kincheloe had been selected as one of the first three test pilots to fly the new X-15 rocket plane, but before he could move on to this coveted assignment, he took off at Edwards in an F-104A to chase another Starfighter piloted by Lou Schalk. Shortly after takeoff, Kincheloe's engine failed at low altitude. Seats in the early models of the F-104 ejected downward, so Kincheloe rolled inverted and ejected, but the plane was too low for his chute to fully open.

Less than a year later, some of the first operational F-104s were assigned to the Tennessee Air National Guard unit in Knoxville, Tennessee, to defend the nearby Oak Ridge National Laboratory, a key installation in the federal government's nuclear weapons program.

"When I heard about that, all of a sudden I knew what I wanted to do," Gilliland said.

He was bored. His father was gone. He was single again. And he was having a hard time getting fired up about finding a conventional nine-to-five job in Memphis. But the thought of flying the world's fastest jet excited him, undeterred by the reality that Kelly Johnson's latest creation had already killed an American hero.

Of all the turning points that shaped Gilliland's career, perhaps none loom larger than his decision to move to Knoxville in 1959 and talk his way into becoming an F-104 pilot for the Tennessee Air National Guard. It was a conscious choice to chase his passion. It was a deliberate migration from one world to another. It was a prerequisite for something he could not yet imagine.

While studying economics at the University of Tennessee, Bob dedicated himself to learning everything he could about the F-104. His education started on one of his first flights, when his engine flamed out.

"Same problem Kincheloe had," he said.

Fortunately, he was at a much higher altitude and had more time to deal with the emergency.

Trouble at 40,000 feet.

Determined not to eject, Gilliland attacked the complete loss of thrust by carefully initiating a series of maneuvers to control the craft while plotting a course for the nearby runway. A red warning light flashed on the instrument panel amid the sound of eerie, haunting silence. Several harrowing minutes later, he calmly touched down with a thud—the first of those five dead-stick landings he would suffer with the F-104.

"Any time the engine quit entirely was a close call," he said.

During one of his Air Guard trips to the Mississippi Gulf Coast, Bob stopped by a favorite restaurant for dinner. He noticed the woman seated next to him at the bar. She was beautiful and engaging, the daughter of a man who had once played football at Notre Dame on the same team with George Gipp. They started chatting and having a good time. She found Bob handsome and charming. One thing led to another, and he got her number. Soon a relationship blossomed, initially of the long-distance variety, because she headed off to San Francisco to become a teacher. They were married the following year.

Because of the expertise he gained in the F-104—and his friendship with Lou Schalk, who worked for Kelly Johnson—Gilliland came to the attention of Lockheed. After undergoing an extensive battery of tests at the company facility in Atlanta just before Christmas in 1960, Gilliland was hired as a production test pilot in the F-104 program and eventually moved with his new wife to Palmdale, a little town on the edge of the desert.

"Bob was very personable," said fellow Starfighter test pilot Bill Weaver. "You'd never know . . . he was from a wealthy family. He didn't act like he came from money. He enjoyed being one of the guys."

Working out of Edwards and the small facility in Palmdale known as Plant 42, Bob was living his dream. Some weeks he flew all seven days, just because he could.

More than a decade after Yeager launched the supersonic age, Edwards exuded a different vibe. Pancho's place was long gone, the victim of a fire, and the erstwhile owner had already spent years engaged in a series of lawsuits with the federal government that felt more like a feud. The once-sleepy outpost gradually assumed the usual trappings of a modern air force base, including a maze of new buildings and hangars and a bureaucracy to manage the various projects. "There was a permanence to it that wasn't there in 1947," Bob Cardenas said. "It felt more civilized."

But the skies above Edwards remained as untamed as the Wild West.

The parade of F-104 losses continued, none more infamous than the mission Yeager piloted in a modified version of the aircraft, which featured a combination General Electric J70 engine, the one that so often flamed out, and a liquid-fuel rocket. Yeager took the plane to the edge of space but lost control and was forced to bail out as his craft crashed in the desert.

Four more times, Gilliland experienced the ominous silence of his burner shutting off above the Antelope Valley, presaging yet another dead-stick landing. Aware of his skill in overcoming the problem, Lockheed officials sent him to a nearby base to advise the air force pilots who were still learning to fly the Starfighter.

Statistically, he told the pilots, they were better off bailing out, under certain conditions, than trying to land with a dead stick. But like Gilliland, the other pilots wanted to avoid the parachute except as a last resort.

In contrast to the handbook, which advised slowing the aircraft down to achieve longer range, he favored a counterintuitive solution: "With a dead engine, I want to have extra speed."

He then proceeded to explain how he liked to simulate a dead stick by putting his landing gear down and executing a full-slip maneuver, which made the plane fly sideways and in a circular motion, giving him greater control on descent. (To make sure this solution was viable, he had spoken with the contractor in charge of the landing gear, who advised him that he had "some margin" before damaging the gear at such a speed, but no one knew where the line was, until he extended it to at least 300 knots with this technique.)

"Of course, you've got to get to the damn runway," he explained. "That's where a lot of people got in trouble. They couldn't put it down, and they waited too late to step out."

Lockheed proved very successful in marketing the F-104 to NATO countries, including West Germany, the Netherlands, and Italy, and to far-flung allies, including Taiwan and Pakistan. A large part of Gilliland's job was serving as an instructor pilot for foreign customers.

Three years after setting the altitude record in a Starfighter, which won him the coveted Collier Trophy, Howard C. "Scrappy" Johnson returned to Edwards for six weeks as an advisor to the West German Air Force. "I came away impressed with Bob as an instructor," Johnson said. "A lot of guys in that situation, they want to give you a bunch of baloney. Bob didn't try to overteach us."

Among his protégés was Gunther Rall, one of the greatest aces of all time. After amassing 275 victories for Nazi Germany in World War II—third behind colleagues Erich Hartmann and Gerhard Barkhorn—Rall became one of the most admired figures in the postwar West German Luftwaffe.

Before their first training sessions in separate F-104s at Edwards, Gilliland noticed that Rall's left thumb was missing, the result of being shot down by an American P-47 during the war. Because in close formation, the throttle-speed brake switch had to be activated immediately with the left-hand thumb upon the flight leader's signal, Bob asked, "Since you don't have a thumb, I want to know if you'll be able to handle that?"

Rall insisted he could and proceeded to demonstrate how he compensated with his remaining digits. "Believe me," Gilliland said, "that guy had no problem doing anything."

Gilliland came away from the experience with a great admiration for Rall and carefully studied what made him and the top-tier pilots so good. "I noticed that they would use their vision better than most . . . jumping around and reading things real fast," he said. "The best ones have the ability to look at something and interpret it in their brain very fast and move on to the next thing. That's so important." He also reviewed the gunnery attributes of the high achievers, the way they were able to know just how much lead to give a target. "You could tell right away somebody who had special skill, and Rall was certainly in that category."

For many West German pilots, the learning curve proved steep. As it became the country's primary fighter at the height of the Cold War, the F-104 continued to fall out of the sky, causing more than one hundred deaths. Outraged Germans started calling it the Widow-Maker. The crashes eventually diminished, as tactics were altered, and the Starfighter remained active for the next two decades, mirroring its longevity in other countries.

"It's true the 104 killed a lot of guys, because a lot of 'em just didn't know how to handle it," Gilliland said.

Early in 1962, after Lockheed consummated a deal to produce the F-104 through a licensing agreement with Italy's Fiat Aviazione, Gilliland moved to Torino, where he began teaching the best pilots in the Italian Air Force how to fly it.

"I remember explaining to those guys, 'Just think. You can bend it over and pull 5 g's and not bleed any speed!' They couldn't believe that. That's one of the reasons that plane was so great."

Life in Italy was good. Bob bought a Fiat convertible and raced through the countryside as fast as he pleased. Despite benefiting from both a maid and a nanny, some American-style domestic conveniences remained elusive. He and Mary and their two small children, Anne and Robert Jr., lived in an apartment without a standard refrigerator or a washing machine, which meant, like most Italian wives of the time, Mary went to the market nearly every day. "We washed all the clothes in the bathtub," Mary recalled, "so on those days when we washed clothes, nobody got a bath or shower."

It was one of the happiest periods of Bob's life, teaching those Italians how to fly the fastest plane in the world, going out on the town for lavish dinners, seeing the sights, and making great friends, including Luigi Barbera, a leading Italian pilot and heartthrob who was romantically linked with Gina Lollobrigida. (Later, Barbera spent several weeks training at Edwards, and the beautiful movie star showed up in a chauffer-driven limousine looking for him, causing a stir among the American pilots, who lustily referred to her as Gina Lollipop.)

The posting allowed him the opportunity for several ski trips, including a weekend outing in the Alps with some of the men he had checked out on the 104 at Edwards. Writing to his brothers, Frank and Jim, he said, "They treated me royally. I trained them in the USA and they are now considered the outstanding fighter wing in the whole GAF . . . the only nuclear fighter wing in the GAF!"[12]

While flying the F-104, Bob sometimes took the time to

explore the area around the Matterhorn, the majestic mountain straddling the border between Italy and Switzerland, rising like a pyramid to a peak of 14,692 feet. During one such excursion, he lowered the flaps and descended over Breuil-Cervinia, the village nearest the base of the mountain on the Italian side. Aware that he was not allowed to cross the Swiss border, he immediately executed a maneuver that sent the jet zooming straight up. The silver bullet vertically pushing toward Mach 2 caught the eye of stunned villagers.

An avid hiker since his childhood days in Elkmont, Gilliland decided to mount an expedition to the top of the Matterhorn, well aware that several hundred people had died trying to reach the summit.

"I knew how dangerous it was, but I liked doing dangerous stuff," he said.

Accompanied by an experienced guide, Gilliland started up the Italian side of the mountain on a mild day in September 1962, carefully traversing the steep vertical cliffs while attached to a rope. He was wearing new boots bought especially for the climb, shoes with a special sole that gave him added traction. One false move and he could be in trouble. When night fell, they sheltered in a hut a few hundred feet from the summit, alongside several climbers from West Germany who were intrigued by his connection to the controversial F-104.

Eager to reach the top and experience one of the most breathtaking vistas in Europe, Gilliland's expedition started out early the next morning. A snow shower quickly turned into a blizzard, reducing visibility to near zero and rendering the footing especially treacherous. Soon they were forced to turn back. While spending another night at the shelter, they drank wine and shared stories as sleet pounded the walls.

"It was disappointing not to make it to the top, but it was one great adventure," Gilliland said.

FIVE

The Man in the Brooks Brothers Suit

GILLILAND WOULD ALWAYS REMEMBER THE FIRST TIME he was summoned to Kelly Johnson's office. It was in early 1962, before he knew what he didn't know.

"We used to call it 'going behind the Iron Curtain,'" he recalled, an apt description dripping with a certain irony.

The precursor to this seminal moment happened several days earlier while he was riding in Lou Schalk's car, getting a lift home after putting his Mercedes in the shop for repairs.

The son of an Iowa veterinarian, Schalk was an amiable West Point man, class of 1948, who had transferred to the air force and distinguished himself as both instructor and test pilot. He joined Lockheed in 1957 and was assigned to the Skunk Works, where he eventually became chief test pilot.

While driving down the road, Schalk looked over toward his buddy. "I think you need to come over with us."

Bob was rather stunned to hear this sentence. Despite their close friendship, he knew nothing about the secret project Schalk was testing.

"What is it?" Bob shot back.

"I can't tell you."

"How do I know I want to do it?"

Schalk grinned. "You don't."

Gilliland was intrigued but suspected it had something to do with helicopters, and he had no interest in testing anything that went straight up.

Without his knowledge, Schalk and Tony LeVier had been lobbying Kelly on his behalf, demonstrating their extreme confidence in his abilities.

LeVier was nearing the end of his brilliant career, which included flying 260 different types of aircraft and logging more than ten thousand hours. He remained the standard by which all Lockheed test pilots were judged. "A lot of people think Chuck Yeager was the greatest American test pilot," Gilliland said. "I say it was Tony LeVier."

Among his many aviation friends was Charles Lindbergh, who had inspired his career. When Lucky Lindy came west for a banquet, LeVier wrangled an invitation for Bob and introduced the men, who had a nice conversation that concluded with Lindbergh's promise to send him a copy of his recently published autobiography.

A year or two later, when the legendary aviator returned to Los Angeles and Gilliland once again made the guest list, Bob started peppering him with questions and marveling at his ability to stay awake for nearly thirty-four hours while crossing the Atlantic.

"I don't think I was ever awake that long in my life!" Bob said.

Lindbergh flashed a puzzled look. "Did you read my book?"

Though Bob deflected the question, the truth was that he had not read a word of the book, and as Lindbergh began explaining one of the most important threads of his story—that he had gotten no sleep the night before the 1927 flight, leaving him sleepless for fifty-five straight hours—Gilliland tried to conceal his profound embarrassment.

In later years, Bob enjoyed telling this story on himself, demonstrating his tendency toward self-deprecation, which belied the stereotypical image of the arrogant pilot incapable of being wrong or looking like a fool. He was always secure enough in who he was to make himself the butt of his own jokes, especially if the punch lines derived from real life.

After Schalk told him Kelly wanted to see him, Bob made an appointment and drove to Burbank at the scheduled time. It was the first time he had ever been allowed into the cloistered atmosphere of Building 82, and when he walked into the plant and exchanged pleasantries with Vera Palm, Johnson's secretary, she said, "He's in there waiting on you now."

Inside his small office, Johnson wasted no time getting to the point, telling Gilliland that he had been investigating him and had heard good things about him from two of his best pilots and an unnamed engineer. (In time, Bob would believe the other man who recommended him was Gene Reynolds, whose judgment was deeply valued by Johnson.)

"I know you like that 104 and those 104 guys like you," he said, "but I've got something here that's faster than the 104, goes higher than the 104, and goes farther than the 104."

Bob was intrigued, especially when Johnson stood up, shoved his chair back, motioned him to the doorway, and said, "Let's go out and take a look at it."

His first glimpse of the machine, which was still being built on the adjacent hangar floor, was memorable, because it was unlike anything he had ever seen. It was a dull metallic color. It looked futuristic and fast. "This came as a complete surprise," Bob said. "I knew nothing at all about the project, because it was being kept a total secret."

He didn't even know what to call it.

The thought of flying the new bird excited him, but after Johnson made clear that he wanted Bob to join the project as a test pilot right away, Gilliland began explaining that he had been assigned to Italy and would be leaving soon. The F-104 was a big moneymaker for the company, and revenue equaled corporate power. The Italians were paying Lockheed (and General Electric, which manufactured the engine) millions to produce the Starfighter, and the executives wanted Gilliland on-site to make the deal work. The mysterious new plane would have to wait.

Kelly was not happy, but he appreciated the pilot's dilemma.

About six months later, Schalk placed a long-distance telephone call to Italy and told Bob, "Kelly would like you to come home at once."

This he greeted with all the unbridled enthusiasm of an ambitious Minor Leaguer being called up to the Show.

Johnson had not tried to stop him from moving to Italy, probably because the new plane was still in the early stages of development, but now he was prepared to exert his considerable influence to get him back.

After less than two years with Lockheed, Gilliland's expertise with the Starfighter made him a very valuable asset to the executives who were selling it around the world, and they were willing to do anything to keep him. In the ensuing corporate tug-of-war for his services, Archie Folden, who managed the program, took him to dinner and began lobbying Bob to stay, banging the table with his fist. "You don't want to be leaving now. It will be bad for me! Bad for you! Bad for Lockheed!"

The F-104 people managed to delay his departure, but ultimately, he made the decision to head back to California, which required the intervention of the Lockheed CEO. He had been offered something he could not resist, something the Starfighter people knew nothing about, because, even at the highest levels of the company, it remained a closely guarded secret.

When he set the wheels in motion, LeVier called to ask, "Who do you think should replace you?"

After considering the all-important question for a moment, he said, "How about Greenamyer?"

Onetime air force pilot Darryl Greenamyer had been on the payroll as a production test pilot in Palmdale for a few months and was just starting his long association with the F-104. On a bitterly cold December day, he arrived on a commercial flight at the Torino airport, dressed like a man who had just flown in from sunny California. Bob met his plane, shook his hand, and said, "The first thing you need to do is go get some winter clothes!"

When Bob touched down at Los Angeles International Airport, he drove straight to Burbank. He had flown through the night and needed a shave. It was a Sunday, the plant was quiet, and Johnson was alone in his office, waiting for him. There was precious little small talk before the man seated behind the neatly ordered desk got right to business. "I've looked over your record and your background," he said, "and I cannot see how you could be anything but a patriot."

Not quite sure where Johnson was taking the conversation, Gilliland nodded his head and interjected, "Kelly, you're absolutely right about that!"

Johnson was the sort of man who liked to cut through the red tape, and even though Bob had not been subjected to the sort of rigorous security investigation typically required by the people in Washington who wrote the big checks, he was willing to leverage his immense clout to avoid any additional delays.

"I've never vouched for anybody with the CIA before," he said, looking Gilliland squarely in the eyes, "but I'm vouching for you."

He pounded his fist on the desk, and it was done.

In the years after the USSR exploded its first atomic bomb, the American intelligence community became obsessed with obtaining the sort of knowledge about the rival superpower's capabilities and activities that could only be gleaned from the air. The first attempts at aerial reconnaissance were made in the early 1950s in modified B-36 bombers, stripped of armaments and loaded with the most sophisticated cameras of the day. Such incursions carried a very high risk, operationally and politically, especially as Russian technology advanced, and they were mostly limited to areas around the border before being abandoned altogether. This weakness tied Washington's hands, leaving much of the vast Soviet heartland invisible to U.S. intelligence at a time of mounting tension and fear, as teachers across America led school children through duck-and-cover drills, parents dug bomb shelters, and politicians warned of a "missile gap."

To solve this problem, Washington turned to Kelly Johnson.

Presented with the challenge of designing a high-altitude reconnaissance aircraft capable of evading Soviet radar and missiles while capturing high-quality photographs, he responded with the U-2, which featured distinctively long wings, skin made of ultralight aluminum, and operational characteristics that in some ways mimicked a glider. Landing could be very tricky, because of a tendency to float when flaring in ground effect, with its slow landing speed causing it to be susceptible to variable winds. At a maximum altitude of more than 70,000 feet, the aircraft was deemed invulnerable to enemy defenses—at least for a few years.

The covert program was directed by the CIA, the spy agency founded after World War II to keep an eye on the Soviets and other potential enemies. No man more profoundly shaped the agency's culture or cultivated its influence than Allen W. Dulles, who served as director from 1953 to 1961. Dulles once told a reporter to think of the CIA as "the State Department for unfriendly countries."[1]

When the CIA approved the design and awarded a contract to Lockheed for the production of twenty spy planes, the Skunk Works swept into action, racing the alarm clock in Johnson's head. (Lockheed actually came in about $2 million under budget.) In the spring of 1955, Kelly called LeVier into his office and told him to close the door.

"Listen, you want to fly my new airplane?"

"What is it?"

"I can't tell you—only if you say yes. If not, get your ass out of here."[2]

LeVier, who saw his boss as a father figure, nodded, and Kelly unfurled a blueprint, told his most trusted pilot what he needed to know, reminded him not to say a word about it to anybody—even his wife—and gave him an immediate assignment: locate an isolated place where we can test the plane.

Several weeks later, Johnson and LeVier escorted CIA official Richard M. Bissell Jr. to a desolate, uninhabited patch of land in the Nevada desert centered on the massive dry lake bed known as Groom Lake. Just over the horizon, to the southwest, lay the Nevada Test Site, where the military exploded hundreds of nuclear bombs to gauge their potency and impact during the Cold War, filling the surrounding skies with ominous mushroom clouds. Bissell, the Yale-educated economist who had been placed in charge of the U-2 program, approved the location and quietly acquired the land and restricted the surrounding airspace for more than five hundred square miles, turning the massive land mass populated with rattlesnakes and scorpions into a classified fortress. Through a dummy corporation, to prevent the activity from being traced back to the CIA, Johnson hired a construction company to build the first semblance of an infrastructure, including a control tower, two hangars, and a mess hall, and arranged with another contractor to haul in a series of portable trailers to house the pilots and other workers. (In the years ahead, after the evening meal, the mess hall was converted into a makeshift movie theater, by reassembling the chairs and unfurling a portable screen.) It took just 243 days from concept to first flight.

The program was approved at the highest level. Realizing he was playing with fire, President Dwight Eisenhower demanded that only civilians be sent on missions that violated the USSR's airspace. Eisenhower wanted some measure of plausible deniability if the Russians ever got lucky and Premier Nikita Khrushchev accused him of committing an act of war.

Starting in the summer of 1956, without the knowledge of the American public, the CIA began conducting overflights of the Soviet Union. The U-2 campaign proved very successful, allowing U.S. officials to identify and assess Russian strengths and weaknesses as never before.

Heading into a highly anticipated summit meeting with Khrushchev, Eisenhower approved one last overflight, aiming to strengthen his informational leverage. Just after dawn on May 1, 1960—which happened to be Gilliland's thirty-fourth birthday—a U-2 piloted by Francis Gary Powers, who had once flown F-84s in the U.S. Air Force, took off from a base in Pakistan and moved into the skies high above the USSR. His mission was scheduled to take him more than 4,800 miles, near the plane's operational limits, in order to photograph several military installations before exiting the country to the north. He was not, however, invisible. During the four years since the first U-2 overflight, the USSR had achieved great strides in its defensive capabilities, and the Russians carefully tracked the plane on radar as it moved into the heart of the country. As news of the incursion spread up the military chain of command, a high-ranking general woke Khrushchev, who gave an unambiguous order: destroy the American invader.

When Powers was shot down near the city of Sverdlovsk, by the combined blast of several surface-to-air missiles (SAMs), the Cold War careened off in a dangerous new direction. Captured alive and identified as an employee of the CIA, when most Americans remained blissfully unaware of the agency's existence, he was tried for espionage as the world watched and sentenced to ten years, humiliating the U.S. government, pushing East-West tensions to the brink, and closing a front in the covert war.

The United States was once again blind.

Even before Gilliland joined Lockheed, Johnson was already working this problem.

In the autumn of 1963, Bob and Mary bought an ultramodern, 6,500-square-foot, hilltop home in the upscale La Canada Flintridge community, located on the western edge of the San Gabriel Valley near Pasadena. The view from 244 Inverness Drive was spectacular. The floor of the entry hall was covered in black terrazzo. The furniture in the dining room and the master bedroom was custom-made. Palm trees surrounded the large swimming pool, and the garage and carport could accommodate seven cars. The Gillilands hosted lavish parties, including an Armenian-themed dinner featuring a ballet dancer.

The house, which cost about $100,000, an enormous sum for the day, made an unmistakable statement. Clearly, Bob had arrived in his chosen profession. Of this there could be no doubt.

Several months before they moved in to the La Canada house, he stepped into a shadowy world. His job was now classified. He said nothing about his work, and family and friends knew better than to ask questions. They were allowed to know that he was employed by Lockheed but not what he did or where he did it.

"When he became involved with the Skunk Works," Mary recalled, "it was like a curtain came down on all the information. No, come to think of it, it was more like a steel door."

Bill Weaver, who joined the F-104 program in 1961, noticed that three highly regarded Starfighter pilots "sort of disappeared."

"They were still around, and we still socialized. But we couldn't talk about what they were doing," Weaver recalled. "They went over to the dark side, and nobody had a clue what they were doing."

In contrast to his days flying the F-104, when he went to work wearing a pilot's jumpsuit, Gilliland now walked out the door every morning in a perfectly tailored Brooks Brothers suit, carrying a small overnight bag, which contained toiletries and a set of thermal underwear.

His wife did not know where he was going or if he would be home that evening.

After driving to Burbank, the man in the Brooks Brothers suit stepped onto a Lockheed Constellation, one of a small fleet that served a specialized clientele. He was surrounded by similarly attired men who looked like they were headed to Cleveland for a sales conference, perpetuating an illusion deemed necessary for national security.

Around the cabin there was very little chatter and absolutely no shop talk. "You knew better than to talk business, because everything was strictly on a need-to-know basis," recalled T. D. Barnes, a tracking specialist who regularly flew on the Connies. Like many others, Frank Murray took the opportunity to close his eyes and catch a nap. "You're living in a world where you're told, 'Don't talk about anything,'" Murray said.

When the aircraft headed east, veered off the radar into restricted airspace, and touched down about an hour after takeoff, Bob and the other passengers stepped into the clandestine world created specifically for the U-2. To some, it was Groom Lake. To others, it was Watertown, Paradise Ranch, or simply the Ranch. The name was of little consequence, because they were forbidden to speak of the secret base in the outside world—because it did not exist. It did not appear on any maps. Only later would Area 51 gather a mystique that launched a thousand conspiracy theories.

As the base became the murky epicenter of various top secret projects, the obsession with maintaining absolute secrecy colored everything. After living for several years with his family in Las Vegas, which allowed him to drive to work, using a very specific pass to traverse the various military checkpoints manned by men with automatic weapons, pilot Frank Murray shifted to a new program and was told he needed to move. "They didn't want any connections between my home life and Area 51," he said. "And to them, Las Vegas was too close. [They] told me, 'You'll have to go in through the backdoor with the rest of the guys out of Burbank.'" So he moved his family to Palmdale and commuted on the Connies.

"You have to remember what those times were like," Gilliland said. "The threat from the Russians was very real, and we knew they had people snooping around trying to learn our secrets."

While having lunch with some of the other pilots' wives in Lancaster, a young lady mentioned something about the secret base. "Yeah, it must be in Nevada," Mary interjected, just guessing, based on a combination of her husband's travel schedule and geography.

"I don't know who turned me in, but Bob came home that night and he was not happy! He said he had been pulled in and questioned, because they thought that he had told me something. Well, he hadn't told me anything. It was just deductive reasoning on my part."

She learned to keep her guesses to herself.

Even though Gilliland was allowed to begin his new work without a background check, the CIA eventually conducted several rigorous investigations of him, which included paying personal visits to many of his relatives and friends. Toof Brown learned to recognize the sign that the agency was renewing his friend's security clearance. Two stern-looking men in dark suits repeatedly showed up at his Memphis office and started peppering him with questions, which began with a familiar refrain:

"You're a friend of Bob Gilliland?"

"Yes."

"Do you know what he's working on?"

"No. Can't tell you anything about it, 'cause I don't know anything."

Brown knew only that his friend worked for Lockheed and that he was assigned to something secret.

In preparation for his new job, Gilliland made the first of several trips to the Worcester, Massachusetts, headquarters of the David Clark Company, where he was fitted for the first of his pressurized so-called moon suits.

Several months after Gilliland began working out of Groom Lake, Yeager put the suit to the ultimate test when he lost control of his specially designed F-104 at 108,700 feet. On the way out, he collided with what was left of his seat, which caused a nasty gash around his eye, and suffered burns on his shoulder and neck. But the pressure suit helped save his life.

"The moon suit was uncomfortable and a lot of trouble," Gilliland said, "but it sure made the difference in what we were doing."

When Robert Jr. was about five, a photographer captured a memorable photograph of the test pilot's son standing in the distinctive silver boots that formed the bottom of his father's suit. "It was so funny," Robert said. "They came all the way up to my waist."

During his trips for fittings in Worcester, Bob always returned with something extra: a nylon envelope containing two new bras, compliments of Clark, whose main business was manufacturing ladies' underwear. "I'm sure all the astronaut wives got them too," Mary said.

Six years after the Soviet Union ignited the space race by launching Sputnik into the earth's orbit, leading to the formation of the National Aeronautics and Space Administration (NASA), Americans saw the Mercury astronauts as the ultimate Cold Warriors. The former military aviators who survived the rigorous selection and training process and then strapped into cramped capsules atop massive rockets, facing the possibility of instant death as the world watched on live television, became the public face of a geopolitical struggle.

Like Bob, his old air force friend Gordon Cooper survived those formative days of jet fighters in Germany to write his name in the history books. Not long after Gilliland began his new assignment, Cooper completed twenty-two orbits of the earth in his *Faith 7* capsule, accumulating more time in space than all the previous five Mercury astronauts combined. He was paraded down Broadway amid a blur of confetti, cementing his legend in a tribute reserved for American heroes including Charles Lindbergh, Howard Hughes, and John Glenn.

In time, the public would learn that the road to the moon began much earlier, with the accumulation of practical knowledge gained by the rocket-propelled aircraft and other high-altitude testing.

Project Manhigh was the brainchild of Colonel John Paul Stapp, a physician whose pioneering research included inventing techniques to help pilots overcome decompression sickness. When Stapp started working with escape systems and balloons to determine the various impacts of high-altitude travel on the body, he recruited test pilot Joe Kittinger, one of Gilliland's closest friends, who had recently survived bailing out of an F-100 that caught fire soon after takeoff.

On June 2, 1957, while wearing a pressure suit that weighed more than he did, Kittinger rode a specially designed balloon to an altitude of 96,784 feet—shattering the previous record by more than three miles. Looking down into the morning sky, Kittinger could see the curvature of the earth, where blue blended to "the blackest black I'd ever seen . . . blacker than ink."[3] Having accomplished his goal, the air force officials on the ground ordered him to begin his descent, warning that he would soon be running out of oxygen. He quickly tapped a reply in Morse code: "Come up and get me!" They worried that he had lost his mind, in that netherworld beyond the clouds, but in fact, Kittinger had already started his preparations to return to the ground. He was just having a little fun.

When Project Mercury was announced, several people encouraged Kittinger to apply to be one of America's first astronauts. Stapp felt certain that Kittinger would be selected, but with another high-altitude test in the works, Kittinger felt an obligation to continue with Stapp, who told him, "If you leave, I'll have to start all over again."

"I would have loved to have been an astronaut, but I was committed to working the objectives that Dr. Stapp had defined," Kittinger said. "I never regretted that decision, because I figured we helped get the program off the ground with the work that we did."

Kittinger's lofty flights continued with Project Excelsior. On August 16, 1960, he rode a similar balloon-lofted gondola to a new record altitude of 102,800 feet. Then he jumped out, falling with a small stabilization chute, reaching 614 miles per hour, a man transformed into a bullet, before denser air gradually slowed his speed. At four minutes thirty-six seconds and 17,000 feet, his main chute opened, gliding Joe safely to earth.

"It was a glorious period in our country's history," he said. "We had the leadership, the spirit, and the will to dream big and work on challenging problems, including what Bob Gilliland was doing with the Skunk Works."

While NASA moved on to Project Gemini, the next step in the decade-long race to beat the Russians to the moon, Gilliland and his colleagues at Groom Lake were waging their own Cold War in the shadows.

Two years before the ill-fated Powers flight, Johnson started planning for the future. Anticipating the U-2's eventual obsolescence, he drew up the first proposal for its successor on April 21, 1958, according to his project diary. Two months later, he presented the plan to the CIA and began working his way through the bureaucracy. A competition among defense contractors ensued, and just three months before the U-2 was shot down, the Skunk Works was awarded the contract to begin developing an aircraft code-named Archangel under the auspices of the top secret Oxcart program. Johnson promised delivery in twenty months.

Later in 1960, as Washington scrambled to paint the Powers disaster in the best possible light, Johnson was convinced to participate in an NBC News television broadcast concerning the U-2. Writing in his diary, he conceded, "I don't want any more publicity on the U-2, for the obvious reason that it might center attention on what I'm doing now."[4]

As the new Kennedy administration debated the political ramifications of future overflights of the Soviet Union—which had been completely curtailed after May 1, 1960—Johnson's revolutionary plane began to take shape inside the Skunk Works. At first, they informally called it the Article. When Gilliland saw it for the first time, it was still a dull metallic color.

Much like his other creations, the aircraft began with Kelly thinking big. He imagined what it would take to create a plane capable of exceeding Mach 3 and reaching a ceiling above 90,000 feet, well beyond the reach of the most advanced SAMs. Such a plane would give the United States the eyes and ears it needed, especially when it was equipped with even more sophisticated surveillance equipment than was available on the U-2. Such a plane might just make the difference. But it took a lot of math and a lot of outside-the-box thinking to bring the new plane to life. Week after week, month after month, Johnson and his team worked through a series of enormously complex problems related to all-important issues including temperature, airflow, engine capacity, metal stress, radar reflectivity, camera stability, and fuel.

Exploiting a series of engineering breakthroughs, the plane that would eventually be known as the A-12 departed radically from the U-2 and every other aircraft previously built. Ben Rich, the senior engineer who would one day succeed

Johnson, said, "In complexity the U-2 was to the Blackbird as a covered wagon was to an Indy 500 racer."[5]

But it took a test pilot to prove it would fly.

On April 26, 1962, Lou Schalk guided the only working A-12, known officially as Article 121, off the runway at Groom Lake. It wobbled dramatically. He worried about being able to fly around the pattern necessary to set it back down on the runway. "I was probably about 3 to 4 percent past the aft limit for the center of gravity, so it was unstable," he recalled.[6]

After traveling less than two miles, he abruptly landed the craft on the lake bed, where it was immediately swallowed in a cloud of dust. The tower called to make sure everything was all right, and he radioed back in the affirmative. But they could not hear him, because the positioning of the UHF radio antenna on the bottom of the fuselage was not intended to allow communications from the ground. The tower called a second time and then a third, unable to see the plane or hear from its pilot.

"Everyone was having a heart attack," Schalk said, "but when I finally made the turn and came out of the dust, [they realized] I hadn't run into the mountain and blown up the plane. There was a big sigh of relief."[7]

Kelly understood how critical it was to have test pilots he could trust. No matter how brilliant the design, every aircraft was an unproven fusion of various technologies. Only a certain kind of experienced aviator could put a plane through its paces and determine the problems that needed to be solved, and Johnson was determined to have complete control over the selection process.

When an air force delegation led by General Don Flickinger showed up at the Skunk Works and proposed creating a Project Mercury–style screening program to select A-12 pilots, Kelly quickly shot him down. "He said they could help me design the plane! The last thing I need around this joint is an assemblage of pilots, and I told them so strongly."[8]

In addition to Gilliland, who joined the program in early 1963, the A-12 team featured two other Korean War fighter pilots: Jim Eastham, who moved to Lockheed after a decade-long career at Hughes, where he became an expert in air-to-air missile technology, and Bill Park, who flew the F-102 Delta Dagger for Convair before being recruited to the Skunk Works.

"We had all sorts of problems with [the A-12], which was understandable because it was right on the cutting edge in so many ways," Gilliland said. "One time, I couldn't even go 5 miles an hour [taxiing out] because the whole frame was shaking."

Mary kept noticing that the dirty long johns Bob brought home in his overnight bag always included a rip in the same area. She repeatedly sewed it up and wondered why the same place kept getting torn. When his wife's dutiful repairs came to the attention of the pilot, he told her, "Don't bother with that." He explained that the hole was necessary to insert a sensor underneath his underwear.

In time, his wife grew accustomed to his unpredictable schedule, which often kept him away overnight. She knew nothing about the plane, but she understood that experimental equaled dangerous. She knew he was risking his life. She knew he could die at work. She knew much more than she wanted to know.

"So much of the time, I was just scared to death," she said.

Emergencies were frequent and sometimes catastrophic.

Park, a native of South Carolina who answered to the call sign Dutch 50, lost control of his craft on approach in the summer of 1964. He was forced to bail out at a low altitude but parachuted safely as the plane crashed into the lake bed.

One of the most memorable scenes involving the aircraft happened several years later, when an A-12 flown by Mele Vojvodich thundered off the runway. The noise caught Frank Murray's attention.

Murray happened to be standing a few hundred feet away.

He had just completed a flight in an F-101. The familiar sound of the A-12 caused him to look up from his paperwork, because he always loved to watch the magnificent beast pull itself into the air. This time, however, he was unnerved by what he saw.

"When it came off [the runway], it went all over the place, like it was doing acrobatics," he said. "The flight path was absolutely nuts. It pitched up, and then it went sideways and pitched up again."

Moments after takeoff, the plane crashed into the lake bed and exploded into a massive fireball.

Rushing to the scene across the icy lake, the fire truck swerved to keep from hitting Vojvodich, who had once mounted the dangerous reconnaissance raid deep into China during the Korean War. He had ejected safely from the A-12 and was walking back toward the hangar.

Several months after Schalk took the A-12 to Mach 3 for the first time—a historic feat that required more than a year to achieve—Gilliland headed out on a mission to hit Mach 3.15.

"We were taking turns pushing it up [on the Mach scale], in case somebody got killed," Gilliland said. "It was my turn to take that next incremental step."

The flight went just as planned. Bob plotted a course toward the Canadian border and moved through the various procedures to hit his number, setting a new speed record. Then he headed for home.

"I had a great feeling coming in," he recalled. "It was a great flight with no emergencies."

After he shut the plane down, one of his colleagues came running up. "I guess you haven't heard?"

"What do you mean?"

"We just heard that they shot JFK and Governor Connally of Texas."

They rushed to the hangar, where several others were crowded around a radio, for there were no televisions at Groom Lake.

Like many fighter pilots, Bill Park was known for dark humor, and at one point, as tension gripped the room, he blurted out, "I don't know what everybody's getting so exciting about! It's nothing but another Texas shoot-out!"

Everybody laughed.

When the awful truth was confirmed, the jokes stopped.

In his debriefing the next day, when he reported the details of his flight, Bob could tell Kelly was impressed not just by the goal he achieved but by his restraint. "I easily could have let it go to 3.2, but by this point, I had already learned from him to do what's on the card [which detailed the flight plan] and nothing but what's on the card," he said.

It did not take Kelly long to feel vindicated in his decision to bring Gilliland into the program.

Four years after leaving Memphis, Gilliland could look back and say without any hesitation that he had made the right decision. He loved his job. He was engaged in something that stirred his patriotism and was vital to national security. He was intellectually stimulated by the various operational challenges he was helping to solve in a craft whose very existence was a remarkable feat of modern technology. He was learning what it took to be a successful test pilot—what to do and what not to do.

"I was so grateful to Kelly for that opportunity," Gilliland said.

Frank never understood his eldest son's obsession with flight, but Bob was searching for something that could not be found in the security and predictability of upper-crust Memphis. He found the missing piece of himself in experimental testing, in a place few others could ever truly appreciate, because, like Area 51, it did not appear on any maps. It was a frontier that existed as much in the mind as in the sky.

Gilliland was at the controls for the A-12's first night flight and night landing; was the first to fly it at design speed, Mach 3.2, at night; the first to demonstrate controllability at night, with induced unstarts; the first to land with the center of gravity aft of the aft limit; and was the first to experience a double flameout and dead-stick ride.

After losing both engines at near 80,000 feet, Gilliland repeatedly tried to restart as he spiraled down toward the runway at Groom Lake.

Bill Skliar was chasing him in a Starfighter, carefully watching his tailpipes for signs of life.

The pilots kept talking with each other and with the tower. At one point, the controllers heard Bob's familiar southern drawl utter an ominous and unfamiliar sentence: "This looks real bad!"

Empowered by his history with dead-stick landings, he kept his cool and maintained enough speed to cause the windmilling engines to turn fast enough to create adequate hydraulic pressure, necessary to maintain the flight controls.

Well aware that a dead-stick landing in this particular craft would not be possible, he was prepared to eject, if he was ultimately unable to reignite. But it was an especially windy day. He was concerned that he might not survive an escape, especially if the high winds sent him hurtling to the ground. "You don't want to shake hands with a cactus doing 40 knots," he was fond of saying.

Finally, at 12,500 feet, Skliar saw a flicker. "You got a light!"

Gilliland would always be grateful for the assistance of his colleague, an accomplished pilot who flew one hundred combat missions in Korea and tested various experimental craft, including the A-12, while on loan to the CIA from the air force. Many years after retiring as a lieutenant colonel, he lost his life when one of the wings of his racing plane snapped off, causing him to crash into the desert near Reno in 1988.

Seconds before Skliar saw the faint red glow, Bob had started one engine at a low-power setting, providing enough pressure for a flare and landing. Knowing not to advance the throttle, which might have caused the engine to once again flame out, he delicately eased the craft onto the concrete strip, achieving a happy ending after one of the closest calls of his career.

About two months after the CIA green-lighted the development of the reconnaissance plane that would become known as the A-12, Johnson approached the air force about adapting the same design to produce an interceptor. The idea bounced around the Pentagon for a while, and when it was finally approved, the second plane in the Blackbird family went into development. It would be known as the YF-12A, featuring two seats, a guided missile system, and several compensating structural changes, including the addition of three stabilizing fins. On August 7, 1963, Jim Eastham made the first flight of the YF-12A, which the air force envisioned as a potent weapon for the Strategic Air Command.

Six years after Kelly started sketching out the plans for the world's first Mach 3 jet, the Oxcart program remained shrouded in secrecy. No one knew when or if President Lyndon Johnson would eventually allow the CIA to resume overflights of the Soviet Union, now that it was in possession of a powerful new tool. The A-12 and YF-12A were headed toward operational status. How they would be used ultimately was a political decision.

Soon after his death, the Society of Experimental Test Pilots (SETP) began presenting the Iven C. Kincheloe Award for "the most proficient test work" conducted during the previous year. It became one of the most coveted honors in the aviation industry.

The winners of the prestigious trophy have included John Glenn, Neil Armstrong, Scott Crossfield, and Dick Rutan.

On a memorable night in 1964, during a black-tie dinner at the Beverly Hilton Hotel attended by the aerospace elite, Joe Tymczyszyn, president of the Society of Experimental Test Pilots, stepped to the podium, alongside Dorothy Kincheloe, the pilot's widow. Dorothy was a beloved figure who helped preside over the presentation for decades, offering a powerful reminder of all those pioneers who paid the ultimate price while leading the country into the future. When Tymczyszyn recognized the team of Lou Schalk, Bob Gilliland, Jim Eastham, and Bill Park, sealing their clandestine achievement in aviation history, the crowd gave the pilots a standing ovation. It had required special permission from the government for the SETP to identify the pilots, even as press outlets including the *New York Times* connected the dots. The scuttlebutt did not affect the organization's deal with Washington.

"I can't tell you exactly what they did to win the Ivan C. Kincheloe Award," Tymczyszyn said, "but believe me they deserve it!"

SIX

Kelly's Masterpiece

THE ROAD TO THE KINCHELOE AWARD BEGAN SEVEN months earlier. On February 29, 1964, during his first general news conference after becoming president, Lyndon Johnson weaponized the covert Blackbird program. Facing charges that his administration was falling behind in the arms race with the Soviets, Johnson announced that the United States had developed a military plane whose performance "far exceeds that of any other aircraft in the world today."[1] He identified the plane as the A-11, which had been the working number of the previous version, and referred to it as an interceptor, which was only partially true. Johnson said that the aircraft could achieve an altitude "in excess of 70,000 feet" and that it was being flight-tested at Edwards, which allowed him to avoid disclosing the existence of Area 51.[2] To perpetuate this illusion, two YF-12As were rushed from Groom Lake to Edwards by Colonel Fox Stephens and Major Walt Daniel, after being briefed by Gilliland. The military hastily placed air force markings on the planes and even allowed the press to take pictures.

"It was all a big lie," Bob said.

The president's unmasking did not affect the tight-lipped

Skunk Works. "We were still forbidden to speak of [the Blackbird]," said engineer Pete Law.

Johnson made no mention of the aircraft's primary purpose, but the most knowledgeable reporters saw through the president's subterfuge. When the *Saturday Evening Post* published an article titled "The Great A-11 Deception"—which included the assertion that "aeronautical experts know that the plane . . . was designed to be a spy"[3]—the president began to lose control of the story. And he was not the sort of man to play defense when he could go on the offensive.

By this time, four distinct versions of the Blackbird were in development.

As his Skunk Works team moved forward with the A-12 for the CIA and the YF-12A for the air force, Kelly simultaneously developed the M-21, a model of the Blackbird capable of launching the D-21 drone on behalf of the agency. The remote technology embodied in the D-21 was far ahead of its time, foreshadowing the sort of capability that would one day become a central function of the U.S. military and intelligence arsenal. But the drone was destined to have an abbreviated lifespan. Like various other black-ops projects that never quite lived up to expectations, its existence was shrouded from public view for decades.

During this period, Kelly also proposed to the air force the dual-purpose R-12/RB-12, capable of utilization as either a bomber or a reconnaissance vehicle. The bomber idea was quickly abandoned, as several high-level officials saw the RB-12 as unwanted competition to North American Aviation's B-70 Valkyrie, already in the pipeline though riddled with problems and ultimately doomed. It was a difficult time to sell strategic bombers, as the advantage appeared to be tilting toward intercontinental ballistic missiles. The missile crowd believed it was better to push a button to ignite the distant furies, a viewpoint that gained strength after May 1,

1960, when the proven threat of Soviet SAMs suddenly colored bombers in a cloud of vulnerability.

But Kelly's reconnaissance idea found a constituency in the Pentagon, where the air force was engaged in a struggle for primacy with the CIA division sometimes referred to as Bissell's Air Force. (Wounded by the Bay of Pigs disaster, which pushed his boss Allen Dulles into an early retirement, Bissell left the agency in early 1962, while the first A-12 was still being assembled.) On December 27, 1962, two months after a U-2 piloted by Major Rudolph Anderson and dispatched by President Kennedy was shot out of the sky during the Cuban Missile Crisis, proving the loss of Powers's plane was no fluke, the air force placed an initial order for six aircraft under the new RS-71 designation. In time this development would be recognized as the birth of Kelly Johnson's most iconic aircraft.

With the election looming and the White House feeling the need for a preemptive strike against hawkish Republican nominee Barry Goldwater, President Johnson made a conscious decision to once again use the country's most advanced aircraft program to his political advantage. On July 24, in a news conference at the State Department, LBJ announced the development of a "long-range advanced strategic reconnaissance plane . . . that will fly at three times the speed of sound."[4] He called it the SR-71.

At the time, many people involved with the program believed the president accidentally transposed the letters. This version of events filtered through the Blackbird community for years, until one man decided to check the facts.

Colonel Richard Graham, who flew 210 combat missions in the F-4 Phantom during the Vietnam War, was assigned to the SR-71 program in 1974. He eventually was promoted to wing commander at Beale and, during his retirement, became a widely acknowledged expert on the aircraft.

In 2000, while researching the second of four books about

the Blackbird, Graham tracked down the ancient scripts and proved that the president read the text as written.[5]

But why?

Some have speculated that the change reflected a calculated decision by the president or someone in the administration to reinforce the preference of General Curtis Lemay, the air force chief of staff and firebrand former head of Strategic Air Command. To avoid embarrassing the president, Lockheed and the air force subsequently renamed the aircraft, the new acronym to represent "strategic reconnaissance," instead of "reconnaissance strike." This required a flurry of corrections to existing blueprints and associated materials. What to call it was not, however, their most pressing concern.

"Kelly was furious," Bob said. "Here we had gone to all these lengths to closely guard this secret, and LBJ just tells the world. He wasn't worried about anything but winning the election."

Around this time, Gilliland was named chief test pilot of LBJ's secret weapon.

"I knew it was to be the big one, and [Kelly's] selection of me was quite an honor," Gilliland recalled. "He knew I could do the job, and I knew it too."

Like every ambitious man who ever turned his thoughts to the sky, Kelly was forced to confront the limits of nature and technology. The birds made it look easy, but contending with the laws of gravity, physics, and motion demonstrated to every aeronautical engineer who ever wielded a T square like a paintbrush that human flight was an unnatural act. It could only be accomplished by harnessing the intricate vibrations of science, by understanding the cause and effect of thousands of actions across several different disciplines. The steady progression of technology allowed Johnson and men like him to prove some once-sacrosanct boundaries to be illusory, but the same achievements of rendered steel and calculated math often revealed ominous roadblocks scattered across the mysterious skies.

On the circuitous road to the SR-71 Blackbird, Kelly faced a long list of engineering problems disguised as stop signs.

In 1937, as storm clouds began to gather on the horizon, Britain's Royal Air Force contracted with Lockheed to build a bomber based on the Electra design. Turning the transport into a bomber sounded much simpler than it turned out to be, because the addition of a massive bomb bay, gun turret, and other combat-necessary equipment significantly altered the aircraft's performance. The daunting task of accommodating all that additional weight without sacrificing the plane's ability to take flight and maneuver and not break apart at the rivets fell to the same man who saved the Electra. Unfazed, Kelly Johnson, then just twenty-eight, locked himself in a London hotel room and spent several sleepless nights hunched over a drawing table. He emerged with a dramatic redesign for the Hudson bomber, just in time for it to become a key weapon in the RAF arsenal at the start of World War II.

In 1938, as the first warplanes neared completion, Prime Minister Neville Chamberlain flew a standard Electra to Munich for his historic negotiation with Adolf Hitler, after which he naively proclaimed he had achieved "peace in our time." Eleven months later, the blitzkrieg of Poland plunged the world into war.

In the years ahead, the various versions of the plane, known internally as Model 14, posed several critical engineering dilemmas that needed to be solved, including its tendency to fall into an uncontrollable roll under certain conditions. The innovative flap system he designed for the Hudson brought him his first taste of industry recognition, demonstrating the sort of resourcefulness that would mark his entire career.

Another defining moment occurred during the development of the Electra-inspired PV-2 Harpoon bomber for the U.S. Navy. During the prototype phase, Johnson discovered that the plane was not generating sufficient power, despite possessing one of the best engines of the day. The culprit, he soon discovered, was the size and placement of the propellers. After several weeks of painstaking trial and error, he ordered the production of significantly smaller props (measuring ten feet six inches in diameter, instead of the standard seventeen feet) and shifted them farther out on the wing, which dramatically improved the Harpoon's performance. "The prop was shorter but wider," he later recalled, "grabbed a bigger bite of air while turning more slowly, and thereby avoided problems with air buildup at the tips."[6]

By this time, he had begun to grapple with a particularly dangerous obstacle resulting from his own progress—the mighty power of colliding air.

The XP-38 Lightning was one of the first aircraft capable of going fast enough to experience aerodynamicists' concerns about the phenomenon known as compressibility, or the buildup of air ahead of the plane. This effect sometimes created a shock wave that LeVier compared to "a giant hand" that "shook [the plane] out of the pilot's control."[7] While testing one potential fix, the wings snapped off, and pilot Ralph Virden crashed to his death. The problem limited the planes' advisable speed and caused many pilots to be wary of straddling what was then the cutting edge of American aviation. After extensive wind tunnel testing, which demonstrated how and when compressibility placed stress and strain on various parts of the aircraft, Johnson developed a series of countermeasures, including external dive flaps that typically brought the nose up and curtailed the shock wave. The compressibility issue proved even worse on the jet-powered XP-80 Shooting Star, but once again, Johnson and his Skunk Works team methodically worked the problem, eventually diminishing the effects of the shock wave with the addition of a damper, a device that allows the pilot to reduce yaw and roll.

"Kelly was a problem solver who was relentless in pursuit of solutions," said longtime Skunk Works engineer Pete Law. "If he couldn't solve a problem himself, he found someone who could."

The U-2 posed a long list of design challenges, most connected to the imperative to make it as light aloft as possible. In order to achieve the desired altitude and range to render it an effective reconnaissance aircraft, the plane featured an aluminum skin roughly the thickness of a tin can, which, combined with the oversize wings, could leave it extremely vulnerable to turbulence. The first versions did not include an ejection seat, which saved thirty pounds, although the CIA eventually consented to a modification. This mandate even extended to the all-important landing gear, which was specially designed to save a few precious pounds but contributed to its difficult handling characteristics. Fuel storage was such a big part of the equation that when the liquid propellant began to burn off, steadily reducing the plane's weight, the U-2 would rise without application of additional burner.

Many solutions required delicately controlled trade-offs, dangerous wagers accepted as the price of flight. Among the various impacts of the revolutionary U-2—which Ben Rich called "a stern taskmaster [that was] unforgiving of pilot error or lack of concentration"[8]—was a rather small margin between the plane's maximum speed and its stall speed at high altitudes, which placed a premium on a pilot's ability to precisely navigate the so-called coffin corner. Too much velocity could produce uncontrollable buffeting, capable of snapping the wings off. Too little was equally perilous. "If you go a little bit slower than [the specifications], it would stall and fall out of the sky," recalled Harry Andonian, who spent several years as a U-2 test pilot at Edwards.

By the time Francis Gary Powers became a household name, Johnson was consumed with confronting a series of engineering problems that collectively represented the greatest challenge of his career.

Six decades after the Wright brothers' first flight, the aviation industry was experiencing explosive growth, enabled by a colliding maze of technological advancements. In addition to the singular achievements of pioneers such as Chuck Yeager and the Mercury astronauts, who risked their lives to extend the frontier into the distant sky, and the mounting demand for increasingly sophisticated helicopters and corporate jets, significant progress in commercial aviation was beginning to reach critical mass. In 1958 Pan Am became the first airline to offer regularly scheduled jet service. The maiden commercial flight of the Boeing 707, which cruised at more than 500 miles per hour, was such a momentous event that it prompted an appearance by President Eisenhower. Soon Douglas's DC-8 joined the race, as the various airlines began converting their fleets, hastening a new era of speed, safety, comfort, and relevance. The long-established jet age became something tangible and transformational when a middle-class consumer could buy a ticket and fly coast-to-coast in six hours.

In 1963, when Hollywood mogul Sonny Werblin acquired a struggling American Football League franchise, he quickly rebranded it in a way that perfectly captured aviation's increasingly prominent role in the zeitgeist. Even before signing Joe Namath, the newly christened New York Jets sounded cool, as if sprinkled with a whiff of the future.

"We were riding this great wave as an industry . . . seeing tremendous advances in aircraft," said celebrated pilot Clay Lacy, who played a leading role in the rise of the Learjet, which revolutionized corporate travel in the 1960s. "And nobody was more cutting-edge than the Skunk Works."

Beyond all the cloak-and-dagger, Building 82 struck a rather ordinary industrial vibe, right down to the birds who sometimes slipped through the big hangar door to terrorize the men in white shirts and skinny ties consumed with advanced calculations and drafting. In this distraction, dive-bombing took on a whole new meaning. Huddled in small offices by specialty group, several dozen smart and dedicated professionals were engaged in a very serious business, driven to strive for goals that others might consider out of reach. "To [Kelly], the word 'impossible' was a gross insult," recalled Ben Rich, his leading propulsion and thermodynamics engineer.[9]

Yet the same man could be "very practical . . . as capable of designing a four-holer latrine," in the words of Lou Schalk.[10] Johnson was so calculating and so intent on promoting efficiency that when he headed off for lunch at the Sky Room on the Lockheed lot, he invariably ran up the stairs, two at a time, explaining to a reporter, later in his career, when he was allowed to speak to reporters, "[It] saves energy. I only have to bend my knees half as many times."[11] He preferred quick oral presentations over detailed charts, and if an employee did not know the answer to a question, he knew better than to try to con the boss. Johnson was a stickler for deadlines. If someone arrived late to one of his 7:00 a.m. staff meetings, the locked door sent an unmistakable message.

The Skunk Works attracted the best and brightest engineers and technicians, every one of them energized by the opportunity to work on the most advanced projects under the guidance of a towering figure whose various honors would eventually include the Presidential Medal of Freedom, two Collier Trophies, the Howard Hughes Memorial Award, and induction into the National Aviation Hall of Fame.

Two decades after forming the Skunk Works, he still commanded a lean operation, managing to avoid the trappings of hierarchy or the creeping complacency so often seen in organizations that experience great success.

"Kelly was all about making quick decisions, because he was completely focused on the speed of development," Gilliland said. "He didn't believe in talking a problem to death. If a decision needed to be made, he made it and moved on."

No decision loomed larger in shaping his legacy than endeavoring to build the world's fastest, highest, most advanced plane—even before its predecessor was blasted out of the shadows.

Like all true innovators, Kelly understood that the path to success often led through failure. Not long after the U-2 became operational, the Skunk Works began developing the CL-400, a liquid-hydrogen-powered plane for the air force, since they desperately wanted in the spy game. Disappointing range and the complications of refueling such a volatile propellant hampered Project Suntan, which was scrapped before it moved beyond the model stage.

Several months later, when Johnson began selling the CIA on a replacement to the U-2, he went a different way but incorporated some of the Suntan research. In a meeting with his top engineers, the Skunk Works' boss proclaimed his ambition to build an airplane that could "rule the skies for a decade or more." Every man in the room knew what this meant and wondered how in the world Kelly could figure out how to take such a quantum leap into the future.

"Kelly's institution was one of taking risks," said Steve Justice, who served as the director of the Skunk Works in the early years of the twenty-first century and has closely studied the work of his celebrated predecessor. "He understood that breakthroughs don't come from the easy path. They come from taking the hard path."

At the time, the U-2, with a ceiling of slightly more than 70,000 feet, was the highest-flying plane in the world. It was, however, rather slow, which was part of the problem as Johnson began anticipating the requirements of trumping the Russians. The only crafts capable of achieving three times the speed of sound were powered by rockets, and they could hit this number for only a few precious minutes before exhausting their fuel. Among the jet-powered planes in operation by the U.S. military, only the F-104 could routinely achieve Mach 2 and only for a relatively short period. Kelly wanted to build a plane that could fly at least 50 percent faster than the Starfighter and climb five miles higher than the U-2, later explaining, "Neither the temperature nor the altitude experience [of previous planes] was much help for the design of the Mach 3 aircraft."

The combination of technological breakthroughs required to build such a craft was no less daunting than those embodied in the NASA rockets then being perfected to shoot for the moon.

"Virtually the entire plane had to be invented from scratch," Gilliland said. "What Kelly was doing was revolutionary in so many ways."

Near the end of his life, Johnson conceded, "The idea of attaining and staying at Mach 3.2 over long flights was the toughest job the Skunk Works ever had and the most difficult of my career."[12]

The long road to the SR-71 began with the A-1, the first permutation of a paper design developed in consultation with the CIA, and continued through eleven more versions, culminating with the A-12. Before the SR-71 could perfect the technology, the A-12 and YF-12A established most of the critical features that would make the SR-71 successful.

"For the longest time, Kelly felt that speed, altitude, and stealth were mutually exclusive—that you could not achieve all three," Justice said.

The biggest obstacle to building such a plane was heat.

After determining that the air friction caused at Mach 3 would push surface temperatures as high as 800°F, hot enough to melt most conventional metals, including the aluminum used on the U-2, Johnson began taking a hard look at stainless steel. The Electra had been a marvel in its day, and the calculations showed that stainless steel could handle the temperature. But stainless steel proved much too heavy to meet the new plane's ambitious specifications. The process of producing the appropriate strain of the metal was also much more complex.

Around this time, the Lockheed team began to consider an obscure metal every bit as strong as stainless steel. It could handle the high heat and was about half the weight. The Skunk Works had been experimenting with titanium for years, but no one had ever made an entire plane out of titanium. It was unproven and unavailable from domestic suppliers in sufficient quantities.

When it became clear to Kelly and his engineers that a titanium alloy was the only way to go, the CIA went to work, creating a series of dummy companies that began acquiring large stocks of the base metal—from miners in the Soviet Union, home of the largest known reserves. This operation would go down among the most fruitful in agency history, exploiting Russian industrial capacity to build the world's most expensive tripod so it could be used against the USSR. Aviation historian Paul Crickmore, one of the foremost experts on the Lockheed spy planes, called this "absolutely one of the greatest ironies of the Cold War."

The metallurgy caused tremendous headaches. Lockheed was forced to invent tools and protocols to fabricate and assemble the titanium, a labor-intensive and delicate process that resulted in costly spoilage rates, sometimes surpassing 90 percent. In certain conditions, the metal was so brittle that it shattered on the factory floor.

"With the titanium, we had a whole new set of problems . . . lessons that had to be learned," Law said. "How do you treat it? How do you form it? How do you drill it? How do you repair it, if there's a crack or something? All of these things had to be learned from scratch."

When the staff began to notice a high failure rate on some of the welded panels, the investigation led to a rather unexpected discovery: the chlorine-laced Burbank city water used to wash the titanium promoted weakness. So they switched to untreated water, and the problem disappeared. As with various other Skunk Works initiatives through the years, the team was driven to constantly improve their rate of metal utilization, for reasons of economics and schedule. In later years, when he was allowed to talk about details, Kelly proudly noted that, over time, his people dramatically increased drill life from an average of 10 holes per grind to more than 119, a stat reflecting the group's ability to turn experience into quantifiable progress (and Johnson's incredibly meticulous, scientific nature).[13]

When President Johnson went public about the program, one of the most disturbing aspects to Kelly was his decision to mention the titanium. Fortunately, by this point, the Skunk Works had stockpiled enough of the raw material to build most of the planes. The Russians never caught on to the deception, which continued for years, and it would be decades before the truth of this brilliant stroke of tradecraft filtered among the professionals who helped bring the Blackbird to life.

The titanium significantly mitigated the heat problem. Ben Rich and Pete Law were credited with an innovation that helped reduce the impact of the fiery friction. Tapping into the principles known as Kirchoff's law of thermal radiation, which deals with the emission and absorption of heat, the two engineers suggested that they cover the plane in a layer of black paint. Although this added about sixty pounds—which caused Kelly, at first, to balk, because he was understandably obsessive about weight—they proved that the color change caused a certain amount of the heat to radiate away from the surface, lowering the temperature by 50°F to 80°F. This differential also allowed them to use a softer, more malleable alloy. Only later would Rich and Law understand that they had conspired to give the plane one of its most distinctive features, enhancing the mythology that would one day make it one of the most iconic and mysterious symbols of the Cold War.

The cultlike fascination that would one day surround the plane resulted largely from its dramatic, futuristic shape, which Johnson likened to "a snake swallowing three mice."[14] Extensive wind tunnel testing provided necessary intelligence on the most efficient design. The determination to maximize aerodynamics, to help the craft glide through the air with minimum obstruction, led to various unusual features, including the addition of chines to the fuselage, which improved lift, critical to a plane that weighed about twice as much as a U-2. Equally important was the attempt to address the CIA's desire to make it invisible to radar, which had been a primary consideration in the heated competition with rival Convair. A team of engineers invested enormous time in the process of learning how to incorporate elements that decreased electronic signatures. The slope-enhanced design, bereft of harsh angles and featuring a convex fuselage and twin tails positioned at a precisely calibrated angle, resulted in a significantly reduced radar cross section. Several areas of the plane were coated with a dielectric material, to prevent the flow of electrical charges, invented by Lockheed physicist Edward Lovick, one of the fathers of stealth technology. It all began with the Blackbird.

One of the most difficult problems was figuring out how to keep the cockpit cool amid all that raging heat. After all, the various innovative features of the airplane would be rendered meaningless if the pilot could not be insulated from the inferno just outside the canopy. The resulting air-conditioning system, powered by each engine's ninth-stage compressor, took more than a year to perfect, every bit as complex as cutting-edge solutions with regard to the electrical grid, hydraulics, navigation, inertial guidance, and ejection.

"The number of incredibly difficult problems that had to

be solved to make the plane work effectively was staggering," Gilliland said. "When you consider the environment it was designed for, all that massive heat and airflow, you have to be amazed at the technological achievement it represented."

Like the surface-metal issue, developing the massive power capable of propelling the machine required an unprecedented level of innovation. Throughout the design process, while waiting for the green light from Washington, Kelly considered several different options, many of which would have pushed Project Oxcart behind schedule. The eventual decision to utilize two Pratt and Whitney J58 turbo-ramjet engines was awash in practicality. It had been developed for a never-built U.S. Navy plane and was available. The J58 featured an innovative approach known as bleed bypass. At Mach 3, it bypassed 20 percent of the air from the fourth-stage compressor around the engine and directly into the afterburner, giving the engine a powerful partial ramjet feature. The engine needed to be able to accept air from the inlets, with compressor inlet temperature (CIT) approaching 800°F (427°C), which required a series of modifications. The Skunk Works team was convinced that the first plane to fly continuously on afterburners—harnessing 160,000 horsepower to produce a 3,400°F blowtorch—could cruise indefinitely at Kelly's magic number of Mach 3.2, or a mile every 1.7 seconds, the Blackbird's best speed for fuel economy.

According to the now-declassified manual eventually written for the pilots, "Mach 3.2 is the design Mach number. Mach 3.17 is the maximum scheduled cruise speed recommended for normal operations. However, when authorized by the Commander, speeds up to Mach 3.3 may be flown if the limit CIT of 427 degrees C is not exceeded."[15]

Everything hinged on the plane's ability to control the ambient air.

When the aircraft zoomed through the stratosphere at three times the speed of sound, air approached the engines at roughly the same velocity. But because no engine was capable of accepting supersonic air, such jets needed a mechanism, known as an inlet, to slow down the air as it entered the compressor.

"It's difficult to explain how tough this geometry challenge was," Justice said.

Future SR-71 pilot Buz Carpenter noted, "Ben Rich said he borderlined on insanity developing the inlets."

The Blackbird inlet, developed by a team led by Rich in collaboration with Dave Campbell, was one of the plane's most crucial features. As the aircraft accelerated and climbed into thinner air, the inlet's cone-shaped spike began to withdraw at Mach 1.6, retracting into the inlet one and five-eighths inches for every tenth increase in Mach. At Mach 3.2, this resulted in a total retraction of about twenty-six inches. As the spike withdrew, the intake area at the front of the inlet increased 112 percent, while the area of the throat inside the inlet decreased 54 percent, forcing the air to be compressed and slowed until the air became subsonic as it passed through the normal shock wave at the throat. The dramatic compression of the air also caused a dramatic increase in air temperature, sometimes approaching 427°C, the redline CIT limit.

"Ideally," Gilliland explained, "the normal shock wave is captured just inside the inlet . . . where the inlet air transforms from supersonic to subsonic flow, accompanied by increases above ambient pressure of as high as forty to one and a sharp rise in temperature. This high-pressure and very hot inlet air is then introduced to the engine between .35 and .55 Mach, which is ideal. The engine thinks it is at low altitude. That is the magic of the complex inlet system."

As a result of all this aerial manipulation, the engines provided just 17 percent of the plane's thrust. The bulk of the energy was drawn from the inlets (54 percent) and the adjoining nacelles and ejectors (29 percent).

"When you are flying along at three times the speed of

sound, the inlet is sort of pulling the airplane forward," Law said.

The symbiosis between the machine and its environment created enormous power, harnessed air transformed into a potent fuel. But this was accomplished only after several years of painstaking trial and error—on paper, on the factory floor, and in the cockpit. "In the whole series of research aircraft . . . there are no power plant problems remotely resembling those we encountered," Kelly said.[16]

During the early tests, Schalk, Gilliland, Park, and Eastham spent much of their time dealing with the various unknowns associated with the extreme temperatures and an unproven engine and inlet system designed to operate in what Bob noted was a "zone that's partially aerodynamic and largely inertial." Everything needed to be tested to see if it would work correctly under the circumstances. "We had to worry about all these melted sensors, which had not been developed to withstand the heat," Schalk said.[17] (This caused Kelly to produce heat-resistant wiring, much of it insulated by asbestos.) After his wobbly first flight of the A-12, Schalk suggested to Kelly, "Why don't we turn on the dampers and see how it works? We can always turn them off." It worked. One problem solved. No one knew for certain what the inlet pressures were or should be, so they flew the plane and created a spike schedule, gathering intelligence and detecting patterns.

Years later, computerization would play a significant role in the airflow process, but in the beginning, the intricate system was calculated using slide rules and was controlled mechanically. The potential for danger forever lurked in the thin air around 85,000 feet, where the outside temperature could vary wildly—from -50°F to -90°F—in a matter of seconds. "The inlet airflow had to match the engine's required airflow," Law said, "and if it didn't and the engine controls couldn't handle it . . . sometimes the inlet would stall, which could be trouble."

The dreaded "unstart" was a reminder that not even Kelly Johnson could tame nature.

"We had a great deal of trouble perfecting our air-inlet engine matching system and encountered numerous 'unstarts,' which involved stark danger," Bob said.

In these instances, the placement of the normal shock wave was not handled precisely enough, requiring the pilot to manually open the bypass doors and adjust the spike. A key change devised by Ben Rich eventually reduced unstarts significantly, and when the advent of digital computers made such violent events exceedingly rare, the technology was able to reach its full potential.

At cruise, the Blackbird consumed an average of about thirty-five thousand pounds of fuel per hour, about four-tenths of a mile per gallon, and like many other aspects of the plane, the choice was influenced by the dangers of heat. The very stable JP-7, a blend invented specially for the Skunk Works, alleviated most concerns about accidental fires igniting in the distant sky. "You could drop a match on it and it wouldn't burn," Bob recalled.

As a further precaution against accidental fire in the hot fuel tanks, space in the tanks was filled with nitrogen gas as fuel was consumed. Because of this, shortly before a flight, fog could be seen eerily venting from the forward fuselage.

The Blackbird used a chemical ignition system featuring triethylborane, a pyrophoric liquid that ignited spontaneously when exposed to air. A small so-called TEB tank, pressurized with nitrogen, was installed on each engine, enough for sixteen injections of TEB per engine. TEB was automatically injected when the pilot advanced the throttle at initial engine start and each time the throttle was advanced into the afterburner position.

For several months, starting in the summer of 1964, Gilliland continued to fly A-12 and YF-12A missions out of Area 51 but regularly commuted to Burbank to check on the progress of his new plane as it began to take shape on the factory floor.

More than a decade after bucking the air force system and angling to fly fighters, despite the arbitrary height restriction, Gilliland continued to deal with cramped cockpits, once noting, "If one's dedication is strong enough, it is easy to put up with extreme discomfiture." But when given the chance, he used his influence to push for more room in the SR-71 cockpit, to accommodate someone of his height. "I knew how it felt to be cramped in [previous cockpits], and I spent a lot of time with the designers, trying to figure out how we could make it a little bit bigger," he said. "Through the years, I've had several guys who were tall like me and wound up flying the SR-71 come up and thank me." Later, when the much shorter Darryl Greenamyer complained about having trouble reaching certain switches, Kelly said, "I have been designing airplanes for over thirty years, and nobody ever accused me of making the cockpit too big before!" The ejection system required modification for the same reason. Subsequent models of the aircraft included an extension to the ring, under the pilot's legs, so it could easily be pulled by more diminutive pilots.

While benefiting from all the lessons learned from the previous Blackbirds, the SR-71 included several significant modifications, making it the greatest reconnaissance plane ever built. In time, it would become recognized as Kelly Johnson's masterpiece.

Stretching 107 feet 5 inches in length, with a wingspan of 55 feet 7 inches, the SR-71 was slightly longer and heavier than the A-12, weighing about 140,000 pounds fully loaded with 80,000 pounds of fuel. In flight, it expanded as much as three to four inches. In contrast to the A-12, it was a two-seat aircraft—like the YF-12A—with the pilot up front and a reconnaissance systems officer in the rear cockpit. With a range of 3,200 miles, a ceiling of 85,000 feet, and a cruising speed of Mach 3.2, it was designed to soar beyond the reach of Soviet missiles and fighters, a bullet streaking across the sky, empowered in the potential showdown with approaching enemy armaments by the complex geometry of speed and distance.

But more than anything else, it was a spy.

As Colonel Roy Stanley, who later worked in photo intelligence for the U.S. Air Force, told Paul Crickmore, "Without the camera system and sensor system, it would just be burning very expensive holes in the sky."

On October 29, 1964, the first SR-71, serial number 64-17950, was delivered to Plant 42 at Palmdale. Because this part of the program was to be operated by the air force, it could not be tested at Groom Lake, which did not exist.

"During that period, I was spending a lot of time working with the engineers, consulting on the progress of the airplane," Gilliland recalled. "We had so many things that weren't ready yet. But Kelly was pushing hard to get in the air, and I was too."

Several weeks later, in early December, Bob and Kelly boarded a Lockheed Jetstar and made the short flight to Palmdale, where Bob Murphy's team was charged with assembling the aircraft.

What they found was not reassuring. Pieces of the plane were still scattered all over the hangar floor.

The first flight had been tentatively scheduled for around December 22, and Bob was well aware that a small group of military brass would be on hand, eager to watch unfolding history.

Pulling Kelly aside, after returning to Burbank, Gilliland said, "Maybe we better postpone this thing till after Christmas. It is liable to be a little embarrassing to you, to me, and to the Skunk Works if we get them out here and we don't go."

Kelly was undeterred. "Nope. If I postponed things every time somebody wanted me to postpone, it would still be in the engineering jigs."

Gilliland remained dubious. "I didn't believe then that we had a prayer of making it before the end of the year."

SEVEN

Warning Lights

ON THE MORNING OF DECEMBER 22, 1964, A LOCKheed JetStar touched down at the Palmdale airport and taxied to a stop. It was a chilly but mostly sunny day in the high desert, and as Kelly Johnson stepped out of the small corporate jet and warmly greeted several high-ranking air force officers, a small team of technicians could be seen making final preparations to the big black plane parked adjacent to a nearby hangar.

The day after a brief taxi test, Gilliland took the time to schmooze the blue-uniformed dignitaries who represented the one and only customer for the new plane. Among the small circle of Lockheed officials in attendance was Archie Folden, who had once tried so hard to keep him on the F-104 program and would one day become a vice president overseeing the L-1011 airliner, which was assembled at Palmdale. By now, he realized Gilliland's decision to return to California had not been "bad for Lockheed" after all.

Bob was wearing an olive drab flight jacket over an orange jumpsuit. Because insurance requirements prevented Lockheed from taking the SR-71 above 50,000 feet on its first flight, Gilliland would not need to strap on his pressurized moon suit. This did not make the flight any less dangerous.

"Any time you do something for the first time, there is exceptional risk," Gilliland said, "especially when you rush to meet a deadline and some things aren't working properly."

In the urgency to get 17950 in the air—and live up to its contract with the air force, which called for the plane to be flying by the end of 1964—the Skunk Works was forced to prioritize some needs over others. This left 379 different unresolved problems scattered across the aircraft, a staggering number reflecting the complexities of the unproven technology.

No one understood this delicate balancing act better than Johnson, who had been managing such calculated gambles for decades, exercising complete control over the sometimes-difficult decision to launch or scrub, relying on a combination of metrics and educated gut.

Soon after arriving at Plant 42, Kelly sent one of his aides on an urgent mission. He needed to speak with Gene Reynolds.

Bob always remembered one conversation about the early days of Lockheed, when the pilot asked his boss, "Is it true Hall Hibbard designed the Electra?"

"Yes," Kelly responded. "He designed it. And I redesigned it."

That was Kelly, a blunt-speaking man who possessed an extreme aversion to obfuscation, not unlike the man he was addressing.

If you asked him a straight question, he responded with a straight answer, often laced with an undercurrent of attitude, which lingered in the ether half a century later, still capable of eliciting a hearty laugh from the test pilot.

Bob liked Kelly very much and respected him immensely. The man he called "the Leonardo de Vinci of American aviation" exerted an enormous impact on Gilliland's life, pushing him toward the pivot point of December 22, 1964, toward a prominent place in aviation history.

"Kelly was a brilliant guy, one of the smartest men I've ever met," he said. "He was also a super patriot. I considered myself very fortunate to have the opportunity to work with him."

In Gilliland, Kelly saw a pilot who "thought like an engineer," in the words of Pete Law. His intricate knowledge of every system—often gained in direct consultation with the Skunk Works' engineers and contractors—gave him unusual insight into the problem-solving process, making him an airborne extension of Johnson.

"Kelly had all sorts of confidence in Bob, and that was quite an accomplishment," said Gilliland's longtime friend U.S. Air Force colonel Jesse Jacobs, who was testing the U-2 at Edwards in those days. "You're talking about a man who had his pick of the best pilots in the business."

Bill Weaver, a Naval Academy graduate who became acquainted with Bob while working as a pilot on the F-104 program, said, "In addition to being a design genius, Kelly was a managerial genius. He picked the right people for the right jobs and let them do their jobs. He could see all these great qualities in Bob."

Johnson admired his ability to think and act quickly, his strict adherence to the flight plan, his thoroughness in gleaning intelligence about an aircraft's performance, his skill in pushing a plane toward the edge without losing control, and his good judgment in avoiding unnecessary risk.

After every flight, Kelly carefully studied the data yielded by a collection of sensors installed on his various aircraft, which measured everything from stick position to engine performance. "He wanted to be able to look at the information as soon as possible after the flight so he could identify any problems and get a clear picture of what happened [on the mission]," said Hal Weber, the Skunk Works' longtime head of instrumentation. The system gave him a window into the way his pilots performed in various situations.

This is how, in the early days of the Mach 3 program, he first began to see the precise way Gilliland handled an aircraft.

To understand the man who was headed for a defining moment in 1964, it helps to flash forward, to two flights beyond the distant horizon, two flights his son would never forget.

For many years, Bob and his friend Jim Stewart owned a twin-engine, eight-seat Beechcraft turbo prop. Robert Jr. began flying with his father at a young age. He shared his dad's sense of adventure, taking a special thrill every time Bob banked the plane hard, twisting it over on one wing, while preparing to land at the strip in Bishop, near the Northern California mountain resort of Mammoth Lakes, where they often rented a condominium, before later buying a unit.

One day in the early 1970s, Bob was at the controls of the Beechcraft, returning from a quail-hunting trip. On approach to Burbank, the landing gear malfunctioned. Eight-year-old Robert, seated in the copilot's chair, watched his dad methodically work through every conceivable procedure to lock the gear into place—including trying to manually crank it—while communicating with the tower about a possible emergency landing.

"I never sensed any sort of panic or concern," Robert recalled. "He was very calm, very professional."

Bob began circling the airport to burn off fuel, which would make the plane less combustible on impact, less likely to explode in a fireball if they were forced to scrape across the runway in a belly landing. He kept tinkering, at one point turning the controls over to Robert—"Just hold it steady, son"—so he could use both hands to investigate the busted switch. Finally, they heard a familiar vibration from below as the wheels locked into place, allowing them to land safely.

"I didn't fully appreciate the situation until I looked out the window and saw all these flashing lights from the fire trucks lined up on the runway," Robert said. "I'm thinking, 'Wow. That could have been a problem.'"

More than a decade later, when Robert was in college, he and one of his buddies were returning from a trip with Bob to Arizona, where they had attended an Arizona State–Oregon State football game. The weather turned bad, reducing visibility nearly to zero in the plane they were using—a four-seat, single-engine Cessna R182, known as the Skylane RG II—as the little craft bounced violently in the clouds, rain pounding against the windshield "like somebody was spraying a gigantic fire hose."

While Bob switched into instrument flight mode and began communicating with air traffic control, plotting a course around the worst of the weather and redirecting their destination from the small Whiteman Air Park in Pacoima, which did not have a tower, to Burbank, Robert knew enough to keep his mouth shut. He did not want to distract his father.

Seated next to his dad and wearing headphones while looking out into a sea of white, he could hear another pilot frantically talking to the tower. The man was out there somewhere, lost in the storm. "You could hear the stress in the guy's voice," Robert said. "He was freaking out." Every so often, the pilot's son turned toward the rear of the cabin, where his nervous friend was making the first flight of his life. The look on his face suggested he was not enjoying the severe turbulence.

Bob's cool demeanor never changed. He just kept flying the plane, eventually starting his descent and moving into a glide path for a runway he could not see. When the Cessna popped out of the clouds during the final minute of flight, just a few hundred feet above the ground, it was lined up perfectly over the runway, and Bob executed a textbook landing. No big deal.

Several minutes later, while helping his dad tie the plane down, Robert heard a powerful roar in the distance. He turned toward the skyward sound. At first, he saw nothing. Then he saw a jetliner breaking through the low-flying clouds, heading toward the same runway where they had just landed. The big plane was out of position, beyond the edge of the tarmac, and descending fast.

It was too late for the pilot to make a course correction, so as Robert watched, the airliner suddenly roared back into the clouds at full thrust, nose extended at a sharp angle, to circle the airport and set up for a second approach.

In that moment of vivid juxtaposition, Robert experienced a touch of the professional acumen Kelly saw in his father—the man of 1964 brought into sharper relief by a powerful object lesson in 1983.

"That whole experience made a real impression on me," he said. "It was yet another confirmation that Dad was truly an elite pilot."

Except for his navy service during World War II, Gene Reynolds spent his entire professional life working for Lockheed, forty-two years in all. Eventually rising to director of quality control, the Civil War buff had been a valued member of the Skunk Works team since the days of the P-38. Kelly trusted him, relying heavily on his judgment.

When someone found Reynolds and brought him to the boss, three days before Christmas in 1964, Kelly wasted no time in getting to the point.

"Is this airplane ready to fly today?"

"Yes, sir. It is."

Gilliland was standing nearby, well aware of his colleague's influence. "If he had said, 'No,' it would not have flown."

Seven weeks after LBJ won a landslide victory over Barry Goldwater, Beatlemania was sweeping through the culture, NASA was racing to the moon, and the country was prosperous, optimistic, and awash in patriotism. But a change was stirring. The Kennedy assassination had been a point of demarcation, though no one fully understood it yet. American boys were starting to die in Vietnam, and it was only a matter of time before the issue divided the country. It was only a matter of time before 1964 was viewed through a nostalgic lens.

The Pentagon saw the SR-71 as a game changer in the battle for Cold War secrets, and the brass who showed up in Palmdale—including Colonel Leo Geary, the director of special projects who worked in conjunction with the CIA—were eager to see if the great Kelly Johnson could deliver on his most audacious plan. The scope of the first flight was completely at Kelly's discretion. Especially with all those unresolved issues, the troubling 379—"an astonishing, unbelievable" number, Bob said—no one wanted to push the plane too far, too fast. "The criterion was supposed to be 'safety of flight,'" Bob recalled, "but as anyone knows who has experience in experimental matters, that leaves a lot of latitude for honest differences of opinion."

On its maiden voyage, the A-12 was airborne for less than three minutes, because Lou Schalk encountered a significant operational flaw. "We didn't know what the problems were until we started flying the airplane," Schalk said.[1]

When it came to the first flight of the SR-71, Bob said, "The engineers could debate the pros and cons of each item and finally 'decide,' but the truth is, I was the final arbiter."

Several weeks before takeoff, Kelly and Bob determined the limited parameters of the first flight, which included taking the aircraft up to 25,000 feet, conducting stability tests on the three axes—pitch, roll, and yaw—and returning fairly quickly to the ground. These details were enumerated on the official flight card, which both men signed, along with Dick Miller, a retired air force colonel who served as the Skunk Works' director of flight test engineering. Kelly was a stickler for many things, especially the sanctity of the flight card, which, in his mind, carried the weight of a binding contract.

"Maybe this was just because he thought the airplane wasn't ready yet," Gilliland said. "He was thinking, 'Let's just take off and leave the gear down and take a big swing around and come in and land.' That would have been thought a great success . . . and he would've had the money for the first flight by the thirty-first."

But Kelly slowly began to reevaluate his caution.

About two weeks after signing the card, he pulled Gilliland aside. "How would you feel about raising the gear?"

Bob considered the question for a moment, understanding that this ratcheting up of the flight plan altered the dynamic in an important way. After all, Bob once noted, "The purpose of the first flight—any first flight—is to land." If the landing gear did not perform properly, he would be forced to eject from a suddenly doomed aircraft.

"I have great confidence in our escape system," he told Johnson. "I don't care whether we raise it or not. How do you feel about it?"

The possibility of losing the prototype gave both men pause, but within a few days, Kelly approved the gear-up idea and also decided to add fuel, enabling Gilliland to make a longer flight than originally planned.

The date of the first flight was uncertain until the morning of Tuesday, December 22. At one point, Kelly had tentatively scheduled it for the twenty-first, and it might have shifted even further if the taxi test had not gone off smoothly, if the weather had been problematic, or if Gene Reynolds had given a different answer.

"There were all sorts of issues we were dealing with right up to that morning, but we had the essential systems working," Gilliland said.

After climbing the ladder, strapping himself into the cockpit, slipping on his white helmet, which featured a painted red F-104 silhouette on each side, and closing the canopy, Gilliland slowly taxied east to Runway 25. For this flight, the back seat was empty. "If I need to step out," he told Kelly, "I don't want to have a committee meeting." He turned the aircraft around, pointed toward the Pacific Ocean.

Monday's taxi test, which involved major systems including engines, instrumentation, and brakes, had gone well, leaving the air force representatives "very much impressed," according to Kelly's project diary.[2] The test gave the team a chance to experience what amounted to a runway simulation, which revealed some issues. Of particular interest was the way the burners had performed in a slightly asymmetrical manner, which could affect thrust.

Bob revved both engines, carefully monitoring and modifying the fuel flow. "The engines were still so new and unreliable, you had to do that . . . so I wouldn't overtemp on takeoff."

Two fire trucks and an ambulance were stationed near the end of the runway.

While still on the ground, he was focused on checking to make sure every detail was as it should be, later noting in his classified debriefing, presented orally, that the exhaust nozzle position indicators "need calibration" and the sliding louvered plastic sunshades "need a slight adjustment."[3] It was a meticulous process, gathering the information that the Skunk Works' engineers and contractors required about the performance of the various systems, so they could make any necessary tweaks before the next flight. No pencil. No tape recorder. He committed every detail to memory, leaning on the skill that had become an especially powerful asset after the CIA's prohibition against writing anything down. He noted that the fuel flow indicators produced a higher reading coming out of the right-hand engine at idle. He checked the two-way radio, the brakes—which seemed to be performing better than the day before, "probably because we bled them"[4]—the instrumentation system, and the fuel tanks.

Three different F-104s were already in the air to give chase, piloted by Lockheed's Jim Eastham and two air force men,

Fox Stephens and Walt Daniel. The USAF planes included back-seat cameramen who were prepared to film and photograph the flight. "I told them not to get too close . . . I didn't want to have to worry about a midair [collision]," Bob said.

This represented a serious concern. On June 8, 1966, one of two F-104s chasing a still-experimental XB-70 for a photo shoot drifted too close, was sucked into the wake of the Valkyrie, and collided with the bomber. The crash killed two veterans of the X-15 program, the latest rocket-propelled craft blurring the lines between high-altitude, high-speed flight and spaceflight: NASA chief research pilot James Walker, at the helm of the F-104, and air force major Carl S. Cross, the copilot of the B-70.

Once the chase planes moved into position, the launch order was relayed to Dutch 51, Bob's call sign, and he initiated takeoff procedures, lighting the burners, which emitted two bright-orange flames. At 1:30 p.m. a deafening roar thundered across Plant 42 and the surrounding countryside as the SR-71 glided down the runway for 4,800 feet—achieving a knots-indicated airspeed (KIAS) of 220 (approximately 253 miles per hour), while encountering a 28-knot wind—and soared into the air.

Among those assaulted by the jarring sound were Gilliland's wife and two children.

Initially, Kelly planned to conduct the first flight of the SR-71 in the controlled secrecy of Groom Lake. But LBJ made this too risky. No longer able to deny the existence of the SR-71, the power structure decided that it was more important to protect the anonymity of Area 51. This is why the SR-71 was launched out of Plant 42. The Lockheed facility was completely locked down, the gates patrolled by armed guards. But it was adjacent to several public roads and the small desert town of Palmdale, where many civilians were bound to see the classified plane flying overhead.

After obtaining permission from Kelly, Bob carefully scouted a nearby area where his family could see the takeoff and landing without violating any rules or becoming vulnerable to any potential hazard resulting from a problem with the aircraft.

"If I decide to step out," Bob told Mary, "I don't want to think you all are underneath me."

Because of the fluidity of the schedule, Bob arranged with Lockheed colleague George Andre to relay a message to his wife, Lenene, who would call Mary. After Mary and the children spent part of Tuesday morning at the Andres' home, the go signal was passed along, and Gilliland's wife loaded four-year-old Anne and two-year-old Robert into her Lincoln Continental and drove off to Palmdale with Lenene. They plotted a course for a vacant lot just beyond the western end of the runway Bob would be using. The children lingered next to her in the front seat and stepped out into the morning air when they arrived at the appointed place. All those years before he became a regular in the cockpit with his father, Robert was so unnerved by the sound, he started sobbing while clutching his mother's leg. While Robert was too young to retain any memories of the event, Anne vaguely recalled sitting by the side of the road and hearing "the loudest, most awful noise."

"What a horrible sound!" Mary said. "I had no idea it would be that loud."

Feeling the weight of history, Mary subsequently penned a letter to members of the family, preserving many of the details of their experience. "The previous flights had never seemed quite as dangerous to me," she wrote. "A new plane—untried and untested . . . The number of unknowns in a first flight is so great."[5]

Aware that the most dangerous times for any aircraft, especially an experimental one, are takeoff and landing, Mary recalled "willing that plane off that runway with every fiber of my being." She carefully trained her binoculars on the Blackbird as it approached and quickly faded from view, soaring into the cloudless blue sky. "The glasses had become a blur," she wrote, "and I realized that tears of relief were streaming down my face."[6]

One of the challenges facing any pilot of the aircraft was managing the flow of fuel from the six tanks, because the burning-off process produced a shifting weight differential, constantly affecting the all-important center of gravity. Because he was carrying only a partial supply of fuel, producing a total weight of ninety-five thousand pounds, takeoff performance was a question mark. "I had been a little concerned about the [center of gravity] as far forward as it was," he said in the debriefing, which remained classified for decades, "but I had no difficulty lifting the nose to the angle I wanted."[7]

Once in the air, he was able to contrast the SR-71 with the previous Mach 3 aircraft. "I definitely got the sensation that it is heavier and longer," he said.[8]

As the landing gear retracted on cue, he headed north, climbed in stages to 20,000 feet, and began working through the requirements of the card, including a successful test of the Honeywell-designed stabilization system. High above the Sierra Nevada, after completing a 180-degree left turn, he experienced some turbulence and what he described as a "lurch,"[9] followed by a series of indicator lights signaling problems with the stabilization system, yaw, and master control. He repeatedly tried to reset the lights, but they kept reilluminating. Bad sensors, he surmised.

Commencing his speed run, he shifted into afterburner, experiencing a slight fishtailing effect as one engine ignited and then the other. "You know everything's normal when you feel that," he said.

Among the systems not working properly was the triple-digit indicator, requiring him to measure airspeed and altitude through the less-precise pitot-static system. Accelerating to Mach 1.5, his maximum speed for the test, while closely monitoring the "slightly nose heavy" center of gravity,[10] he encountered a particularly ominous indicator light around 30,000 feet: CANOPY UNSAFE.

Gilliland's mind immediately flashed back to the Korean War, when he was confronted with a similar situation in his F-84. In that case, the canopy was slightly ajar. It was a problem common to the model, as designers struggled to deal with the impact of increased altitude, speed, and air pressure. "I could feel the wind coming in," he said.

More than a decade later, he was well acquainted with the men who designed and installed the canopy in the SR-71. "They were among the best in the business," he said. He craned his neck to closely examine the hooks holding the hatch in place. They all looked fine, and he felt no draft. "I assumed [the canopy] was lifting up slightly, just enough to [trip] the indicator . . . or it was a malfunctioning of the switch. I wasn't 100 percent sure. But I decided to go that route."

Acutely aware that a canopy suddenly flying off could cause significant, potentially catastrophic problems, Gilliland chose to ignore the warning. He trusted his gut.

"The engineers used to joke with me, 'Why do you think we put that big red light right in front of your face?'"

The decision reflected one of the qualities central to Gilliland's success. Bob indeed thought like an engineer, fully invested in the power of all those colliding numbers. But the controlled rigidity sometimes yielded to the imperatives of instinct and nerve, because he was well aware that a big part of his job was shouldering risks that the professionals on the ground might consider unwise.

The trick was knowing when to listen to each of these sometimes-contradictory voices.

"If Kelly had known about [the canopy warning light], I think he would have been critical of me, for not aborting the flight," Bob said. "But after he saw I got away with it, he was thrilled."

When he learned about the way his friend dealt with the warning light, Greenamyer was not surprised. "That's a judgment thing, and Bob just made a judgment and went on with the flight," he said. "That's the way Bob operated."

The first flight and the man in the cockpit would be closely studied by the various SR-71 pilots who followed in his footsteps, and the way he dealt with the canopy situation was understood as a defining moment. "In a flight like that, there's always going to be some unknowns," said Colonel Buz Carpenter, who would spend more than a decade flying the SR-71 for the air force. "One of the measures that shows what a great pilot Bob was, was his ability to analyze something very quickly. Was a problem something he could live with? The canopy deal was a good example. He could see it was mechanically locked, and he determined that he didn't need to abort. There was a logic to it, given his extensive knowledge of the airplane, but also . . . he had to make a very calculated judgment."

Soon Gilliland moved on to other business, skillfully handling the multitasking required to monitor the various indicators and control the complex machine as it streaked into the distance, reaching a maximum altitude of 46,000 feet. As he began his deceleration while heading south, Bob noticed a left-side exhaust gas temperature (EGT) of 844°C, which called for him to tap the EGT reduction mechanism to keep the engine from overheating. Around this time, he felt the center of gravity shifting, which required him to delicately control the pitch axis by trimming the stick. After calculating his remaining fuel and shifting the contents of one tank to another—while dealing with some inconsistent fuel indicators—he began communicating with the F-104 pilots to coordinate additional film and photographs. They drew close, but not too close, capturing the historic flight across the California sky for posterity.

When he approached Palmdale, Bob heard Kelly's voice over the radio: "How's your fuel level?"

Bob clicked a switch. "Fuel's fine, sir."

"How about a flyby?"

Encouraged by the smooth flight, Kelly wanted to show off.

This represented a deviation from the card, but the man who buzzed every place he was ever stationed happily slowed to 300 knots and descended toward the runway. Every eye on the tarmac closely followed the Blackbird as it roared just above the surface, while the last of the F-104s, piloted by Eastham, followed in chase formation.

When Kelly asked for a second pass, Bob circled the field and zoomed over the edge of the taxiway at 330 knots. The maiden voyage was beginning to feel like a very private air show. No barrel rolls or scissor maneuvers. Just raw power in a sinister-looking package, close enough to feel the vibration of all those titanium molecules.

"The plane handled very well," Bob said. "It was exciting to see it respond just like it was supposed to."

After the Blackbird started venting fuel, Kelly explained to one of the air force officers that it was no big deal—just a small problem that needed to be fixed. But he immediately regretted the second flyby, for exposing a flaw. He wanted to be perfect.

By the time Bob started his final descent, he was unsure of his actual fuel level, so he decided not to dump. "I thought it prudent to land a little heavy, since we had a 30-knot breeze down the runway."[11]

Around this time, the canopy light suddenly went out, convincing him that it was just a bad indicator the whole time.

When he lowered the landing gear, he noticed that the main gear was slow to indicate down and locked, and the nose-gear light flickered momentarily before indicating down and locked. No imperfection was too small to escape his notice.

Touching down at 180 knots, Bob held the stick aft to hold the "heavier than normal" nose up while cruising down the runway,[12] eventually deploying the drag chute, which helped bring the aircraft to a stop. After jettisoning the chute, he rode the brakes while moving onto the taxiway, where Kelly and the dignitaries greeted him enthusiastically.

The flight, which lasted fifty-six minutes, was an unqualified success, the crucial first step in the SR-71's development. Kelly noted that the speed of more than 1,000 miles per hour was "some kind of record for a first flight." He said the air force people were "highly pleased."[13]

Gilliland knew he had achieved something important.

"It was a very high honor for me to make the first flight of such a remarkable aircraft," Bob said. "I was sure glad it was me and not somebody else."

He did not know he had permanently attached himself to an aircraft destined to cast a shadow across aviation history.

The shroud of secrecy surrounding Plant 42 included a complete media blackout until after it was over. The Department of Defense released a short statement confirming the flight, asserting that "all test objectives were met" and disclosing the name of the Lockheed pilot,[14] less out of a desire for transparency than a need to pay off the narrative unleashed by President Johnson. The news became the lead story in the *Antelope Valley Press*, which noted, "[The paper] Tuesday afternoon began receiving calls from Valleyites who reported seeing the SR-71 aloft."[15]

After Gilliland completed his debriefing, Kelly boarded his JetStar and flew off to Area 51, where, later that afternoon, he joined a small group from Washington to witness the successful first flight of the M-21 Blackbird, piloted by Bill Park. No statement was issued. Two years later, a midair collision off the coast of California killed launch control officer Ray

Torick. Soon the technology was deemed impractical, and the program was cancelled. It would be years before the drone program was disclosed publicly.

Sometime later, Johnson obtained a color photograph of the SR-71 on its maiden flight, with Jim Eastham's F-104 chase plane closely trailing. He carefully inscribed it:

> To: Bob Gilliland—
> First Flight of the SR-71
> Dec. 22, 1964—Thanks for
> A fine flight!
> C. L. "Kelly" Johnson

When he saw the picture, Tony LeVier, the most prolific of all Lockheed test pilots, knew he was no longer Kelly's golden boy. "I did all those first flights, and he never signed one of those for me!"

To Bob, this reaction from his friend and mentor was almost as good as the inscription. In the rarefied air of the elite test pilot community, LeVier's envy was a hard-won prize.

Bob remained close to his family and frequently returned to Memphis to see his mother and brothers.

They knew nothing about the secret plane, until LBJ told the world.

"I found out when everybody else found out," said his brother Jim, who had resigned his navy commission and entered private practice in Memphis. "Bob never said a word about it. I was pretty shocked about the whole thing."

Bob's jobs as a fighter pilot and test pilot had always generated significant pride and excitement within the family. But when everyone learned about his role in developing the hot aircraft of the day, he became the family's rock star.

"He was living this very exciting life and having a ball," said Jim, who was headed for a distinguished legal career, eventually serving as chief counsel for the U.S. Department of Agriculture during the Clinton administration.

"Bob was this glamorous figure," said his sister-in-law Tandy.

Flying the world's fastest plane gave him cachet and entrée, even as he was obligated to remain discrete about the details of the program, which remained classified.

When Frank and Tandy began planning a trip to California in the early 1960s, Bob wrote his brother a letter and started listing the various places he wanted to take them. Bob's enthusiasm for California's various attractions was palpable, demonstrating the sense of adventure and exploration that marked his entire life. "Considering the cost of coming out here, and the infrequency," he wrote, "you ought to stay an absolute minimum of three weeks."[16]

Frank was too busy and too conscientious to close his law office for three weeks, but the adults and their children packed an enormous amount of fun into one week. There would be other trips. His nieces and nephews grew up seeing Bob as the fun uncle; he always took the time to converse with them and ask questions about their lives.

Their family outings often included some sort of physical activity.

During his post–air force years in Memphis, Bob took up handball, introduced to the sport by his childhood friend Giles "Bull" Coors. By the time they moved to California, he played regularly and was known among the pilot community as a very good player. "I really liked playing handball, and I was damned good," he said. Using the game to stay in shape, important for his job, he became a regular at the Hollywood YMCA, where he often played against Jimmy Jacobs, a boxing manager and documentary filmmaker who captured several American championships and was proclaimed by one *Sports Illustrated* writer as "the finest player of all time."[17]

Jacobs later became a central figure in Mike Tyson's rise to the heavyweight boxing championship.

Gilliland found regular games among his Edwards colleagues, including F-104 pilot Roger von Grote, a distant relative of Manfred von Richthofen, the World War I German ace better known as the Red Baron. "Bob was an excellent player," von Grote said. "He had an advantage being tall and having long arms. We had very competitive games, but I very seldom ever beat him."

The man who took pride in twice hiking to the top of Mount Whitney, the tallest mountain in the contiguous United States (elevation 14,505 feet), and three times to the summit of Telescope Peak, the highest point of Death Valley National Park (11,049 feet), encouraged an appreciation for nature and outdoor activities in his children. Anne and Robert learned to snow ski at age four, under his supervision, and spent many hours hiking with their father through the wilderness. "I attribute my love of the Sierra and the outdoors to my dad," Anne said. "He cultivated that in us." But she was never fond of the food. For their lunch, Bob typically packed tin cans filled with sardines and Vienna sausages, along with saltine crackers and cheese. "It was nasty food, but my dad loved it."

Trout fishing remained a constant in his life, tapping into the memories of the young boy back in Elkmont who enjoyed getting up before everyone else and heading off to Jake's Creek. "I liked the solitude, the scenery . . . trying to outsmart the trout," he said once, ending a long letter to his mother with a telling line: "I sure would like to retire and do more trout fishing!"[18]

Sometimes the kids accompanied him on fishing expeditions. Sometimes he went off by himself to a favorite spot along the San Joaquin River. One memorable time, Robert saw his father returning from a solo outing wearing a green flight suit and Chuck Taylor Converse All-Star sneakers.

"Did you catch any trout, Dad?"

"A few."

A broad smile rose across the pilot's face as he began unzipping pockets filled with fish.

Like his own father, Bob demanded academic achievement in his children. Both started out in the community's well-regarded public schools, where Mary often substituted, before transitioning to prestigious prep schools. "Our mother and father expected us to work hard and make good grades," Robert said. "We were taught to believe the sky was the limit, as long as we worked hard." Theirs was a house filled with books and the emphasis on edification they represented. Bob was especially interested when his daughter chose to study Latin, giving them a point of intellectual connection. "Dad thought that was the greatest thing," she said. "He enjoyed discussing Latin with me."

After several years of driving a Mercedes originally acquired overseas by his brother Jim, Bob bought a brand-new silver 1966 Ford Mustang, which enabled his need for speed. The test pilot who loved instruments installed an altimeter on the dash, watching carefully as the dial spun rapidly while negotiating the steep approach between Bishop and Mammoth known as the Sherwin Grade. "I thought that was the coolest thing," recalled his niece Carol. "Who has an altimeter in their car?"

His regular morning drive out of La Canada Flintridge took him along the picturesque Angeles Crest Highway, a winding, two-lane road traversing the San Gabriel Mountains, which reached a peak of more than 7,000 feet before descending into the Antelope Valley. "It was a fun drive to work," Bob said, adding, "I learned just how fast I could take those curves."

One morning, while heading up the mountain, he rounded a curve and saw a deer standing in the middle of the road. It was near a particularly treacherous cliff overlooking the sprawling Los Angeles Basin. He braked slightly but hit the animal, which bounced off the left side of the car, as he struggled to maintain control. As the Mustang thundered into the distance, he caught a glimpse of the deer in his rearview mirror, wounded and lying on the pavement.

"I didn't stop because I didn't want to be late for work," he said. "Working for Kelly Johnson, you knew you'd better not be late."

This sense of mission made him popular with the highway patrol. Once, Robert opened his father's glove compartment, which was overflowing with yellow speeding tickets. Even as a young boy, he was not surprised: "If you're flying an SR-71 that goes Mach 3, how big of a deal is it to go 80 miles an hour?"

No activity on the ground could quite measure up to the thrill of commanding a massive metallic monster into the distant skies, feeling the power of the roaring engines, juiced by the reality that he was the master of some little corner of the universe, motivated by the knowledge that one wrong move could spell disaster.

The same raging intensity that caused him to punch it around the sharp curves of the Angeles Crest Highway also led to a little contest with his colleague Bill Park.

According to a tale spun by former Lockheed ground crew member Jim Norris, on a spring morning in the early days of the Blackbird testing, Gilliland set out to prove that his beloved F-104 could outclimb the faster but much heavier SR-71, his new ride.[19]

This was the Skunk Works equivalent of two Old West gunfighters counting out twenty paces in front of the local saloon, determined to test the Colt Peacemaker against the Winchester rifle.

The machines were very different, with strikingly distinct purposes, but these two very disciplined and accomplished pilots had been spoiling for a duel for months. They wanted to prove a little something about the airplanes and about themselves.

This was one of those outings Bob kept to himself. No need to tell Kelly that two of his key Skunk Works employees were pulling out metaphorical rulers in the skies above Edwards.

Squinting into the cloudless blue sky as the combined roar of the competing engines shrieked across the desert, Norris and several others watched from outside a nearby hangar.

Writing about the scene many years later in *Air and Space* magazine, he said, "The two airplanes were together briefly. Then the lighter F-104 pulled slightly out front. Gradually, the Blackbird caught up and began to pull ahead. . . . While the F-104 was still in view, the SR-71 became no more than a dark pinpoint, long gone and still pulling away."[20]

No one recorded the nature of the wager, but among the Lockheed pilots, no prize could possibly match the sweet taste of victory.

After the first flight, Gilliland continued the testing program for 950, which for several months remained the only SR-71. The first aircraft was highly instrumented, because they were testing so many attributes and functions. It also featured a distinctive white strip about a foot wide extending around the nose. The aviation and maritime artist Stan Stokes, who has painted three scenes featuring Gilliland, has called it the Blackbird's "Band-Aid."

With each successive flight, he guided the plane faster, higher, and farther, working through the specifications of a succession of cards, one incremental step leading inexorably to the next. He established various protocols that would be utilized by air force pilots for the next quarter century.

"The greatest thing Bob did was create a safe airplane for us," said Colonel Jim Shelton, a longtime SR-71 pilot for the air force. "With his testing and knowledge about what needed to be in the cockpit . . . he got us to where the average pilot could fly the airplane and fly it safely."

Especially given the aircraft's relatively limited range and the expectation that it would be called on to fly long missions around the globe, refueling needed to be mastered. The necessity of slowing down to the KC-135's speed, about Mach .75 at 25,000 feet, and maneuvering into position slightly behind and beneath the tanker but close enough to be reached by its boom could be very tricky. "You could feel it on the airframe when [the boom] went in," Bob said. Communication between the two planes was prohibited, given the covert nature of the Blackbird, which made a strict adherence to established patterns critical in the fueling process. The slightest miscalculation could spell trouble. After hookup, communication was allowed through the interphone.

As the Blackbird took on fuel, the pilot needed to constantly lift the plane's nose, eventually reaching 100 percent throttle. All future SR-71 pilots learned to air refuel in the manner pioneered by Bob. When full military power was not enough, the left throttle was placed in minimum afterburner and the right throttle was retarded and modulated to maintain position. That asymmetric thrust resulted in about a 20-degree left bank while refueling, requiring skill and full concentration, especially in weather, at night, and with turbulence.

Gilliland usually took off from Edwards, immediately refueled, and headed toward the middle of the country or north toward Canada while testing various systems. He might hook up with a second tanker, depending on the mission.

After every flight, he sat down for an extensive debriefing with the various contractors and Colonel Fox Stephens, the air force liaison pilot for the program, who represented the next link in the chain of getting each aircraft ready to be deemed operational. Always looking for ways to speed up his system, Kelly Johnson collared his chief test pilot one day and asked if he thought he could make his debriefings shorter. "I can make 'em zero," Bob said. "'Cause the story of the flight is in the instrumentation."

Later, Kelly reversed himself, upon learning that the contractors believed they gleaned valuable and timely information from the oral presentations, which helped them solve problems more quickly. "He was very pragmatic," Bob said.

One routine flight early in the program very nearly ended in catastrophe.

Tom Wolfe memorably talked about the "demon" lurking out near Mach 1 taunting Yeager and the other souls brave enough to resist nature's limits.

Like Yeager, Crossfield, Apt, Schalk, Kincheloe, and various others, Gilliland was engaged in a continuing struggle to redefine the invisible boundary line in the sky.

The Blackbird program endeavored to build on the accumulated knowledge while also perfecting the technology required to routinely operate in an environment of extreme speed, altitude, and heat.

No one could say with any certainty exactly where the tolerance line was for bank angles while traveling in excess of Mach 3 or how a slight adjustment to the center of gravity could affect the pilot's ability to maintain control.

If the delicate symbiosis between power plant, aerodynamics, and pilot ever broke down, the sky could turn into a brick wall, as it did for Gilliland and 950 on that day in early 1965, which was forever seared in his memory.

Cruising along at Mach 2.8 at an altitude of about 60,000 feet, working through a series of so-called pulse tests related to pitch and balance, the aircraft suddenly became unresponsive.

If Gilliland could not quickly regain control, several potential outcomes loomed, including the Blackbird snapping into pieces and tumbling violently to the earth—and the likely death of the pilot and his RSO (reconnaissance systems officer), Dick Miller. The aircraft included the most sophisticated ejection and parachute systems available, but the improbability of surviving a bailout at such a high speed and altitude, while being buffeted by severe g's, was understood by all.

In this primal clash between man and nature, far above the clouds, far above any other living thing, the SR-71 was teetering precariously between lifeboat and time bomb. It all depended on which force ultimately managed to control Kelly's masterpiece.

Leaning on his encyclopedic knowledge of the aircraft and how it performed, Gilliland pushed the stick full forward and to the left. For a few moments, nothing happened. Then, slowly, the nose began to drop.

"I knew then that I had it back," Bob recalled. "If I hadn't done that, we easily could have lost that plane."

The decision likely saved his life.

During his postflight analysis of the instrumentation tape, Kelly recognized the severity of the event. "He saw exactly how close we came to a disaster," Bob said.

The incident demonstrated one of Gilliland's fundamental strengths.

"Kelly knew I was the kind of guy who wasn't going to get rattled up there," he said.

The man who always seemed a bit detached and unemotional in his private life was deeply connected to the pilot who never lost his nerve in the stress of experimental flight. "Mr. Cool," that's how Frank Murray thought of Gilliland. When Bob was testing the earlier Mach 3 aircraft at Area 51, Murray was often chasing him. "You get to know a guy when you fly in formation with him," Murray said. "Bob was one of the chosen few, and one of the reasons was because he was so unflappable."

Like other premiere test pilots, Gilliland thrived because he was able to maintain a kind of force field around himself, especially in the heat of the moment, shielding himself from the sort of fear that could prove debilitating. He calmly worked a problem without losing his ability to focus and perform, never very interested in how this mysterious quality allowed him to stare death in the face without flinching.

Reflecting on the incident a half century later, he said, "Sure, I realized I might have been killed. But everybody dies."

While working to alleviate the center of gravity problem at the heart of the malfunction, Kelly approached his pilot with a critical question: "For continuity purposes, who would you like to get in there?"

The wording struck Gilliland, who understood that the boss was asking him to choose a backup test pilot—in the case of his own death.

Not long after this conversation, Bill Weaver and Darryl Greenamyer joined the team, just in time for the next models of the aircraft to start rolling out of assembly. Eventually, the group also included Art Peterson.

On January 25, 1966, Bob was dressed in his moon suit and strapped into the cockpit of one of the newer SR-71 models, on the runway at Edwards, preparing for takeoff. Suddenly, he heard the voice of Dick Miller on the intercom.

"It looks like we're gonna have to abort!" Miller said.

Startled, Bob quickly surveyed his instruments, his eyes darting around the panel. "What do you mean we have to abort?" He was little testy. "I don't see any reason we have to abort!"

When he learned that another Blackbird had crashed, Gilliland quickly concurred and began taxiing back to the hangar, realizing that Miller would be in charge of the investigation.

Because he knew the crash might make the news, Bob broke protocol and called home, telling Mary only, "I'm OK."

Indeed, the catastrophic failure could not be hidden from the media. It wound up on front pages across the country the next day, including the *Commercial Appeal* in Memphis, where the headline no doubt caught the attention of the Gillilands: "Super Secret Spy Plane Crashes."

The aircraft had been piloted by his good friend Bill Weaver.

Weaver had been to his house many times. In fact, it was during a party on Inverness Drive about two years earlier that Gilliland and his colleagues Lou Schalk and Bill Park had first suggested that he might be a good fit for their black program, not that they could talk about it, whatever it was. Weaver was their sort of guy—tough but cerebral. He started work with the Mach 3 Oxcart program at Area 51 on the very day Bob took the SR-71 up for the first time, and Weaver eventually shifted over to the air force version.

Noticing his buddy's street clothes hanging in his locker, Bob saw two cigars in his shirt pocket.

"I thought he was probably dead," Gilliland recalled. "I knew he would be high and going fast. Maybe he broke up?"

He decided to smoke one of those cigars to celebrate his friend's memory and handed the other one to Miller.

Several hours earlier, after 11:00 a.m., Weaver and his RSO, Jim Zwayer, had taken off from Edwards and headed east in Blackbird 952, the third airplane in the series and one of several being tested at the time. They were tasked with two primary mission objectives: evaluate the reconnaissance systems and establish a procedure to improve the airplane's performance range by reducing trim drag, flying with center of gravity farther aft than normal, thus reducing longitudinal stability.

Like everything else concerning the Blackbird, its optical, radar, and so-called ELINT (electronic intelligence) sensors represented the state of the art. The camera system—one in the nose and another in the belly—captured photographs in much greater resolution than possible with the comparatively primitive U-2's equipment. The ASARS (advanced synthetic aperture radar system) provided a remarkable level of high-resolution imagery.

The challenges of speed, heat, and reflection proved every bit as vexing as the revolutionary inlet system. Among the solutions was a window shielded in quartz, which helped produce crystal clear images. "We all knew [the Blackbird] was the greatest airplane ever built and it carried the world's greatest cameras," said Norman Nelson, a CIA engineer who worked inside the Skunk Works.[21] The aircraft could photograph a staggering one hundred thousand square miles in a single hour.

Once the film was developed, the air force interpreters could see "the stripes on a parking lot" from maximum altitude, Nelson said.[22] The ability to photograph deep into enemy territory—at least forty-one miles, with clarity—while staying on the right side of the border promised enormous benefits bereft of risk, along with the most sophisticated electronic surveillance equipment ever designed, which yielded a wealth of intelligence, hundreds of miles beyond the photographic imagery.

"Where the SR really had [superiority] over the A-12," explained Jim Shelton, "was the multisensor capability . . . [including the ASARS] which really paid off on bad-weather days," allowing the crew to closely monitor naval and other asset activity despite otherwise debilitating cloud cover. "Most crews liked radar missions better," observed Colonel Rich Graham, "because they were not dependent on target weather and were always a go."[23]

Long before Graham and his colleagues could start collecting data, the Lockheed pilots needed to test and perfect the reconnaissance systems.

Zwayer, a retired air force colonel, was one of the backseaters brought in by Kelly Johnson for this purpose. "Jim was a very sharp guy," Weaver said.

The first leg of the flight was uneventful. Several minutes after rendezvousing with a tanker and getting the Blackbird back up to speed, hitting Mach 3.2, and reaching an altitude of 78,000 feet over New Mexico, the right inlet's automatic control system malfunctioned. This caused Weaver to switch to manual control, after which he entered a preprogrammed 35-degree bank turn to the right. Then they experienced a dreaded unstart, a sudden loss of thrust resulting from a shock wave that overwhelmed the inlet, compromising the pilot's ability to control the aircraft.

"The unstarts were very violent," Weaver recalled, "but normally, it could be controlled [by the pilot]. In this case, it was so severe that within two or three seconds, the airplane exceeded control authority and departed from controlled flight in an erratic manner."

As the plane pitched up wildly and fell into a hard right turn, Weaver pushed the stick all the way forward and to the left. "There was no response at all," he said. "I knew at that point we were just along for the ride."

The last reading he remembered seeing on his triple-digit indicator was Mach 3.18. Doubting their ability to survive an ejection at such a high speed, he tried to tell Zwayer that he intended to stay with whatever remained of the aircraft. The message was garbled, his ability to speak severely hampered by the high g's assaulting his body. Then his whole world faded to black.

At first, it all felt like a nightmare, savage sights and sounds swirling through his brain. "I thought, 'Man, that's a horrible dream. I hope I wake up soon,'" Weaver recalled. Then he remembered losing control of the aircraft, figured that he could not have survived such a catastrophic event, and concluded that he must be dead, a feeling enhanced by his ice-covered visor, which completely obscured his view. "I wasn't feeling any pain. It was not a bad feeling at all."

Around this time, H. R. Smith heard two explosions in the sky.

Smith, who worked for the New Mexico State Planning

Office, stopped his car and caught a glimpse of the plane before it "went down in spirals and left a big trail of smoke."[24]

When he started to regain full consciousness, as the air whooshed past, Weaver realized he was indeed alive and falling rapidly. The calm he felt when he thought he was dead quickly faded as his mind rebooted. How did he get out? He had no memory of ejecting. Would his parachutes open? What about Jim?

Not long after his main chute opened around 15,000 feet, he began fumbling with his malfunctioning visor, which kept falling shut, so he just held it open with his left hand. In the distance, he could see Jim's chute drifting toward the snow-covered ground in the distance, which was "a wonderful feeling."

"I didn't think either one of us would survive," he said. "To realize that both of us had was a feeling of great relief."

After landing safely and encountering a bewildered antelope, who galloped away, Weaver started trying to collapse his chute, which was billowing in the wind, with his right hand. His left hand was still busy with the visor.

"Can I help you?"

When he heard the voice in the distance, he thought perhaps he was dreaming after all.

"Can I help you?"

This time, the voice sounded louder.

He saw a man approaching him, a man wearing a cowboy hat.

In the distance, he could see the rotating blades of a helicopter.

After the man, who turned out to be the owner of the surrounding ranch, determined that Weaver was in no immediate danger and helped him collapse his chute, he flew off in his chopper to check on the other man who had fallen out of the sky. Bill struggled to get out of his bulky moon suit without the usual help. About ten minutes later, the rancher,

Albert Mitchell Jr., returned with a sad look on his face. "I'm sorry to tell you this, but your buddy didn't make it," he said. Weaver was devastated.

After notifying the highway patrol, Mitchell insisted on flying Weaver to the nearest hospital, in Tucumcari, located about sixty miles away, just to make sure he had not sustained any serious injuries.

The pilot who routinely flew airplanes at three times the speed of sound and had somehow just managed the most remarkable escape in aviation history did not particularly like helicopters. Something about those whirly birds unnerved him, and he could see that his new friend was really punching it, way past the redline. He tried to convince him to slow down. No need to hurry. "I kept thinking how ironic it would be if the guy who saved me after surviving the breakup of a Blackbird ended up killing me in a helicopter," he said.

After a doctor examined him, diagnosing him with only a slight whiplash, Weaver placed a long-distance telephone call to Edwards.

Bob was still in the hangar, still smelling of Weaver's cigar, when Dick picked up the phone.

"Yes," Miller said, his face suddenly aglow, "I will take a collect call from Bill Weaver!"

Elated to hear about Weaver but saddened by Zwayer's death, Gilliland soon drove to Burbank to meet the surviving pilot, who was summoned to Kelly's office. When he arrived at the front gate, Bill realized he did not have his top-secret security pass, and he knew no one was admitted to the Skunk Works by the CIA guards without the proper credentials. He offered to go home and retrieve it, but when the matter reached Kelly, a stickler for security but very eager to debrief his pilot, he told Gilliland, "I'll take care of this."

"I never heard of anyone else getting in without a pass," Bob said. "This was unheard of. Kelly was the only one who could make that happen. He walked out there and told those guys to let him in, and they did."

The postmortem began in earnest with those three men and continued for months, including several different simulations and a careful examination of the wreckage, which concluded that a center of gravity pushed too far aft was one of the main reasons for the loss of control. The Skunk Works team went to work to alleviate the problem, making a series of modifications to the structure, including slightly elongating the nose. The issue of recommended bank angles became a matter of significant study. Eventually, the SR-71 flight guidelines allowed a maximum of 45 degrees during supersonic cruise, but with a manual inlet, they allowed a maximum of 35 degrees of bank below 75,000 feet and 20 degrees above 75,000 feet and a maximum of Mach 3 and 80,000 feet.[25] These limits were shaped by the lessons of the Weaver-Zwayer crash.

No one wanted to lose another man—or another plane.

Slightly less than one year later, on January 10, 1967, Art Peterson taxied out of the hangar at Edwards in the white-striped prototype. The Gillilands had once rented Peterson's house, while he was on temporary assignment overseas with the F-104 program and Mary was still searching for the mansion on the hill. Peterson was testing the antiskid braking system that day when a tire blew and his aircraft caught fire. He escaped unharmed, but the Blackbird was destroyed. In time, this would be understood as a particularly bitter loss, for model 950, which put Gilliland in the history books, would never be available to take its place among the great aviation artifacts.

The government's determination to cloak the entire Blackbird family in secrecy had been significantly undermined by President Johnson's public pronouncements.

In the early days, the pilots were not required to talk with civilian air traffic control, which contributed to the mythology concerning the Blackbird. Sometimes, however, practicality and safety dictated a certain level of communication. When he was still flying the A-12, Greenamyer completed a refueling rendezvous with a tanker over the Gulf of Mexico and began ascending back to his standard altitude above 80,000 feet, necessitating a series of very rapid radio check-ins.

"Passing 46,000 feet," he said.

Pause.

"Passing 48,000 feet."

Pause.

"Passing 50,000 feet . . ."

Eventually, some snarky controller who knew enough not to ask any questions responded to the pilot of the mysterious, high-flying plane: "Wow, you must be an F-84!"

Around the time of the first flight of the SR-71, Greenamyer took off from Groom Lake in an A-12 and headed east on a routine mission. Somewhere around the border of Texas and New Mexico, he lost an engine, which required him to make an emergency landing at Nellis Air Force Base in Las Vegas. The secret plane was carefully shuttled into a distant hangar, amid a large contingent of armed guards, but it was not invisible, an inconvenient truth that sent shock waves throughout the chain of command. When a colonel arrived to handle the matter, he insisted on meeting personally with every enlisted man and officer who saw the Blackbird, to remind them all to keep their mouths shut.

When a major told him that "everybody on the base" saw the plane, the colonel knew he had a big problem.

"Well," he said, "schedule the auditorium."

Gilliland understood the need to protect the Blackbird's secrets, but in one memorable instance, he used the cloak-and-dagger bubble to scare the devil out of his oldest friend.

While flying missions out of Florida's Eglin Air Force Base for several weeks, Bob learned that Toof Brown was in the

Warning Lights

area visiting clients. By this time, Toof had moved his family's business into check printing, working with nearly two thousand banks scattered across the country and utilizing a big plant located near the Mississippi Gulf Coast.

At the appointed time, Brown, wearing a dress shirt and a tie, having ditched his jacket in the warm Florida sun, showed up at the front gate and asked the guard, "Where's the SR-71?"

"It's over there," the young enlisted man said, pointing toward a hangar in the distance.

It did not dawn on Brown that the MP had let him in without much trouble and directed him toward one of the most closely guarded assets in the American strategic arsenal. What if he had been a Russian spy?

When he arrived at the appropriate hangar, Toof parked his car and walked through a door, experiencing for the first time a Blackbird up close. "I was just astounded," he recalled. "Amazed at how large it was."

His excitement quickly faded into sheer terror, when he felt an automatic weapon poking him in the back.

"What are you doing in here?" the air force guard demanded.

"I'm looking for the guy that flies that plane!" Toof said, while following the guard's instruction to raise his hands.

"Who would that be?"

"Robert Gilliland."

"Never heard of him."

Never heard of him?

"I have to tell you," Brown related a half century later, "when you have a gun up against your back and the guy says he doesn't know Bob . . . I was pretty concerned that I had made a big mistake walking through that door."

"You gotta come with me," the guard said, leading Toof toward a glass-fronted office at the rear of the hangar, where several men in civilian clothes were gathered around a long table. He noticed a set of blueprints spread across the table.

The man in charge flashed a stern look. "What do we have here?"

The guard said, "This guy was prowling around the SR-71!"

Brown, who still looked like a referee signaling a touchdown, began trying to explain. "I was not prowling!"

They all insisted they didn't have a clue who this Gilliland fellow was. After a few minutes of back-and-forth, the man in charge told the guard to "take him away."

The guard and his prisoner were walking toward the door, headed for the base brig, when the man yelled out, "Wait a minute!"

Toof turned around and noticed that the group were now cracking smiles. "If you'll go out to this motel on the beach," the man said, citing a specific establishment's name and the appropriate room number, "you'll find Bob."

The guard retracted his weapon and let him go on his way.

"They really had me going," Brown said. "I was starting to wonder if they'd give me a phone call and who I'd call to help get me out of this mess."

Bob and Toof wound up at dinner at some place near the beach, where the Memphis boys encountered the men from the hangar, who apparently worked for Lockheed. They began reliving their little joke: "We kinda scared you, didn't we?"

While the Skunk Works continued to assemble new models to be tested—a total of twenty-nine of the two-seat SR-71As; two SR-71Bs used in training; and a hybrid SR-71C trainer, constructed partially of the shell of a never-used YF-12A, known as the "Bastard"—the first planes began to move through the air force pipeline, becoming operational as the 9th Reconnaissance Wing headquartered at California's Beale Air Force Base, north of Sacramento. In time, aircrews would rotate on temporary duty, usually for six weeks, to the U.S.-controlled Kadena Air Base in Okinawa, Japan, known as Detachment 1, and the Royal Air Force Base in Mildenhall, England, known as Detachment 4.

Eight years after the U-2 incident, the CIA and air force operated similar aircraft with similar objectives, struggling for primacy in the battle for secrets. The first A-12s began flying out of Kadena in May 1967, in an operation code-named Black Shield, ten months before the first SR-71 sorties. When North Korea seized the USS *Pueblo* in January 1968, an A-12 piloted by Frank Murray ventured into enemy territory, too high and too fast to be touched, and located the ship. It was a validating moment for Kelly Johnson's baby.

However, the A-12—a victim, many believed, of the lingering effects of the U-2 debacle—was soon mothballed in favor of the SR-71. "The Powers deal poisoned the State Department against Oxcart," Murray said. "They didn't want to ever risk that kind of embarrassment again." In June 1968 the White House decommissioned the CIA's Blackbird program, ceding the reconnaissance operation over North Vietnam and across the globe entirely to the air force. Oxcart would not be declassified until the 1990s, leaving the short list of pilots who tested the A-12 (including Walter Ray, who died during a crash over Utah in 1967) and the six men who flew operational missions in Black Shield (including Jack Weeks, who died when his plane disappeared over the South China Sea in 1968, as well as Frank Murray, Jack Layton, Ken Collins, Dennis Sullivan, and Mele Vojvodich) as uncelebrated as the various other covert operatives of the Cold War.

President Johnson became the second of seven presidents to live up to Eisenhower's private commitment not to overfly the Soviet Union, but the Blackbirds played a large role in the Vietnam War. "We learned precisely the locations of missile and antiaircraft batteries, what ships were in the harbor unloading, and obtained up-to-date targeting intelligence for our bombing missions," said Walt W. Rostow, Johnson's national security advisor.[26]

In the summer of 1968, several weeks after being wounded in combat, Staff Sergeant Billy Alford of the U.S. Army Green Berets was convalescing at the military hospital in Okinawa when a connected acquaintance approached him. "Come with me," he said. "I want you to see something."

After the pair made their way to the nearby airstrip, where a steady stream of B-52 bombers could be seen taking off and landing, the man who knew the big secret pointed into the distance. Alford followed the strange-looking craft closely as it landed and taxied down the runway. It was escorted to a distant hangar by four jeeps, each mounted with a .50-caliber machine gun.

What the hell is that?

Alford was stunned.

"I'd never seen an aircraft like that. It looked like something from outer space."

The Okinawans who watched in awe as the mysterious-looking plane flew overhead gave it a nickname, after a deadly black viper indigenous to the Ryukyu Islands: "Habu." The pilots and crews embraced the distinctive sobriquet, which became deeply embedded in the Blackbird identity.

The number of SAMs fired at Blackbirds during the Vietnam War remains a source of significant debate, but the aircraft operated with complete impunity. The closest call happened to agency pilot Dennis Sullivan. On October 30, 1967, after Sullivan successfully completed his eighteenth mission, to Hanoi and back to Kadena, the ground crew discovered two small pieces of missile debris, which had penetrated but not significantly damaged the lower right wing, apparently from a SAM that had detonated one hundred to two hundred feet away.

On July 26, 1968, while conducting a surveillance mission above Hanoi, Lieutenant Colonel Tony Bevacqua achieved a dubious distinction: piloting the first SR-71 to be shot at by a SAM.

In the first leg of a so-called double looper mission—two passes over the same territory, with a refueling over Thailand sandwiched in between—RSO Jerry Crew alerted Bevacqua that he had detected two SA-2 missiles locked and headed their way. Bevacqua initiated a turn, secure in the belief that the evasive maneuver and the overwhelming advantages of speed and altitude would keep the aircraft far beyond the missiles' range.

"Based on what we knew about our aircraft and the SA-2 missile, we felt very safe," said Bevacqua, a former U-2 pilot. "We were just too fast."

With the SA-2 requiring approximately forty-five seconds to reach the Blackbird's cruising altitude, in which time the SR-71 could travel approximately twenty-six miles, "it came down to geometry," Jim Shelton said. "We were confident that they could never get the geometry right, to hit you."

The Blackbird's evasive capabilities were strengthened by the addition of a revolutionary electronic system that allowed the RSO to temporarily capture the radar signal being emitted from an enemy ground station, effectively delaying the blip and further tilting the math. "You're actually in front of where they think you are," Shelton said. "That was another huge advantage."

Eventually, the North Vietnamese stopped wasting their missiles.

For Gilliland, the war was not a distant abstraction. On April 24, 1968, his friend Colonel Bobby Vinson, a onetime West Point football star, went down in his F-4 Phantom during a night raid against an enemy storage facility near Van Loc. Both Vinson and his back-seater, First Lieutenant Woody Parker, were declared missing in action and later confirmed as killed in action.

Two other friends were shot down and captured. Colonel Norman Gaddis served nearly six years in the infamous Hoa Lo prison camp, known as the Hanoi Hilton, including one thousand days of solitary confinement. Near the end of the war, Colonel Joe Kittinger spent eleven months in captivity, including the final three months at the Hanoi Hilton alongside his colleague from Nieubiberg.

"Sixty-four hours. That's how long they interrogated me, right after I was shot down," Gaddis said. "And in that sixty-four hours, I was tortured three times. Two of the times, I lost consciousness. The pain was so intense, so severe, that I lost consciousness."

Gilliland was marked deeply by his friend's suffering. "Norm went through hell," he said. "But he was tough, and he never gave up."

On May 2 and 4, 1972, the air force dispatched two SR-71s to fly over the North Vietnamese capital as part of Operation Thunderhead, an elaborate mission to rescue some of the long-suffering POWs. At precisely noon each day, the lead pilot was instructed to go supersonic over the city and release three successive sonic booms. Exactly fifteen seconds later, the second plane's distinctive triple shattering of the sound barrier could be heard. This combination was intended as a signal to the prisoners that their escape plan—hatched through Morse code tapped onto cell walls and relayed through cryptic letters and smuggled radio equipment—had been approved by Washington. A SEAL team, a submarine, and various other military assets were dispatched to the North Vietnamese coast at the agreed time, but the operation failed. No prisoners were repatriated until the hostilities ended eight months later.[27]

Still, the sound of freedom lifted many POW spirits.

For Gaddis, it was like his old friend reaching down from the sky.

"We knew our country hadn't forgotten about us," Gaddis said. "That was a huge thing."

Like many children of the day, Robert Gilliland Jr. collected bracelets with the names of POWs, including his father's two buddies as well as Commander Harley Hall. Bob and Mary had met Hall at an air show, when he was the leader of the vaunted Blue Angels. Hall had autographed a color photo of himself for the pilot's son.

Several months later, Hall was shot down—on the very day the Paris Peace Accords were signed, ending America's war in Vietnam. He became the last U.S. POW of the conflict and the last U.S. Navy casualty.

While the Cold War raged hot in Southeast Asia and the Skunk Works continued to perfect the Blackbird as the ultimate intelligence trump card, Gilliland's colleagues at NASA were redefining what it meant to be test pilots, leveraging remarkable technological achievements, extending the frontier, and emerging as worldwide celebrities.

"I'm not sure I would have wanted to be an astronaut," Bob said. "Those guys waited months and years for a single flight. In my line of work, I got to go up and have fun all the time."

Still, his admiration for the NASA boys was forever evident.

When frequent handball partner Jim Irwin invited Bob and Mary to Cape Canaveral for the launch of *Apollo 15* in July 1971, they flew out from California and joined another couple from Memphis as well as Libby. Bob's mother had arranged for them to borrow a friend's summer home near Cocoa Beach.

Mary always carried a small flashlight in her purse. When she woke up in the middle of the night and started to go to the bathroom, she heard a rustling. Not wanting to turn on the table lamp and risk waking up her husband, she flicked on the flashlight, aimed it at the floor, and was shocked to see a large number of cockroaches scurrying around.

"There was no way I was getting out of that bed!"

The next day, as the nation's eyes turned toward the Cape, Irwin repeatedly called Bob to talk shop.

After watching the launch from the friends-and-relatives area, feeling overwhelming pride and relief as the massive

Saturn V rocket thundered into the distance, Bob and Mary flew off to Jamaica.

Four days later, lunar module pilot Irwin became the eighth man to walk on the moon. He and Commander David Scott wrote their names into the history books as the first astronauts to ride around in the lunar rover.

By this time, with a Blackbird model preserved under glass, occupying a place of honor on Inverness Drive, Robert Jr. was beginning to understand that his father had a rather unique job too. Bob maintained his tight lip, but Robert picked up just enough to want to brag on his father, once telling several of his friends, "My dad flies this superfast plane! It goes so fast he could fly to Florida and be there in an hour!"

"Yeah, right," one of them responded, sealing Bob's secret in a patronizing blur.

EIGHT

Out of the Shadows

AS THE AMERICAN AIRLINES BOEING 777 BOUNCED violently on a stormy night in March 2010, Tom Lee knew enough to be concerned.

Many people on the plane were "puking their guts out."

By this point in his life, the middle-aged aerospace engineer had logged several million miles as a paying customer, encountering his share of bumpy rides. Fascinated with aviation from an early age, Lee had already achieved a rare distinction—riding along on the first commercial flights of the Boeing 747, the Airbus A320, and the Boeing 787 Dreamliner, three signature airliners of the modern age. In time, he would add the Airbus A350 to his list of firsts, further demonstrating his passion for cutting-edge experiences.

But this flight was historic in a different way.

In one row of the first-class cabin sat Neil Armstrong, the first man on the moon.

Jim Lovell, one of the first astronauts to circumnavigate the moon on *Apollo 8* and the commander of the ill-fated *Apollo 13* mission, which transformed him into a folk hero immortalized by Tom Hanks, was strapped in across the aisle.

Nearly four decades after becoming the last man to walk

on the moon, helping cement a ubiquitous image of dusty, pressurized weightlessness during those heady days when Apollo reflected America's noblest instincts, Gene Cernan felt a familiar sensation as his body gyrated in the choppy air.

Steve Ritchie, the only U.S. Air Force pilot ace in the Vietnam War, who once shot down two Soviet-made MiG-21s in the space of eighty-nine seconds, could tell the pilot was having a hard time controlling the airliner as it descended through the clouds on approach to New York's John F. Kennedy International Airport. "The crosswinds were so bad," Ritchie said, "and I remember thinking to myself, 'I hope to hell the captain flying this airplane doesn't try to land it.'"

Like his colleagues, Bob Gilliland felt increasingly weary from the long journey and was eager to start making his way back home to California. All those years after writing his name into the history books with the first flight of the SR-71 Blackbird and accumulating more experimental hours above Mach 2 and Mach 3 than any man alive, the eighty-three-year-old Gilliland flashed back to his conversation with the captain before takeoff at London's Heathrow Airport.

"I knew the weather was going to be bad, and I asked him, 'What's your alternate airport?' He said, 'Montreal.' So as it got very, very bumpy when he tried one approach . . . and he pulled off and tried another and it was bumpy as hell, I thought for sure we were going to Montreal."

Among the other passengers of this very special flight was David Hartman, the affable longtime host of ABC's *Good Morning America*, who happened to be sitting next to Armstrong, the calculating engineer turned astronaut who had pushed the *Apollo 11* lunar module to within seconds of running out of gas while searching for Tranquility Base on that memorable July night in 1969, when the world held its collective breath.

Like the other aviators surrounding him, Armstrong was trained to view the severe turbulence through a detached, scientific lens. "Neil was looking out the window, analyzing the wind shear," Hartman said. "On the second approach, when the wind shear was still bouncing us all over the place, he turned to me, shook his head, and said, 'We're not going to get down.'"

For five men who had spent their careers routinely placing their lives in jeopardy in the distant skies, the big 777 seemed about as safe as a Volvo station wagon. After all, the pilot did not have to worry about the various perils of zipping through the stratosphere at three times the speed of sound, blazing a trail through outer space, or avoiding the deadly aim of Soviet-made air-to-air missiles.

But the unpredictability of the weather was something they all understood as the great equalizer, especially after Scott Crossfield, the first man to go twice the speed of sound, lost control of the Cessna 210A he was flying during a severe thunderstorm over northern Georgia in 2006. The plane, a slightly larger version of the model Gilliland sometimes flew, broke apart in the winds and tumbled to the ground, spreading a debris field over a quarter-mile area. Crossfield died on impact.

And the so-called Miracle on the Hudson was still fresh in the minds of all.

Just fifteen months before the famous aviators took flight, the U.S. Airways A320 that struck a flock of Canadian geese immediately after takeoff from LaGuardia Airport served as a reminder of all the little things that could go wrong— and, ultimately, offered a powerful object lesson about how one skilled and quick-thinking pilot could avert disaster. By carefully guiding the fast-sinking jetliner onto the Hudson River, Captain Chesley "Sully" Sullenberger saved the lives of 155 passengers and crew.

In the otherwise comparatively monotonous life of an airline pilot, the decision to try to land or divert during dangerous weather always looms large, and this particular situation was embroidered with an additional level of pressure. No one needed to remind the American Airlines captain that he was personally responsible for five legendary aviators who had already survived spaceflight, experimental testing, and combat before reaching the rather prosaic threat of a nasty storm parked over New York.

"Can you imagine what was going through his head?" Hartman said.

The tension of the moment also fell heavily on Tom Lee. He was the man who had brought them all together.

In 1975, when Kelly Johnson retired from the Skunk Works, company president A. Carl Kotchian said it was "like losing a cornerstone of the Lockheed structure."[1] His departure was greeted somewhat like a great coach walking off the sidelines after a remarkable run of championships, and it was hard to say what the Skunk Works would be without the man who invented the place. As the country moved into the post–Vietnam War era, with the Pentagon forced to deal with significant budget cuts, the Advanced Development Projects division faced an uncertain future, forever shadowed by the old boss's remarkable achievements.

No aircraft loomed larger in Burbank than the SR-71, and the final versions of the plane had long since been delivered to the air force. With no more Blackbirds to test and nothing else like it moving through the Lockheed pipeline, Gilliland, pushing fifty and restless, decided to follow his mentor out the door. For several years, he accepted a succession of contract assignments flying high-performance aircraft for clients scattered across the globe, including missions to Taiwan and Iran, while it was still controlled by U.S. ally Mohammad Reza Pahlavi, better known as the Shah.

In 1977 he assisted his friend Darryl Greenamyer when he set a new world low-altitude speed record of 988.26 miles per hour in a modified F-104, which he nicknamed *Red Baron*.

Darryl had methodically built the plane from spare parts. The attempt required FAA approval, because of the sonic boom it caused. Gilliland successfully lobbied the government to green-light the attempt by arguing for the importance of the data it would glean on sonic boom overpressure. Four months later, the plane's landing gear locked, and Greenamyer was forced to bail out, leaving it to crash in the Mojave Desert.

Increasingly, Bob felt the tug of more earthly pursuits. He formed a partnership with his brothers, Frank Jr. and Jim, and Greenamyer, to build a Holiday Inn on a dusty patch of California desert near Palmdale. Their timing was bad. Buffeted by a deep recession and the impact of a decision by civic officials to scuttle plans for a new airport in northern Los Angeles County, the hotel struggled financially. They eventually sold the property.

When Frank Jr. died suddenly of a heart attack in 1983, Bob and the entire family were devastated. "Only time I ever saw Dad cry," Robert said.

Bob tried to be an especially good uncle to Frank's children and took charge of a key family asset.

In the 1940s, Frank Sr. and several Memphis friends bought a 5,200-acre tract of Louisiana timberland. Eventually, the partners of what became the Desoto Oil and Gas Trust sold the surface of the land but retained the mineral rights, which the geological experts considered virtually worthless.

"We were told the mineral rights might be worth $25,000," Bob said. "I told [the partners] I'd be willing to buy it for $35,000 and take my chances."

They all decided to hold on for a while and see what happened.

Demonstrating many of the same qualities that had propelled his aviation career, Bob endeavored to learn the business. "Bob is a very shrewd guy and very diligent," said Tom Arceneaux, Desoto's Louisiana attorney. "He always does his homework and always thinks long-term." Under Bob's direction, Desoto began acquiring the mineral rights to other land, while posting steady royalties on the original patch of dirt. When the shale revolution transformed the industry, Desoto became extremely profitable. During this period, the family's minority investment in the Empire State Building, which had grown out of Frank Sr.'s friendship with Lawrence A. Wien, also proved increasingly lucrative.

While Bob was focused on business interests, the aircraft he helped develop was busy waging the Cold War at 80,000 feet.

The details of the SR-71 program remained shrouded in secrecy. The general public knew practically nothing about the plane's operational characteristics or its missions. It was rarely seen, but like many other aviation aficionados, future Skunk Works director Steve Justice tacked a Blackbird poster up on the wall of his college dorm room. It was a constant reminder of his raging ambition, reduced to a single image. Someday, he was going to follow in Kelly Johnson's footsteps.

In the early years of the Reagan military buildup, Paul Crickmore wondered how the SR-71 was being used in the war of secrets between East and West.

Crickmore, who worked as a civilian air traffic controller in London, had developed an affinity for aircraft at an early age. He was also good with a camera. Using industry connections, he managed to talk his way onto several Royal Air Force and U.S. Air Force planes, giving him the chance to use his photographic skills. In September 1981 he was granted permission to ride along aboard a KC-135 as it refueled NATO fighter aircraft over West Germany. It was an eye-opening experience, to observe the fighters up close and witness the delicate midair tethering. When the big tanker touched down back at Mildenhall Air Force Base, located in England's Suffolk region, Major Jim Morrow of the Royal Air Force, the officer assigned as Crickmore's escort, wanted to know how he enjoyed the show.

"I got some pretty good shots," Crickmore said.

Just then, as they taxied toward the hangar, something caught the photographer's eye.

Something big, black, and mysterious.

It was the plane he had heard about but never seen up close.

Pointing into the distance, he turned to Morrow. "What's the chance of getting a tanker mission to refuel that over there?"

Morrow was a heavy smoker, and his voice sounded like two sheets of colliding sandpaper. "Well, that would be something a bit different."

Crickmore thought nothing more of the conversation, until about two weeks later, when one evening, his home telephone rang. He immediately recognized the gruff voice, even though the man did not identify himself.

"Paul, you know that airplane we were talking about the other day?"

Suddenly, the young man who made his living staring at radar blips began to feel like a shadowy character in a James Bond film.

"Yes."

"Can you be at Mildenhall main gate tomorrow morning at seven o'clock?"

His heart raced. "Yes. Can I bring my camera?"

"Yes," the voice said, before the phone went dead.

Fortunate to have asked the right question at the right time, as the Pentagon began to see the value of pulling back the veil, just a bit, Crickmore became one of the first civilian photographers allowed to take pictures of the Blackbird in flight.

Soon he was asked to write an article about the aircraft for a British aviation journal, to accompany his photographs. This led to a book deal, which eventually spawned several books, each successive volume benefiting from the passage of time and the eventual end of the Cold War, which caused many of the secrets associated with the aircraft to be declassified. Crickmore became recognized as one of the foremost experts on the SR-71.

"It didn't take me long to understand that many people across the world were as fascinated by the Blackbird as I was," he said. "It was always surrounded by such mystery. The crews were not allowed to talk about where they went or what they did, which got people speculating about many things, including how fast it went and how high."

Forever stung by the embarrassing shooting down of Francis Gary Powers, a succession of U.S. presidents refused to send the SR-71 over Soviet territory. It mattered not that the Blackbird's designers and pilots felt secure in their ability to outrun any potential enemy missile, enabled by the overpowering math of altitude and speed, and demonstrated by periodic incursions across the SAM-infested enemy territories of North Vietnam, North Korea, and Libya.

"Mathematically, the odds of getting a hit against the SR-71 are almost nonexistent," Gilliland told journalist Warren Thompson some years later. "It would not have even raised my blood pressure, back in the Cold War days, to have known that a SAM was being fired at me. As a matter of fact, you could have announced in advance when and where you were going to fly over—altitude, speed, etc.—and there was absolutely nothing the Soviets could have done about it. They might have gone broke sooner by shooting more SAMs, as those weapons are very expensive. I know for a fact that the Russians and their satellite countries have fired between 4,000 and 5,000 SAMs at the Blackbird without even a close hit."[2]

The decision to limit the plane's operational theater was all about politics and the desire to avoid antagonizing the Soviets with what they considered an overt act of war. It was a strategic choice made easier by the advent, and steady improvement, of satellite technology, which gave the Pentagon a wealth of remote-control intelligence bereft of risk.

In addition to its enormous value as a high-tech insurance policy, capable of overflying Soviet territory with presumed impunity in the event the Cold War ever turned hot, the SR-71 proved extremely effective in the sort of reconnaissance that remained beyond the reach of stationary satellites. The aircraft's ability to carefully skirt the border of the Soviet Union and other Communist Bloc countries brought vast areas within view of its powerful cameras and sensors. Communist radar frequently detected the SR-71, but thanks to its first-generation stealth capabilities, the blips often vanished.

While on missions out of Mildenhall, crews carefully traversed the eastern border of West Germany and gathered intelligence deep into East Germany and Czechoslovakia. These flights nearly always headed over the Baltic Sea as well, for reconnaissance of the USSR's Baltic States. The planes turned south before reaching Finland and never flew over neutral Sweden.

The Blackbirds also flew with regularity out of Mildenhall on sorties that took them over the Arctic Circle. The crews knew that if something went wrong and ejection was required, the odds of surviving the frigid waters in tiny one-man life rafts long enough to be rescued were not very good. At those latitudes, the Blackbird often left a fingerprint in the sky—the sort of long contrails typically produced only at much lower altitudes.

Heading east across the Barents Sea, which brought the vital submarine base of Murmansk into view, along with other important strategic sites beyond the northwestern coast of the Soviet Union, the pilots and RSOs were engaged in a very precise business. There was little margin for error as the map turned red, but they trusted implicitly in their carefully calibrated guidance system.

The Blackbird became a valuable instrument in Washington's mission to closely monitor the movement of the USSR's large fleet of attack submarines, constantly prowling the oceans in a game of nuclear cat and mouse with their U.S. counterparts.

"When the Soviets developed [submarine-launched]

missiles with far greater range capability, the whole strategy changed," Crickmore said. "It became even more critical to know where the subs were at any given time, and [in the climatic years of the Cold War] the SR was very important in that role."

Because so little was known about the aircraft's top secret development, one con man was able to convince a series of aviation clubs that he had been a Blackbird test pilot. The speech he delivered was inspiring but completely untrue. Only after an aviation magazine printed an article about the man did the close circle of people who knew the truth put an end to the fiction.

Among the old guard at Lockheed, President Johnson's decision to announce the secret program to gain political advantage will forever remain a source of consternation, but a quarter century later, the controversy was awash in the sort of irony that could only be appreciated from the long march of military history.

Fascinated with airplanes from an early age, fifteen-year-old Ed Yeilding was an Eagle Scout and a rising sophomore at Coffee High School in Florence, Alabama, in 1964, when the news of the revolutionary aircraft was splattered across newspapers and television screens. "That really grabbed my attention," he said. "I remember thinking, 'I would love to fly that airplane someday.' It immediately became one of my life's goals."

Several years later, while Ed began pursuing an undergraduate engineering degree at Auburn University, his father, who had served as a U.S. Navy Seabee during World War II, suggested he consider naval aviation. "But the air force has that SR-71," the son insisted, determined to pursue his ultimate ambition, which had been spurred by LBJ's unmasking. The father, his most ardent supporter, understood.

By aspiring to fly the world's most mysterious aircraft, Ed was chasing a man he didn't know.

Piloting the SR-71 became one of the most coveted of all air force assignments, and like most of the other hotshot aviators who dreamed of someday flying through the stratosphere at Mach 3, Yeilding started out in fighters, first the RF-4 and then the F-4E Phantom. "Through that nine years, I always tried to achieve the best record I could, thinking someday I would apply for the SR-71. I knew it took a really good record to be considered," he said.

Three years after getting his first look at a Blackbird while flying out of Kadena, Yeilding visited Beale for the first time. He saw the object of his obsession parked in a hangar several hundred yards away, momentarily exposed by an open door. This was the image that had danced in his dreams. His heart pounded.

Less than a year later, after undergoing a rigorous weeklong interview process, Yeilding was chosen to join the SR-71 wing at Beale, where the squadron commander, Al Joersz, had set the absolute speed record in the aircraft: 2,193 miles per hour.

From 1983 to 1987 Yeilding flew ninety-three missions in search of Cold War secrets, often tasked with tracking the movement of Soviet submarines in and around the Barents Sea. The cameras and sensors operated by RSOs Steve Lee and Curt Osterheld captured nuclear missiles being loaded and unloaded and other vital intelligence.

"You felt like you were doing something special for the cause of freedom," Yeilding said.

In the early hours of April 15, 1986, local time, the United States launched coordinated air strikes on military and terrorist targets in Libya, long a troublemaker on the world stage. The attack by more than one hundred different aircraft by the U.S. Air Force, U.S. Navy, and U.S. Marines was ordered by President Reagan in retaliation for a list of provocations by the Muammar Qaddafi regime, including the recent bombing of a West Berlin discotheque. The next day, the Pentagon dispatched an SR-71 out of Mildenhall to assess the damage. The Libyans fired several SAMs at Blackbird 960, but none came close to impeding its long reconnaissance sweep across the country, which confirmed the details of the successful operation.

Born in the age of Beatlemania, the SR-71 remained every bit as relevant and untouchable in the time of Michael Jackson, Bruce Springsteen, and Run DMC.

Gilliland's pioneering work was still paying dividends for the U.S. military.

Long after he moved on to other things, Bob was treated like a celebrity by the pilots, RSOs, and support personnel who followed in his footsteps. They bombarded him with questions about how he learned to deal with unstarts, spike variations, and various malfunctions while pushing the Blackbird to its operational limits.

"Bob was always a hero to me, but because of the circumstances of that time, he was a largely unknown hero to the general public," said longtime SR-71 pilot Jim Shelton. "He was a hero who sort of belonged to us."

About two years into his SR-71 assignment, Yeilding was introduced to Gilliland at a 1985 reunion of Blackbird pilots.

"My main memory of that first meeting was how friendly and courteous Bob was to me, even though I was new in the airplane and he was a famous test pilot." Yeilding said. "As I got to know him, I realized he was that way with everybody—no matter what their station in life. He's a very nice gentleman who happens to be an aviation legend."

Out of this meeting, the two native southerners who shared something rare developed a friendship. The bond grew stronger still when Lieutenant Colonel Yeilding was chosen for a very special mission.

On December 20, 1989, just six weeks after the fall of the Berlin Wall, Yeilding, then a Blackbird test pilot, joined RSO Tom Fuhrman to commemorate, two days early, the twenty-fifth anniversary of Gilliland's first flight. The Blackbird descended out of the bright-white haze at Burbank's Bob Hope Airport as a large crowd of current and former Lockheed employees lined up along Runway 15-33. Airport personnel and others gathered on the roof of the terminal building, where they could feel the surging power of the mighty machine assaulting their senses. It was a moment mixed with pride and sadness, because the Skunk Works' signature achievement was being phased out by the air force, for reasons having more to do with politics and budgets than mechanical obsolescence. The crowd included Kelly Johnson, who was seriously ill and confined to a wheelchair. Tears filled the old man's eyes. He would die 366 days later.

It was a measure of the changing times when the Smithsonian Institution approached Secretary of the Air Force Donald Rice, requesting that a Blackbird set an official coast-to-coast speed record to highlight the retiring fleet. Yeilding and RSO J. T. Vida were selected to make the historic flight.

On March 6, 1990, after refueling 972 over the Pacific, Yeilding and Vida departed the Southern California coast on a closely watched transcontinental mission.

Cruising at Mach 3.3, about 2,190 miles per hour, which required special approval through the chain of command, they set four records while heading east, including Los Angeles to Washington DC in sixty-four minutes twenty seconds—averaging 2,145 miles per hour.

After a widely publicized landing at Dulles International Airport, Yeilding and Vida turned the aircraft over to officials from the National Air and Space Museum, part of the Smithsonian. It was now officially a relic of a previous age.

Various key figures showed up to offer their congratulations and bid farewell to an old friend, including Ben Rich, a collection of maintenance technicians, and pilots including Gilliland, Schalk, General Harold B. Adams, who set the London–to–Los Angeles speed record (three hours forty-seven minutes), and absolute speed record holder Colonel Al Joersz.

Blackbird 972 took its place in the hallowed collection of history-making vehicles reflecting man's long struggle to tame the skies, including the Wright brothers' 1903 flyer, Lucky Lindy's *Spirit of St. Louis*, Yeager's *Glamorous Glennis*, and the *Columbia* command module that took Armstrong, Aldrin, and Collins to the moon. In 2003, when the Smithsonian opened the Steven F. Udvar-Hazy Center adjacent to Dulles, the Blackbird quickly became one of the most popular attractions.

Aviation museums across the country began lobbying the federal government for their very own artifact. In time, a total of thirty Blackbirds, mostly SR-71s, found a public home across eighteen states—including the U.S. Space and Rocket Center in Huntsville, Alabama; the Air Zoo Aerospace and Science Museum in Kalamazoo, Michigan; the Museum of Flight in Seattle, Washington; and the Museum of Aviation in Warner Robins, Georgia—as well as the Imperial War Museum in Duxford, England.

"Visitors come in to the Smithsonian or wherever there is a Blackbird, and they have a hard time processing it, because it looks like something out of *Star Wars*," said Buz Carpenter, who works as a docent at Udvar-Hazy. "You can hear them wondering: 'Is this an airplane? Is this a spaceship?'"

Something remarkable and unprecedented began to happen. The Blackbird did not fade into the past. It roared out of the shadows to become an American icon, awash in the power of nostalgia, mythology, and aspiration. The aircraft became an enduring symbol of an epic struggle—and the power of audacity and ingenuity enabled by necessity.

"There's something about the Blackbird that touches people in a very visceral way," said Steve Justice, who worked on several black projects inspired by the technological breakthroughs embodied in the SR-71.

Museum visitors of all ages in the twenty-first century crowd around the plane and carefully study its sensuously sloped edges, because it looks so incredibly cool and sinister. Because it was once a creature of a dark world. Because it flew so high and so fast.

Straddling the worlds of science, culture, and fantasy, the real-life plane has inspired fictional portrayals in such Hollywood blockbusters as *The X-Men*, *Transformers 2*, and *Deadpool*.

Especially after the first Gulf War proved the effectiveness of the F-117A Nighthawk's revolutionary stealth capabilities, word began to circulate about the long road the U.S. military had traveled to achieve radar invisibility. The disclosure that this process started with the Blackbird contributed to the plane's aura.

Like the Blackbird itself, Gilliland remained a shadowy figure until the Cold War began to fade into the history books. As interest in the SR-71 surged, he became increasingly popular on the lecture circuit, regaling audiences across the United States and beyond with what it was like to go three times the speed of sound, what it was like to fly off in an unproven machine while headed for a technological frontier, what it was like to work with the legendary Kelly Johnson. Whenever someone asked a question that reflected an attempt to peak beyond the veil of secrets, Bob would smile and say, "Oh, that's classified."

"When he spoke to a group, they realized they were hearing something that they could not near hear from anybody else in the world," said longtime friend Roy Rousch, a former Lockheed employee who accompanied him to several presentations. "Because of the mystique of the SR-71, Bob took on sort of a mystique himself."

Sometimes his inexorable link to the aircraft proved more complicated, such as the time when the popular *Pawn Stars* cable television show featured a customer trying to sell an exterior panel from a Blackbird, which he had signed. The program's expert correctly authenticated Gilliland's signature, while mispronouncing his name. He also incorrectly assured the shop employee that it wasn't titanium, but they still paid $1,500 for the prized aviation relic.

Robert Finnigan, his Naval Academy classmate, watched with a sense of admiration one night as Gilliland captivated a large gathering of technology elites at NASA Ames Hangar One, the cavernous Silicon Valley landmark constructed, during aviation's long-ago adolescence, to house zeppelins. The tech crowd wanted to hear all about the revolutionary inlet system and how the Lockheed team solved the heat problem, and Bob weaved an entertaining tale about the cutting-edge machine. Finnigan let his mind wander to the old days in Annapolis, when they both dreamed big dreams while chafing under all those silly rules. He could not help feeling enormous pride in the accomplishments of a man he thought of as his "blood brother."

When the time for questions arrived, Finnigan stood up and raised his hand.

"You've talked about your successes," he said. "Now tell us about one of your failures. Tell us about when you thought you'd lost it and what you did to stay alive."

At this suggestion, Gilliland began talking about that frantic moment in 1965 when model 950 began buffeting wildly near maximum speed, headed for the same aerodynamic vortex that swallowed Bill Weaver and Jim Zwayer. He told the rapt crowd about the g-forces confronting him. He told them about his stick position and the attitude of the aircraft and the likelihood of immediate calamity if he did not quickly make the appropriate decision.

"Bob's greatness as a pilot was demonstrated by that fact that he was standing there talking to us, that he survived all that time on the edge," Finnigan said.

Active as a fellow in the Society of Experimental Test Pilots, one of the most exclusive of all aviation fraternities, Gilliland emerged as a mentor and friend for a long list of younger pilots.

Airline pilot Donna Miller happened to be seated next to him at an Aero Club of Southern California dinner in 1999 celebrating space shuttle pilot Eileen Collins. They struck up a conversation and have been friends for decades. "Bob has been such a great mentor and so supportive of my career," Miller said. "He has a way of making everybody feel special."

When Dick Rutan completed his remarkable around-the-world flight in the Rutan Voyager, designed by his brother, Burt, without stopping or refueling, Gilliland was one of the first people to congratulate him and his copilot, Jeana Yeager, on the runway at Edwards. Years later, Bob made the presenting speech for Rutan's induction into the National Aviation Hall of Fame.

Membership in the Adventurer's Club of Los Angeles introduced Bob to various interesting and accomplished people, including Jean Boenish, the cofounder of the BASE-jumping movement. (Participants qualify by leaping from buildings, antennas, spans, and earth. Her husband, Carl, the father of BASE, died during a 1984 jump in Norway, as portrayed in the 2014 documentary *Sunshine Superman*.) Jean often accompanied Bob to lectures at the Altadena Library, sometimes featuring scientists from Cal Tech and NASA's Jet Propulsion Laboratory. "Bob has a real intellectual streak," Boenish said. "He loves to talk about ideas and learn new things."

Finnigan, who developed the first commercial mass spectrometer and founded the Silicon Valley powerhouse Finnigan Instruments, admired his friend's "great curiosity, whether it was directly related to his work or not."

In those days, he often showed up for breakfast at a little delicatessen down the street, sipping coffee while reading the *Los Angeles Times*. Soon he noticed that two other men were doing the same, which led to conversations about the day's news. Eventually, they started sitting together and became friends: computer specialist Jamie Markowitz, Burbank police officer Roger Mason, and Bob, who could not imagine where this random connection would lead.

Like many test pilots, Gilliland struggled with matrimony. After going through the first of two more divorces, he moved into a condominium in Burbank. He was frequently on the go, headlining major corporate or aviation functions all over the world. Bob and neighbor Lonnie Felker, a senior prosecutor for the Los Angeles County District Attorney's Office, often shared a soak, sometimes with their lady friends, in the community hot tub—carefully calibrated by the test pilot to bubble up to the maximum of 104°F. At the end of the day, they could look down into the surrounding lights of the San Fernando Valley. "Bob was always a lot of fun to be around," Felker said. "He has such a quick mind and can talk about so many different subjects."

When Felker arranged a coveted seat for his buddy for one day of O. J. Simpson's murder trial, the hottest ticket in the world in 1995, Gilliland delighted in the opportunity. Several long, boring hours into the proceedings, as he carefully listened to the legal sparring, a bailiff approached him, having noticed his closed eyelids.

"Sir, we don't sleep in here."

"I'm not sleeping! I'm listening," he said forcefully. "Sometimes I close my eyes when I listen."

One of the most fulfilling moments of Gilliland's life started with a blank sheet of paper.

Two years after launching Morale Entertainment, a foundation dedicated to bolstering the spirits of U.S. troops stationed overseas, Tom Lee and his partner in the enterprise, retired U.S. Marine colonel Mike Whalen, were starting to talk about their next big trip. The planning also included their mutual friend Jamie Markowitz.

They had already taken several tours of prominent sports figures to U.S. military bases around the globe. The success of the trips demonstrated a hunger among service members and the military establishment for such high-profile meet and greets.

While seated at his desk at Zodiac Aerospace in Los Angeles toward the end of 2009, Lee took out a sheet of white paper, the meticulous engineer determined to bring a measure of tangibility to his latest brainstorm. On top of it he neatly wrote, "Legends of Aerospace."

"The first name I wrote down was Neil Armstrong."

But could he actually convince the aging, famously reclusive Armstrong to go?

Soon Lee was furiously scribbling names, enlisting friends and colleagues in the search for the right combination of aviation heroes who might be willing to be the star attractions in Morale's latest goodwill tour.

More than a decade after their unlikely friendship began in a Burbank delicatessen, Markowitz was insistent: "You've got to put Bob Gilliland on the list."

Gilliland's eventual inclusion on their short list, alongside Armstrong, Ritchie, Cernan, and Lovell, reflected the gathering public appreciation for a man who was slowly emerging from the shadows of American aviation.

The eleven-day Legends of Aerospace Tour, which took the aviators and their support personnel to visit more than ten thousand troops and special guests in Germany, Turkey, Kuwait, Qatar, Bahrain, England, and aboard the aircraft carrier USS *Dwight D. Eisenhower*, floating in the Northern Arabian Sea, proved grueling, especially for an old man who was starting to struggle with mobility issues. But he would look back on it as one of the greatest adventures of his life.

"It was a high honor and wonderful to visit with all those young people serving our country," Gilliland said.

At each stop, the American forces watched a short video about the five legends, followed by a discussion of their experiences, moderated by David Hartman, and the chance to pose for pictures and obtain autographs and handouts. Their days typically started around 7:00 a.m. and often ended near midnight, the aging veterans' desire to visit and share colliding with the realities of gathering fatigue. Nobody was turned away, even when one fire marshal locked the doors when a room filled up, leaving several hundred soldiers standing outside. They simply rearranged the schedule and added a second show.

"The whole tour was a remarkable experience for all of us," Hartman said. "So often [the military personnel] would ask, 'Why are you here?' And the guys would all essentially say the same thing: 'We're here to thank you on behalf of the American people for your sacrifice, for volunteering, for protecting our rights and freedoms.'"

As the war in Afghanistan continued with no end in sight, the veterans were all deeply moved while visiting with critically wounded soldiers at Landstuhl Regional Medical Center, located at the Ramstein Air Base in Germany, where Gilliland had been stationed in the early 1950s. "Every tour we've ever done . . . I can't even describe the emotion everyone feels in that place," Lee said. "You saw tears literally streaming down cheeks."

More than four decades after the momentous events of December 1964, Gilliland was struck by the enduring interest in the world's fastest airplane, which had been retired before many of the troops were born. Some approached with their own books about the fabled aircraft. "They all wanted to know about the SR . . . wanted to know all the details . . . especially the pilots, who wanted to know what it was like to go so fast."

The pilots in the crowd were always impressed to learn that the Blackbird master had never been forced to, in his words, "step out"—a remarkable achievement considering all the experimental craft he flew.

When Armstrong started talking about the treacherous first landing on the moon, invariably someone would ask if he had been nervous about running out of fuel. For this he was always ready with a well-practiced line.

"Well, you know those gauges," he would say flatly, forever the understated midwesterner. "When they go down to empty, there's always an extra gallon in the tank."

Especially memorable for Gilliland was the propeller-plane landing on the *Eisenhower*, the sudden jolt of the tailhook catching, while strapped in next to Ritchie. "I tried to sit next to Bob every chance I got," said Ritchie, who enjoyed chatting about his own days flying the F-104, before moving on to the F-4 Phantom during the Vietnam War. "He never complained about anything. Always had a smile on his face."

The three astronauts, who all started out as navy aviators, found a kindred spirit in Gilliland, who might have followed the same path if he had chosen a different envelope in the spring of 1949. During those long hours on planes and buses, they talked about the various machines they had flown and their operational characteristics, and Bob, forever inquisitive, asked probing questions. "Bob is such an engaging guy and told such great stories," Lovell said. "It was interesting to learn all about the development of the SR-71, which was happening as we were trying to get to the moon."

All five having battled on different fronts in the increasingly distant Cold War, they could now appreciate the various accomplishments that brought them all together in what felt like one last great mission. "Those guys like Bob flying those unproven machines in the shadows, they took enormous risks to prove the technology . . . [and to] extend the frontier of aviation," said Cernan, who died in 2017.

On the way home, the tour stopped in England for a program at the prestigious Royal Society, which bills itself as "the world's oldest independent scientific academy," to be followed by a private celebration dinner.

That morning, at the military base where they were staying, Tom Lee suddenly was confronted with a dilemma—Gilliland wanted to invite two friends to their special dinner.

"I was conflicted, because this was supposed to be a dinner just for our group, with no outsiders," Lee recalled. "But I finally said, 'Okay, Bob, if that will make you happy.'"

Gilliland handed him two telephone numbers, and soon Lee was talking to the first man on his cell phone. "Oh, Bobby's in town! How wonderful! Yes, I'd love to see him for dinner."

When the thirteen-man party convened for dinner that evening, at a big round table in the secluded basement of a French restaurant, Lee learned the identity of his party crashers: Eric Brown, widely regarded as Britain's greatest test pilot, who had flown 487 different types of aircraft, more than any man in history, and Andrew Green, a still-active wing commander in the Royal Air Force. Green had set the speed record in the Thrust supersonic car, becoming the first man to shatter the sound barrier on land.

Hours after suppressing his initial inclination to tell Gilliland that they could not accommodate his friends, Lee watched with wonder as Neil Armstrong, the most famous aviator since Lindbergh, spent the whole dinner under the spell of the aging World War II veteran seated to his right. "Neil is absolutely in awe of Eric Brown," Lee recalled. "They're sharing stories, and he's practically drooling."

Observing the scene, Hartman, the veteran television interviewer of presidents, movie stars, and business titans, a man who was not easily impressed, nudged Lee and whispered, "Can you believe this?"

"The most amazing dinner I've ever been to, truly a once-in-a-lifetime moment," Lee later related, "and it wouldn't have happened if Bob didn't know everybody in the world."

Eleven days after kicking off in Chicago, with a banquet hosted by Mayor Richard M. Daley, the tour was scheduled to end in New York City, where several hundred Boy Scouts and various others were gathering to meet the legendary aviators on the deck of the uss *Intrepid*, the World War II–era aircraft carrier permanently docked at Pier 86 on the Hudson River.

When the weather turned nasty on approach to JFK, Lee felt the full weight of his blank sheet of paper brought to life. But not even a massive storm could deter that bunch.

Fortunately, after making a third pass, the American Airlines pilot diverted, not to Montreal but to Boston. By the wee hours of the morning, the Morale Entertainment crew had arranged a bus to drive the group to New York, where the scouts had adjusted to accommodate the delay, pitching tents and unfurling sleeping bags on the deck of the carrier. It was raining like hell when the aviators and their entourage climbed aboard the old bus, which reminded Hartman of his days as a high school baseball player. They were all tired and wet and just wanted to get home.

About forty-five minutes out of Manhattan, as the sun started to pierce through the clouds, the bus pulled off the Connecticut Turnpike and parked outside a McDonald's. Soon the weary travelers began lining up at the counter, eager to grab a quick bite before getting back on the road toward their final destination. No one recognized them.

Cernan looked over at Armstrong, who was carefully studying the menu board, and whispered to Hartman, "Do you think Neil's ever been in a McDonald's?"

The delay forced Lovell and Cernan to scramble to arrange other flights out of New York, because of prior commitments, but when Gilliland, Ritchie, and Armstrong arrived on the deck of the *Intrepid*, Jamie Markowitz, who had flown out from the West Coast, was surprised by their enthusiasm. "They were all smiling and very energized by the size of the crowd," said Markowitz. "I think a big part of that for Bob and the other guys was the number of scouts on hand. . . . They had all been scouts . . . and believed that the experience . . . had been instrumental in their lives."

Stepping to the podium after a brief introduction, with a menacing-looking A-12 Blackbird parked to his left, Bob could not help flashing back to his first trip to New York, nearly seventy years earlier. He remembered riding the train from Memphis with his own Boy Scout troop. Sleeping in Indian-style tepees adjacent to the World's Fair site. Going up in that tethered balloon. Buying that special coin. Losing his wallet. It all buzzed through his mind in an instant, the circle of his life momentarily connecting.

"I understand there are some Scouts in the audience," he said playfully. "Is that right?"

And the sea of brown shirts and neckerchiefs roared.

"Well, I was a Scout, too, an Eagle Scout. Of course, that was a long time ago."

One morning in the spring of 2011, while attending a Society of Experimental Test Pilots meeting, Bob felt his left side go numb. Soon he faced a very serious choice.

In an examination room at Los Angeles County + USC Medical Center, Dr. Steven L. Giannotta broke the news: Bob was afflicted with a cavernous malformation on his spinal cord.

"If you do nothing," the neurosurgeon said flatly, "it's eventually going to make you a quadriplegic and kill you."

Giannotta recommended immediate surgery but warned, "At your age, surgery is very risky. It could go badly."

Confronted with the choice between almost certain death and the chance of solving the problem, which included the possibility that he could die on the operating table, the old man who had spent much of his life hurtling through the stratosphere toward the outer reaches of American ambition flashed a steely look.

"Let's go," he said, looking his son in the eyes. "I'm ready for surgery."

In this moment, Robert witnessed two characteristics central to his father's success: his decisiveness and his willingness to accept a certain amount of calculated risk.

"I thought there was a high probability he wouldn't make it," Robert said.

The next day, when they wheeled Bob away, Jamie Markowitz, who had become a good family friend, maintained a vigil with Robert in the waiting room. When his sister Anne arrived from Reno, she was crying and fearing the worst.

During the five-hour surgery, the doctors sliced a six-inch incision into his neck, removed the tumor, and sewed him up. After Bob moved to recovery and slowly escaped the effects of the anesthesia, the doctors began to sound optimistic.

When word began to spread, Robert learned just how many people cared about his father. The number of calls and emails from dear friends overwhelmed the family, including Bob Cardenas, Norman Gaddis, Bob Hoover, Bud Anderson, and Joe Kittinger. Neil Armstrong emailed to say he had heard about his illness. "I hope that's just a temporary malady and you are on the road to recovery," he said.

And then there was Louis Zamperini.

He called Robert nearly every day.

"When can I see him?"

"When can I come?"

The special friendship between Bob and Louie was a source of joy to them both, the aging test pilot and the aging Olympian and World War II prisoner of war, whose remarkable story of resilience became the subject of Laura Hillenbrand's blockbuster book *Unbroken*, which spawned two motion pictures.

When the doctors finally allowed Bob to have visitors, Louie rushed to the hospital, the onetime Trojans track star, the Torrance Tornado, wearing his familiar USC ball cap. Though very weak and facing about a month in the hospital and several more weeks of rehabilitation, Bob's eyes lit up when he saw a man he greatly admired.

After Bob moved to a rehab facility in the town of Palm Desert, about 120 miles southeast of Los Angeles, where his son lived, Jamie and his wife, Jane, took Louie for a surprise visit. Robert began telling his father about a new personal trainer they had hired to help whip him into shape. He milked the moment for all it was worth. Bob seemed dubious about this idea—until Zamperini walked through the door.

"Louigi!"

Grinning from ear to ear, Bob traded a fist bump with his buddy.

"You know," Bob said, "I consider you the world's greatest survivor on planet earth! If you can survive forty-seven days on a life raft, this is a piece of cake!"

Avoiding paralysis, Bob slowly recovered much of his strength, but he would require the use of a wheelchair because of balance issues, which hastened a major lifestyle change and the decision to move permanently to the Palm Desert area.

Fifty-one years after Gilliland and his colleagues accepted the Kincheloe Award for a project that could not be disclosed for national security reasons, Robert wheeled his smiling father through a door into a large crowd of well-wishers, many wielding cell phone cameras. It was not 1964 anymore.

Less than ten miles from the Beverly Hilton Hotel and all those memories wrapped in a blanket of shadows, friends and aviation enthusiasts had gathered on a festive night in 2015 at Santa Monica's Museum of Flying to induct Gilliland into the California Aviation Hall of Fame, many of the studious attendees openly chatting about the wonders of titanium. The reason for his veneration was no longer unspeakable.

"At every stop, every one of Bob's pebbles hitting the water,"

David Hartman said in introducing his friend, "he reflected who he was, who he is, a great patriot who has spent his career protecting our freedoms and making our country safer and better."

Previously enshrined into his home state's Tennessee Aviation Hall of Fame and presented with the Godfrey L. Cabot Award and the Flight Test Historical Foundation's Excellence in Aviation Award, Gilliland moved toward his ninetieth birthday and beyond riding a wave of recognition. He took a measure of understandable pride every time the news media wanted him to talk about his unique place in aviation history and appreciated every honor, including serving as grand marshal of the 2015 Palm Desert Golf Cart Parade.

Despite the wheelchair and the various ailments associated with his advanced age, Gilliland remained on the go, dining out for at least one meal each day. He rarely missed the sporting events featuring his grandson Scott (a football and basketball player) and granddaughter Heather (a competitive cheerleader and varsity cheerleader), who attended a nearby preparatory high school. He also cherished the times when his daughter, Anne Hayes, a Reno physician, and her husband, Richard, flew in to town with their children, Laura, Nate, and Stuart. A steady stream of relatives, friends, and former colleagues regularly visited the desert, and he enjoyed playing host, blessed with a sharp mind, a quick wit, and an unbridled curiosity.

One afternoon in 2015 Bob and a friend were having lunch with Norman Gaddis. The ninety-one-year-old retired brigadier general was in from North Carolina. Except for the lingering effects of cataract surgery, he was in good shape for a man who had survived the death of an older brother at Normandy, the Allison time bomb, combat in Vietnam, six football seasons in a Communist prison, several years negotiating the jungles of the Pentagon, and the loss of a beloved wife.

"Did I ever tell you how Norm got the name 'Snap' Gaddis?"

Bob liked to brag about his friends, so he began relating a story about a day back in postwar West Germany when Gaddis's plane was thrown into a dramatic spin.

By the time the food arrived, the conversation had moved on to more contemporary topics, including Norman's late-in-life passion for picture framing and his current living arrangement with his son Tony's family.

"I tell people I'm the superintendent for roads and grounds," he said in his deep southern drawl. "Translated, that means that I cut the grass."

Soon the Neubiberg boys started discussing a baseball game Bob had watched the night before.

Unspoken but understood was the shared satisfaction that these two patriots had both survived to enjoy old age.

One morning in November 2016, Winnie Oburu, Bob's caregiver, wheeled him out of his Rancho Mirage assisted living apartment and locked him into position in his specially designed red sport utility vehicle (license plate: 1STSR71), which offered him a good view of the road. He was dressed, as usual, in a golf shirt and shorts with an SR-71 baseball cap pulled tight over his head—"the uniform," as Robert liked to call it. Off they headed for breakfast at Si Bon, a favorite nearby Belgian restaurant. He had already read the morning paper, clipped several articles to mail to friends, watched the television news, and made a few phone calls, keeping tabs on a large circle of friends scattered around the country.

Jamie Markowitz, who lived in the hills near Los Angeles and was accustomed to the seasonal threat of brush fires, said, "Whenever [the fires get close], Bob is always the first one to call, to make sure I'm okay."

Especially after moving to the desert, Bob relied heavily on Robert and his wife, Kim, who lived just a few miles up the road and handled many of his regular needs. Often Kim could be seen behind the wheel of the SUV, smiling, joking, and talking about the news of the day with her father-in-law as she wheeled him in and out of one of his regular lunch places on swanky El Paseo or to a nearby diner for a hearty breakfast.

Despite the intense demands of his successful law practice, Robert checked in on his father virtually every day, dined with him at least once a week, and spent a significant amount of his time attending to his father's aviation legacy, becoming a repository of knowledge and the keeper of the flame.

When Bob and Mary started going through their bitter divorce in the late 1970s, young Robert found himself caught in the middle. The breakup hit him hard. He loved both his mom and dad and went to great lengths to maintain a relationship with his father, who never stopped being his hero. That they could be so close at the end of Bob's life was a testament to the son's ability to forgive and forget.

Robert's interest in aviation had been stoked from an early age. Among his most vivid childhood memories was sneaking in under the ropes to visit with his dad's buddy Greenamyer on the day in 1969 when he shattered the speed record for a piston engine airplane (483.04 miles per hour) in his F8F-2 Bearcat, *Conquest I*. For this he shared the Kincheloe Award with the *Apollo 11* astronauts. The distinctive yellow plane is now on display at Udvar-Hazy.

The son grew up hearing tales about daring men who ventured off on dangerous missions. Learning to appreciate the delicate balance between risk and reward, he met many of his father's colleagues, including NASA test pilot Bruce Peterson, who had been lucky to survive the crash of his wingless M2-F2 craft at Edwards in 1967. Real-life footage of the incident was familiar to millions of Americans in the 1970s, because it rolled each week during the opening sequence of a popular ABC television series about a fictional government agent who had been rebuilt with bionic parts. Bob always introduced Peterson as "the real *Six-Million Dollar Man*."

Especially in later years, especially after the veil of secrets was lifted, the son began to ask questions about the Skunk Works days. One time, he wanted to know, "Did you ever fly the Blackbird upside down?"

Bob looked at his boy and smiled.

"Yes, I did," he said. As Robert's eyes brightened, his father launched into a detailed description of a time when he went up with Dick Miller in the back seat and rolled the SR-71 on its belly for a few precarious moments.

"But weren't you concerned about Kelly finding out?"

"Oh, I turned off the instrumentation," the old pilot said with a hearty laugh.

In such instances, the son saw brief flashes of the rebel who never much cared for rules and liked to push the edge but was too wise to allow himself to become reckless.

A half century after Bob appropriated the two cigars in Bill Weaver's pocket, believing his friend was dead, Robert delighted in sending Weaver a box of expensive stogies. This was his way of completing the story, which had become part of the fabric of his own life. "Those cigars were much better than the ones Bob took," Weaver said.

In 2002 Robert stood in for Bob and unveiled his father's plaque at the Aerospace Walk of Honor in Lancaster. Bob had a good excuse for not showing up in the little desert town that remains understandably proud of its link to all those pioneering figures at nearby Edwards—he was in England receiving another aviation award from Prince Charles.

And that morning at Si Bon, Robert had a secret.

Not long after Robert and Kim sat down at Bob's favorite table, the son said, "Dad, I have some terrific news to share with you. You have been selected for induction into the National Aviation Hall of Fame!"

Robert watched as a slight smile rose across his father's face as he tried to explain what a big deal this was, finally telling him, "It's like winning the Academy Award!"

"Oh, that is good news," Bob said, before he started peppering his boy with questions about various details of the award, which would be presented nearly a year later.

Reflecting on the scene, Robert said, "That reaction was so typical for dad. He knew what a big deal it was, but he always has that test pilot mentality—never lose your cool. This was not his first touchdown, and he didn't need to celebrate."

The enduring glow surrounding the Blackbird could be seen several months later, in April 2017, at Riverside's March Field Air Museum. In the shadow of Blackbird 975, the centerpiece of one of the country's largest collections of vintage aircraft, March was hosting its biennial SR-71 weekend. Several hundred aviation enthusiasts had gathered to participate in panel discussions with former pilots, engineers, mechanics, and specialists, eager to learn from the experts about secret missions, titanium metallurgy, and unstarts.

They discussed the decision to paint it black.

The inlets.

The fuel.

The heat.

One man asked, "Why haven't we surpassed the technology of the Blackbird after all this time?"

The question proved more revealing than the answer.

The public's continuing fascination with the sixty-year-old achievement was impossible to separate from the reality that it remained a high point in aircraft development, unsurpassed in speed or ceiling.

Long after most of the people who designed it were dead, the Blackbird still looked like a visitor from some murky future.

The first panel of the morning was still in progress when Robert wheeled Bob in, trying to be inconspicuous at the rear of the auditorium. Within a few moments, a young man wearing a Tuskegee Airmen leather jacket approached Bob and politely asked him to autograph his SR-71 model. Writing was no longer easy for his arthritic hands, but he carefully cradled the model and meticulously signed his name. Soon another man approached with a sheet of paper and a pen. Having spotted the celebrity gathering a crowd at the back of the room, the moderator momentarily paused his discussion putting the aircraft into the context of other late-1950s technology.

"On December 22, 1964, someone stepped into an SR-71 for the first time," said Lieutenant Colonel Gerald Glasser, a former Blackbird pilot. "A warm welcome: Bob Gilliland, the best of the best."

Then the crowd gave him a standing ovation.

When Glasser asked Bob a question about the first flight, he launched into a detailed answer involving his instructions from Kelly, including their exchange about possibly raising the landing gear.

"I told him that would be fine, because I have great confidence in our escape system," Bob said, eliciting a chorus of laughter from the sophisticated crowd of aficionados, who instantaneously understood the nuance of the snarky reply.

By this time, preparations were underway for the National Aviation Hall of Fame's next induction ceremony, and Bob was busy counting tickets and writing his speech.

For the first time, the National Aviation Hall of Fame, based in Dayton, Ohio, was taking its elaborate awards ceremony on the road, timed to coincide with Fort Worth's popular Alliance Air Show.

Bob had not flown since becoming disabled and generally turned down all invitations outside Southern California, but he was determined to be in Texas when they called his name. The logistics of such a long trip caused Robert and Anne various headaches, but the American Airlines flight to Dallas–Fort Worth International Airport proved uneventful, until the very end. "This probably is my last hurrah," Bob had said to his friend Donna Miller several months earlier on the telephone, not so much wistfully but in the typical frankness of a ninety-one-year-old man who never believed in conning himself or anyone else.

There was no way Miller would miss the festivities, but after letting that sentence roll around in her head for a few days, she was determined to make Bob's "last hurrah" especially memorable.

When the big day arrived and the Boeing 737 pulled up to the gate, Robert wheeled Bob through the jetway, into a surprise he would never forget.

For a moment, he wasn't quite sure what was happening, as a large crowd of airline employees and various others greeted Gilliland enthusiastically, the thunderous sound of applause and cheers echoing across the concourse. The American Airlines Honor Team, composed of grim-faced veterans and reserves, saluted and held flags at attention. In the distance, hearing the commotion, travelers in transit wondered what was happening. Perhaps some Hollywood celebrity or a sports star arriving in the metroplex?

This reception was Donna Miller's special gift.

The American captain had worked the phone and email for months, motivating the outpouring of respect, which included several chief pilots from her own airline who had taken time out of their busy day.

She carefully watched the angles of Bob's craggy face as it came to life.

"It was fun to see his reaction," Miller said. "It brought me joy to see him so happy."

While checking into his hotel an hour later, the old pilot was still trying to process the scene. "That was some welcome."

The next day, Robert and Anne hosted a private reception for their father, inviting a select group who toasted him with champagne and took turns visiting with the man of the hour, who joked, told stories, and seemed to be having a ball. A total of twenty-three Gillilands showed up for the festivities on October 29, 2017, along with various friends, including aviators Ed Yeilding and Harry Andonian. With the cocktail reception looming, the large delegation stepped into cars and shuttle buses for the half-hour drive to the Fort Worth Alliance Airport, where Bob, sharply dressed in a classic black tuxedo with a red pocket square, was wheeled down the red carpet by Robert.

Ross Perot Jr. had retrofitted his brand-new, spacious hangar for the reception and formal banquet, where hundreds of aerospace and business leaders, icons, and enthusiasts gathered for the gala billed as the "Oscar Night of Aviation."

"It would be hard to top this," said his brother Jim, who had arrived from Memphis with his wife, Lucia, and several other members of their family.

Kay Combs Moore, an aviation enthusiast who had traveled from Kentucky, spoke for many when she said, "This is long overdue."

David Hartman, the longtime master of ceremonies for the event, eloquently connected the dots between America's founders and the march of progress embodied in the aviation industry. "None of this could have happened," he said, "without all of us being so privileged to work in a country, in a petri dish of freedom and opportunities, which were created by a bunch of very smart, gutsy patriots."

Honored alongside the late Scott Carpenter, one of the original Mercury Seven astronauts; Charles Bolden, former NASA administrator and space shuttle astronaut; and the late Frank Whittle, the British man who invented the turbojet engine, Gilliland joined the greatest names in aviation history, officially immortalized in the same sentence as the Wright brothers, Charles Lindbergh, Neil Armstrong, Chuck Yeager, Amelia Earhart, and Jimmy Doolittle.

In speaking about Bob, previous honoree Joe Kittinger, the hero of Project Manhigh, called him "one hell of a fighter pilot . . . a great experimental test pilot . . . and my best friend for over sixty-seven years."

As Gilliland, joined onstage by Robert and Anne, accepted his enshrinement medal and wheeled toward the microphone while the sold-out crowd gave him a standing ovation, he seemed happy and content. Perhaps this was his last hurrah. It certainly had the ring of culmination, completing his long march out of the shadows.

General Bob Cardenas, the man who sent Chuck Yeager into the history books, always viewed Gilliland as "one of the best of the best."

"What he did with the Blackbird program qualified him in the top tier of test pilots."

Dick Rutan saw his friend as a trailblazing figure who "paved the way" for future test pilots, "courageously, safely, and without a scratch."

Gilliland did not bury a myth like Chuck Yeager. He did not die as a tragic hero like Ivan Kincheloe. He did not achieve a cultural milestone like Neil Armstrong or embody the power of resilience in the face of deep-space adversity like Jim Lovell.

But his DNA is sprinkled all over an aircraft that has animated dreams for more than a half century.

As long as wide-eyed crowds parade through museums to experience a Blackbird up close, he will have a tangible place in aviation history.

All too aware of their father's tendency to offer multilayered answers to the most basic questions and feeling pressure from the organizers to keep his remarks to four minutes, Robert had worked with Bob to craft a succinct speech, hitting just the right notes. But soon the man at the mike, his voice scratchy and weak at the end of a long day, veered off script, at one point telling the crowd, "They said we only have four minutes, and I don't know how to do this in four minutes," which elicited a smattering of laughs.

Backstage, Anne and Robert started to sweat. No one cared

that the aging pilot had lingered a bit while trying to explain what the great Kelly Johnson had meant to his life. Soon he brought it in for a landing, and his proud children wheeled him off the stage.

When the applause faded and they moved on to the next inductee, Robert looked at his watch. It was after 11:00 p.m., way past his father's ordinary bedtime, and they were only halfway through the enshrinement. He suggested they slip out and into a waiting courtesy shuttle van.

"No," Bob said, his adrenaline still pumping. "I want to stay till the end."

ACKNOWLEDGMENTS

THIS BOOK HAPPENED BECAUSE OF ONE MAN: ROBERT Gilliland Jr.

For several years, Robert gently pushed his father to tell his story. Bob kept resisting. Fortunately, the accomplished lawyer eventually won the argument.

Robert's encyclopedic knowledge of the Blackbird and his father's career proved indispensable. Robert's wife, Kim, was always eager to help and positively impacted the manuscript in various ways. Robert and Kim always made me feel like a member of the family, as did Bob's daughter, Anne Hayes, and her husband, Richard, who went out of their way to encourage and assist with this book.

We started working on this project in February 2015 and were still tweaking the completed manuscript three days before Bob died, suddenly and peacefully, on July 4, 2019, at the age of ninety-three. Like many others, I felt a sense of loss when I heard from my friend Robert that his father was gone.

We celebrated his life at March Field Air Museum on September 28, 2019.

I'm sorry Bob didn't get to see this book and bask in the glow of his extraordinary life, which offers such a wonderful example about the American virtues of ambition and risk-taking. This project proved to be one of the most challenging and rewarding of my career.

Over the course of four years, Bob and I spent hundreds of hours together, mostly in and around Palm Desert, California. At the start of our collaboration, he was approaching his eighty-ninth birthday and had been confined to his wheelchair for several years, but his mind remained very sharp. We had great discussions about everything from history to football and ate many meals together.

Bob was still able to discuss in great detail the various technical and operational characteristics of the SR-71 Blackbird and other aircraft he flew, never growing weary of my incessant questions about matters of engineering and aerodynamics. He was still able to recall long-ago conversations and pivotal flights and talk about various friends and acquaintances who had crossed his path, which allowed the book to achieve a level of narrative intimacy.

Thanks to Tom Swanson, Taylor Rothgeb, and all the good folks at Potomac Books, who provided a home for this book and nurtured it so carefully.

The project owes a debt to a long list of family, friends, and colleagues who were generous with their time.

Mary Fitz, Bob's second wife and the mother of his two children, was particularly helpful in capturing the anxiety associated with his test pilot days, including the letter she wrote to the family about the first flight of the SR-71.

I'm grateful to the late Jim Gilliland, Bob's youngest brother, and to his wife, Lucia. Our interviews provided great insight into the all-important family dynamics. Also, Jim's family history informed the narrative in several places.

Other members of the family who have my sincere appreciation include Kate Connell, Frank Gilliland III, Heather Gilliland, Jim Gilliland Jr., Liz Gilliland, Scott Gilliland, Tandy

Gilliland, Carol Gilliland Jordan, Laura Hayes, Nate Hayes, Stuart Hayes, Susy Ruddle, Tandy Taylor, and Josie Williams.

The story benefited from the participation of many accomplished aviators who were eager to talk about Bob and the evolution of flight, including Harry Andonian, Tony Bevacqua, Bob Cardenas, Buz Carpenter, Gene Cernan, Wolfgang Czaia, Rod Dykman, Norman Gaddis, Darryl Greenamyer, Pat Halloran, Jesse Jacobs, Shannon Jipson, Scrappy Johnson, Joe Kittinger, Clay Lacy, Jim Lovell, Donna Miller, Frank Murray, Steve Ritchie, Dick Rutan, Jim Shelton, Ken Solomon, Roger von Grote, and Bill Weaver.

Thanks to Pete Law, whose remarkable memory concerning the Blackbird's development proved incredibly helpful.

Fortunately, Blackbird record setter Ed Yeilding helped make sure the complex technology was explained accurately. Thank you, Ed!

Aviation historian Carol Osborne graciously opened her video archives, allowing us to quote from interviews with Tony LeVier and Lou Schalk, two test pilots who were central to the Skunk Works story.

A big thank you to T. D. Barnes and all the good folks with Roadrunners Internationale, Fred Bell and Greg Kenny at the Palm Springs Air Museum, Jean Boenish, Toof Brown, Paul Crickmore, Jamil Dada and the team at March Field Air Museum (especially Jeff Houlihan and Greg Kuster), Nissan Davis of the Aero Club of Southern California, Jimmy Doolittle III, Lonnie Felker, Robert Finnigan, David Hartman, Theresa Hoey at Lockheed Martin, Carroll Johnson, Steve Justice, Tom and Sally Lee, Jamie Markowitz, Jim Matheney, Jim McVoy, Winnie Oburu, Angella Raisian, Roy Roush, Warren Thompson, Hal Weber, and George Welsh and Tony Moore from the Edwards Air Force Base Museum.

A special thanks to my friend and collaborator Gary Powers Jr., who made the connection that brought this project to life.

Thanks to my family and friends, scattered across the country, who encouraged me as I plotted a course for the stratosphere.

Various books proved helpful, including *Lockheed Blackbird: Beyond the Secret Missions* (revised edition) and *Lockheed SR-71*, by Paul F. Crickmore; *Kelly: More Than My Share of It All*, by Clarence L. "Kelly" Johnson with Maggie Smith; *Skunk Works*, by Ben Rich and Lee Janos; *The Complete Book of the SR-71 Blackbird*, by Richard Graham; *Jane's American Fighting Aircraft of the 20th Century*, by Michael J. H. Taylor; *Area 51: An Uncensored History of America's Top Secret Military Base*, by Annie Jacobsen; *SR-71 Revealed: The Inside Story*, by Richard Graham; *The Right Stuff*, by Tom Wolfe; *Yeager: An Autobiography*, by Chuck Yeager and Leo Janos; *Scrappy: Memoir of a U.S. Fighter Pilot in Korea and Vietnam*, by Howard C. Johnson and Ian A. O'Connor; *Beyond the Horizons: The Lockheed Story*, by Walter J. Boyne; *Come Up and Get Me*, by Joe Kittinger and Craig Ryan; *Lockheed Blackbirds*, by Anthony M. Thornborough and Peter E. Davies; *Area 51 Black Jets*, by Bill Yenne; and *From Rainbow to Gusto*, by Paul A. Suhler.

Keith Dunnavant

NOTES

Unless otherwise indicated, all direct quotes were taken from interviews conducted by Keith Dunnavant or from the memory of Bob Gilliland.

1. Two Wars

1. Nick Lloyd, *Hundred Days: The Campaign That Ended World War I* (New York: Basic Books, 2014), 145.

2. Elizabeth Jordan Gilliland, comp., Gilliland family history, n.d., Gilliland family private collection.

3. Frank M. Gilliland, letter to stateside friend, published in unknown newspaper, 1918, Gilliland family private collection.

4. Frank M. Gilliland, letter to stateside friend, published in unknown newspaper, 1918, Gilliland family private collection.

5. Newspaper clipping, *Memphis Commercial Appeal*, n.d., Gilliland family private collection.

6. Jordan Gilliland, Gilliland family history.

7. Jordan Gilliland, Gilliland family history.

8. Jordan Gilliland, Gilliland family history.

9. Jordan Gilliland, Gilliland family history.

10. Elizabeth Jordan Gilliland, personal diary, Gilliland family private collection.

11. Report card from Webb School, Gilliland family private collection.

12. William R. Webb to Frank M. Gilliland, April 7, 1942, Gilliland family private collection.

13. Webb Follin to Frank M. Gilliland, April 8, 1942, Gilliland family private collection.

2. Anchors Away

1. "Chester, Texas Angora Goat, Replaces Razor Bill at Navy," *Baltimore Sun*, September 16, 1945.

2. Bob Gilliland to Jim McVoy, postcard, April 12, 2000, Jim McVoy private collection.

3. Taking Flight

1. Lou Schalk, video interview with Carol Osborne, June 4, 1993, Carol Osborne private collection.

4. Two Worlds

1. Chuck Yeager and Leo Janos, *Yeager: An Autobiography* (New York: Bantam Books, 1985), 47.

2. Daniel Ford, "The Edwards Diaries," *Air and Space Magazine*, July 1997, https://www.airspacemag.com/flight-today/the-edwards-diaries-32471/?page=1.

3. Frank M. Gilliland to James S. Gilliland, July 30, 1954, Gilliland family private collection.

4. Clarence L. "Kelly" Johnson with Maggie Smith, *Kelly: More Than My Share of It All* (Washington DC: Smithsonian Institution Press, 1985), 97.

5. Walter J. Boyne, *Beyond the Horizons: The Lockheed Story* (New York: St. Martin's Press, 1998), 208.

6. Ben R. Rich and Leo Janos, *Skunk Works* (New York: Back Bay Books, 1996), 62.

7. Rich and Janos, *Skunk Works*, 114.

8. Tony LeVier, video interview with Carol Osborne, September 18, 1982, Carol Osborne private collection.

9. Jim Skeen, "Services Set for Famed Aviator," *Los Angeles Daily News*, February 10, 1998.

10. LeVier, video interview with Osborne.

11. LeVier, video interview with Osborne.

12. Bob Gilliland to Frank M. Gilliland Jr. and James S. Gilliland, December 5, 1962, Gilliland family private collection.

5. The Man in the Brooks Brothers Suit

1. Michael Beschloss, *Mayday: Eisenhower, Khrushchev, and the U-2 Affair* (New York: Harper and Row, 1986), 126.

2. Rich and Janos, *Skunk Works*, 131.

3. Joe Kittinger and Craig Ryan, *Come Up and Get Me: An Autobiography of Colonel Joe Kittinger* (Albuquerque: University of New Mexico Press, 2011), 121.

4. Clarence L. "Kelly" Johnson, Lockheed Skunk Works program logs, November 3, 1960, Gilliland family private collection.

5. Rich and Janos, *Skunk Works*, 195.

6. Schalk, video interview with Osborne.

7. Schalk, video interview with Osborne.
8. Johnson, program logs, February 4, 1960.

6. Kelly's Masterpiece

1. Jack Raymond, "Johnson Reveals 2,000-M.P.H. Jet," *New York Times*, March 1, 1964.
2. Raymond, "Johnson Reveals 2,000-M.P.H. Jet."
3. James Atwater, "The Great A-11 Deception," *Saturday Evening Post*, May 2, 1964.
4. Richard H. Graham, *Flying the SR-71 Blackbird: In the Cockpit on a Secret Operational Mission* (Minneapolis MN: Zenith Press, 2008), 5.
5. Graham, *Flying the SR-71 Blackbird*, 5.
6. Johnson with Smith, *Kelly*, 68.
7. LeVier, video interview with Osborne.
8. Rich and Janos, *Skunk Works*, 140.
9. Rich and Janos, *Skunk Works*, 195.
10. Schalk, video interview with Osborne.
11. Don Dwiggins, World Book Encyclopedia Science Services, "'Skunk Works' Airs Smell of Success," October 1, 1964, Gilliland family private collection.
12. Johnson with Smith, *Kelly*, 148.
13. "Kelly Johnson Discusses Inside Story on YF-12A Development," *Antelope Valley Press*, July 17, 1969.
14. Johnson with Smith, *Kelly*.
15. Lockheed, *SR-71 A/B Flight Manual* (Edwards CA: NASA Dryden Flight Research Facility, 1986), 5–8, Lieutenant Colonel Ed Yeilding private collection.
16. "Kelly Johnson Discusses Inside Story on YF-12A Development."
17. Schalk, video interview with Osborne.

7. Warning Lights

1. Schalk, video interview with Osborne.
2. Johnson, program logs, December 22, 1964.
3. Johnson, program logs, December 22, 1964.
4. Johnson, program logs, December 22, 1964.
5. Mary Gilliland to Gilliland family, December 27, 1964, Gilliland family private collection.
6. Mary Gilliland to Gilliland family, December 27, 1964.
7. Bob Gilliland, debriefing, December 22, 1964, Gilliland family private collection.
8. Gilliland, debriefing, December 22, 1964.
9. Gilliland, debriefing, December 22, 1964.
10. Gilliland, debriefing, December 22, 1964.
11. Gilliland, debriefing, December 22, 1964.
12. Gilliland, debriefing, December 22, 1964.
13. Johnson, program logs, December 22, 1964.
14. Department of Defense, press release, December 22, 1964.

15. "New Airplane Program Revealed as SR-71 Flies from Plant 42," *Antelope Valley Press*, December 24, 1964.

16. Bob Gilliland to Frank M. Gilliland Jr., May 31, 1963, Gilliland family private collection.

17. Robert H. Boyle, "Really the Greatest," *Sports Illustrated*, March 7, 1966.

18. Bob Gilliland to Elizabeth Gilliland, October 7, 1969, Gilliland family private collection.

19. Jim Norris, "The SR-71 Was Close to Perfect," *Air and Space*, August 1991, https://www.airspacemag.com/articles/sr-71-was-close-perfect-180963856/.

20. Norris, "The SR-71 Was Close to Perfect."

21. Rich and Janos, *Skunk Works*, 222.

22. Rich and Janos, *Skunk Works*, 222.

23. Richard M. Graham, *The Complete Book of the SR-71 Blackbird* (Minneapolis MN: Zenith Press 2015).

24. Newspaper clipping, *Memphis Commercial Appeal*, January 26, 1966, Gilliland family private collection.

25. Lockheed, *SR-71 A/B Flight Manual*, 5–9.

26. Rich and Janos, *Skunk Works*, 244.

27. Gordon I. Peterson and David C. Taylor, "A Shield and a Sword," declassified report concerning Operation Thunderhead, Central Intelligence Agency, https://www.cia.gov/library/center-for-the-study-of-intelligence/csi-publications/csi-studies/studies/vol-60-no-1/a-shield-and-a-sword.html.

8. Out of the Shadows

1. Associated Press, "Lockheed's Famous Designer Will Retire," news release, November 5, 1974.

2. Warren Thompson, "Spy Planes," *Air and Space Smithsonian*, January 2016.

INDEX

a-1 Blackbird (Lockheed), 143
a-11 Blackbird (Lockheed), 133
a-12 "Archangel" Blackbird (Lockheed): cia's use of, 131, 134; code-name of, 125; crashes of, 127–28; development of, 124–26, 134, 143; and engineering innovations, 125–26, 143; Kelly Johnson's proposal for, 124–25; Nellis Air Force Base emergency landing of, 187; in Operation Black Shield, 190; problems during testing and development of, 126, 127–31, 149, 161; refueling of, 187; RJG as test pilot for, 127, 128, 129–30, 150–51; RJG's first view of, 113; secrecy of, 131, 133–34, 187; sr-71 compared to, 151, 182; test pilots of, 126–32, 190
Adams, Harold B., 209
Aerospace Walk of Honor (Lancaster), 226
Air Force, U.S.: air strikes of, against Libya, 207–8; and Berlin Airlift resupply mission, 55; and the Blackbird program, 126, 133, 135–36; and cl-400 "Project Suntan," 142; during the Cold War, 58, 202–7; and deaths during supersonic testing, 88–89; and deaths during transition to jets, 68; 86th Fighter-Bomber Wing of, 66–74; establishment of, 47; high-altitude testing programs of, 123–24; and missile-bomber debates, 134–35; 9th Reconnaissance Wing of, 189–90, 207; RJG commissioned as second lieutenant in, 52; and RJG requesting assignment to Eglin, 83; RJG resigning from, 94–95; and RJG's flight training at Randolph, 57–62; and RJG's flight training at Williams, 62–66; RJG's impact on sr-71 program of, 176–78; rules of, on fighter pilot height, 60–62; and rushed testing and development programs, 88–89; and sr-71 reconnaissance capabilities, 182; and sr-71 reconnaissance missions, 189–90, 203–8; at sr-71's first test flight, 152–53, 155–56, 161–71; and sr-71's phasing out, 209; and sr-71's unmasking by Lyndon Johnson, 135–36; and struggle with cia for primacy, 135, 190; and testing airsickness pill, 58–59; and testing operational aircraft at Eglin, 92–93; and testing to break the sound barrier, 84–88; 36th Fighter-Bomber Wing of, 66; transitional strategy of, for officer corps training, 47–49; during Vietnam War, 190; and x-1 program, 84–85, 87–88; and x-2 program, 91; yf-12a for, 131, 134
Alford, Billy, 191
American Legion (Memphis), 12, 49
Anderson, Bud, 221
Anderson, Rudolph, 135

241

Andonian, Harry, 90, 93, 139, 230
Andre, George, 165
Andre, Lenene, 165
Apollo 8, 69, 197
Apollo 11, 198, 217, 225
Apollo 13, 69, 197
Apollo 15, 194–95
Apt, Milburn "Mel," 91
Arceneaux, Tom, 201
Arctic Circle missions (SR-71), 205
Area 51. *See* Groom Lake
Arkansas farm (Gilliland family farm), 14–15
Armstrong, Neil: and *Apollo 11*, 198, 217, 225; awards and honors of, 131, 225; friendship of, with RJG, 221; and "Legends of Aerospace" goodwill tour, 197–200, 215–20
Army, U.S., 3, 5–7, 47–48
Arnold, Henry "Hap," 86
astronauts: Jim Irwin, 194–95; Jim Lovell, 69, 197–200, 215–19; on the "Legends of Aerospace" goodwill tour, 197–200, 214–20; of the Mercury missions, 122–24, 140; Neil Armstrong, 131, 197–200, 215–20, 221; RJG's admiration of, 194–95, 217
atomic bombs, 34, 66, 115, 117
Australian infantry (World War I), 6
automobiles: of the Jordan family, 7–8; RJG's Ford convertible, 62, 63–64; RJG's Ford Mustang, 174–75; RJG's Mercedes Benz, 1; RJG's specially designed red SUV, 224
aviation industry: and commercial industry growth, 34, 140; Lockheed's impact on, 97–98; and propeller-powered aircraft, 34, 63, 74; supersonic age of, 76, 88–89, 102; and technological advancements, 140; transition to jet-powered, 63, 74. *See also* jet-powered aircraft; rocket-powered aircraft

B-25 bomber (North American Aviation), 60, 70, 96, 103
B-29 bomber (Boeing), 85, 88
B-36 bomber (Convair), 58, 116
B-70 Valkyrie (North American Aviation), 134, 164
Bainbridge Naval Center, 31–32
balloon ride (World's Fair), 21, 220

balloons (high-altitude testing), 123–24
Bancroft Hall (Naval Academy), 35, 43–44, 48
bank angles, 178, 183, 186
Bankhead, John H., II, 36
Banshee fighters, 69
Barbera, Luigi, 108
Barnes, Pancho, 86–87, 105
Barnes, T. D., 120
barnstormers, 19
BASE-jumping movement, 213
Battle of Shiloh, 9
Bay of Pigs invasion, 135
Beale Air Force Base, 189, 207
Bell Aircraft: and breaking the sound barrier, 84–85; as defense contractor, 91; P-59 Airacomet, 62; X-1 rocket plane, 84–85, 87–88; X-2 rocket plane, 91
Bellicourt (France), 3, 6
Berlin (Germany), 54–56, 208
Bevacqua, Tony, 191–92
Bill the Goat (Navy mascot goat), 44–45
Bill X "Chester" (Navy mascot goat), 44
Bissell, Richard M., Jr., 117, 135
Blackbird program (Lockheed): A-1 Blackbird, 143; A-11 Blackbird, 133; during the Cold War, 202–7; crashes and deaths in, 170–71, 180–86; decommissioning of, 190; ending of testing and development in, 200; engineering and design challenges of, 137, 143–51, 178; impact of U-2 incident on, 190, 204–5; Lyndon Johnson unmasking, 133–34, 186, 206; M-21 drone, 134, 170–71; museums housing aircraft from, 210–11; and RJG's legacy, 231; secrecy of, 133–34, 186–89, 206; versions of, 134–35, 143; during the Vietnam War, 190–93; YF-12A Blackbird, 131, 133, 134, 143, 150–51. *See also* A-12 "Archangel" Blackbird (Lockheed); SR-71 Blackbird (Lockheed)
Black Shield, Operation, 190
Blaik, Earl "Red," 45
Blanchard, Doc, 45, 59
bleed bypass, 147–50
Boeing 707 (commercial airliner), 140
Boenish, Carl, 213
Boenish, Jean, 213

Bolden, Charles, 230
bombers: B-25, 60, 70, 96, 103; B-29, 85, 88; B-36, 58, 116; Hudson, 137; impact of missiles on, 134–35; PV-2 Harpoon, 137–38; RAF contract based on the Electra, 137; RJG flying, 58, 96, 103; YB-49, 88–89
Boyd, Albert, 84, 88
Boyne, Walter J., 100
Boy Scouts, 20–21, 219, 220
Bramlett, Leon, 40
Breuil-Cervinia (Italian village), 109
Brewer, Nicholas R., 10
Brown, Eric, 218–19
Brown, Toof, 15, 95–96, 121–22, 187–89

California Aviation Hall of Fame, 222–23
Campbell, Dave, 148
Camp Sevier (Greenville SC), 6
canopies, 68, 70, 167–68, 169
Cardenas, Bob, 83–89, 105, 221, 231
Carpenter, Buz, 148, 168, 210
Carpenter, Scott, 230
Carvel Hall (hotel), 50–52
Cernan, Gene, 198–200, 215–19
Chamberlain, Neville, 137
Charles, Prince, 226
Chennault, Claire, 73
Chennault, Claire Patrick, 74
Chennault, John S., 73
Cherry Mansion (Savannah GA), 8–9
Chester (Navy mascot goat), 44
CIA (Central Intelligence Agency): A-12 reconnaissance program of, 124–25, 131, 134, 190; under Allen Dulles, 116; and background investigations of RJG, 121–22; and Bay of Pigs invasion, 135; and decommissioning the Blackbird program, 190; early aerial reconnaissance programs of, 115–16; and Kelly Johnson vouching for RJG, 115; M-21/D-21 drone project of, 134; obtaining titanium, 144; relation of, with the U.S. Air Force, 135, 161, 190; and Skunk Works security, 115, 185–86; U-2 reconnaissance program of, 116–19, 139
Civil War, 9
CL-400 "Project Suntan" (Lockheed), 142
coffin corner, 139
Cold War: aerial reconnaissance during, 115–19; and Berlin Airlift resupply mission, 54–56; and the Blackbird program, 133–35, 161; impact of, on aircraft development, 91; and the Korean War, 71; and Soviet capabilities, 75–76; and the space race, 91, 122–24; SR-71 missions during, 202–7; tensions during, 54–55, 66–67, 75–76, 116, 121; and U-2 incident, 118; and U.S. bomber capabilities, 58
Collins, Eileen, 213
Collins, Ken, 190
commercial aviation, 34, 97–98, 140
compressibility, 138
Connally, John, 128
Conquest I (F8F-2 Bearcat), 225
Constellation airliner (Lockheed), 98, 120
Convair, 58, 116, 127, 146
Cook, Everett, 95
Cooper, Gordon, 123
Coors, Giles "Bull," 18, 172
Copenhagen (Denmark), 46–47, 54
Crew, Jerry, 192
Crickmore, Paul, 144, 152, 202–4, 206
Cross, Carl S., 164
Crossfield, Scott, 91, 131, 199
Cuban Missile Crisis, 135

D-21 drone, 134, 171
Daley, Richard M., 219
d'Angleterre, Hotel (Copenhagen), 47
Daniel, Walt, 133, 164
David Clark Company, 122
Davis, Glenn, 45
Davis, Mel, 35–37, 40, 43–44, 47
DC-8 airliner (Douglas), 140
dead-stick landings, 104, 105–6, 130
Desoto Oil and Gas Trust, 201–2
Detroit Aircraft Corporation, 97
Doolittle, Jimmy, 60
Douglas Aircraft: C-47 "Gooney Bird," 56; D-558-11 Skyrocket, 91; DC-4 airliner, 34; DC-8 airliner, 140; as defense contractor, 91; start of, 101
drone program, 134, 170–71
Dulles, Allen W., 116, 135

Earhart, Amelia, 86, 98
East Berlin (Germany), 55, 208

Eastham, Jim: as A-12 test pilot, 127, 132; awards and honors of, 132; at Hughes, 127; during SR-71's maiden flight, 163–64, 169, 171; as SR-71 test pilot, 149; and YF-12A maiden flight, 131

Edwards, Glen, 88, 89

Edwards Air Force Base: naming of, 89; RJG's work out of, 105; SR-71 testing at, 1–2; X-1 program at, 91; YF-12As testing at, 133. *See also* Muroc Army Air Base

Eglin Air Force Base: RJG as pilot at, 89–91, 92–93; RJG requesting reassignment to, 83; RJG's SR-71 joke at, 187–89; testing operational aircraft at, 92–93

86th Fighter-Bomber Wing, 66–74

Eisenhower (aircraft carrier), 215, 217

Eisenhower, Dwight, 117–18, 140, 190

ejection system: F-84 Thunderjet, 70; F-104 Starfighter, 103; John Paul Stapp's research in, 123–24; SR-71, 151, 162, 178–79; U-2, 139

Electra (Lockheed), 97–98, 137, 143–44, 156

Elkmont (Gilliland family cabin), 17–18, 173

Empire Test Pilots' School, 92

engines: and dead-stick landings, 104, 105–6; failures of, during beginning of jet age, 63, 67–70; failures of, during testing, 101–2; J35 Allison, 67–68; J70, 105; of the SR-71 Blackbird, 143–45, 147–50; turbo-ramjet, 147–50; and unstarts, 130, 150, 183

Excelsior, Project (high-altitude testing), 124

F-4 Phantom (McDonnell), 192, 207, 217

F8F-2 Bearcat (Grumman), 225

F-80 (Lockheed), 67, 76. *See also* P-80 Shooting Star (Lockheed)

F-84E (Republic Aviation), 67–68

F-84 Thunderjet (Republic Aviation): compared to the MiG-15, 76; crashes of, 68; at Eglin, 92; engine and canopy issues of, 67–68, 70; flown at Fürstenfeldbruck, 66; flown at Neubiberg, 67–68, 70; and gunnery competitions, 70–71; in the Korean War, 72, 76, 77–79, 167; RJG as pilot of, 70–71, 76, 77–79, 90, 92, 167; sweptwing version of, 92

F-86 Sabre (North American Aviation): aerial reconnaissance mission with, 77; crashes of, 77; at Eglin, 92–93; introduction of, 76; in the Korean War, 76–77; RJG piloting, 81, 92–93

F-104 Starfighter (Lockheed): crashes and deaths in, 103, 105, 107, 122, 164; dead-stick landings in, 104, 105–6; development of, 102–3; ejection system of, 103; Lockheed's testing of, 104–5; records set by, 103; RJG as instructor pilot for, 105–8, 113–15; RJG piloting, 104–5, 108–9; and RJG's contest against the SR-71, 175–76; sold to NATO countries, 106–8; speed limitations of, 143; as SR-71 chase aircraft, 163–64, 168–69; in the Tennessee Air National Guard, 103–4

F-117A Nighthawk (Lockheed), 211

Faith 7, 123

Favreau, Miss, 18

Felker, Lonnie, 214

Finch College (New York City), 10

Finnigan, Robert, 37, 39–40, 44, 45–46, 212, 213

fishing, 81–82, 173–74

Fitz, Mary Gilliland (RJG's second wife): divorce of, 214, 225; and expectations of children, 174; and gifts from David Clark Company, 122; in Italy, 108; and move to La Canada Flintridge, 119; and move to Palmdale, 104–5; repairing RJG's work clothes, 127; and RJG's time at Skunk Works, 119–21, 122, 127; watching launch of *Apollo 15*, 194–95; watching SR-71 first flight, 164–67; and the Weaver-Zwayer crash, 180

Flickinger, Don, 126

flight cards: for A-12 test flights, 129; Kelly Johnson's adherence to, 129, 161; for the SR-71's first flight, 161–62, 166, 169, 176

flying wing aircraft, 88–89

Folden, Archie, 114, 155

Follin, Webb, 23–24

football, 32, 44–45, 140

Forbes, Daniel, 88

Ford convertible, RJG's, 62, 63–64

Ford Mustang, RJG's, 174–75

Forrest, Nathan Bedford, 9

France: during World War I, 3–4, 5–7; during World War II, 22

Fuhrman, Tom, 208–9

full-slip maneuvers, 106
Fürstenfeldbruck Air Base (Germany), 66

Gaddis, Norman: during the Berlin Airlift, 55; on characteristics of pilots, 57, 72–73; on F-84 crashes, 68; friendship of, with RJG, 73, 221, 223–24; nickname of, 223–24; on the transition to jets, 74; as Vietnam prisoner of war, 192–93
Gaddis, Tony, 224
Galloway Drive house (Memphis TN), 13, 15, 17
Geary, Leo, 161
Gemini, Project, 124
General Electric engines, 105, 114
Germany: Fürstenfeldbruck Air Base in, 66; Legends of Aerospace goodwill tour in, 216; Neubiberg Air Base in, 66–74; Ramstein Air Base in, 81–82, 216; RJG as instructor pilot in, 106–7; SR-71 missions over, 202, 205; during World War I, 3–4, 5–7; during World War II, 22, 26–27, 62
Giannotta, Steven L., 220–21
Gilliland, Anne (RJG's daughter). *See* Hayes, Anne Gilliland (RJG's daughter)
Gilliland, Elizabeth "Libby" Jordan (RJG's mother): ancestry of, 8–9; birth of, 8; character and personality of, 16, 18; childhood of, 7–10; education of, 10; expectations and parenting style of, 15, 19–20; and family automobile outing, 7–8; on Frank Jr.'s disposition, 97; and Frank Jr.'s graduation, 50; and fur coat story, 79–80; during the Great Depression, 14–15, 93–94; honeymoon cruise of, 12–13; and husband's death, 96; relationship of, with husband, 26; relationship of, with RJG, 16, 17–18, 171; and RJG's Korean tour of duty, 75; and RJG's Naval Academy appointment, 33; and sons' Webb School education, 21; volunteer work of, 10–11; watching launch of *Apollo 15*, 194
Gilliland, Frank, Jr. (RJG's brother): birth of, 14; business partnership of, with brothers, 201; career of, 97; childhood of, 14, 16–17, 20; death of, 201; and father's war experience, 26; graduation of, from Vanderbilt, 50; naval service of, 97; parents' expectations for, 17, 20; personality of, 24, 97; relationship of, with RJG, 17, 97, 171–72; at Webb School, 24
Gilliland, Frank Marshall (RJG's father): business ventures of, 13–14, 93–96, 201–2; character and personality of, 15–16, 17, 38; death of, 96; education of, 4, 5; expectations and parenting style of, 14, 15–17, 20, 21, 62; friendship of, with Felix Stump, 49–50, 52; during the Great Depression, 14–15; health and illness of, 5, 96; helping RJG join the military, 27–28; honeymoon cruise of, 12–13; impact of Frank Jr.'s death on, 201; law career of, 5, 12, 13–14, 18; letters from Webb School to, 22–24; military service of, 5–7, 26; military support group work of, 12, 49; relationship of, with RJG, 15–16, 20, 26, 29, 94, 96; RJG resigning from U.S. Air Force for, 93–95; on RJG's love of flying, 95; watching RJG's Naval Academy graduation, 50, 52; at Webb School, 4, 21; during World War I, 5–7
Gilliland, Heather (RJG's granddaughter), 223
Gilliland, Jim (RJG's brother), 94; birth of, 14; business partnership of, with brothers, 201; buzzed by RJG's F-84, 90; childhood of, 14–15, 16–17, 20; and father's war experience, 26; at National Aviation Hall of Fame induction, 230; naval service of, 97; parents' expectations for, 17, 20; relationship of, with RJG, 17, 171–72; at Webb School, 50
Gilliland, John (RJG's uncle), 5
Gilliland, Kim (RJG's daughter-in-law), 224–25, 226
Gilliland, Lucia (RJG's sister-in-law), 230
Gilliland, Mary (RJG's second wife). *See* Fitz, Mary Gilliland (RJG's second wife)
Gilliland, Robert, Jr. (RJG's son): at California Aviation Hall of Fame induction, 222–23; childhood of, 108, 122, 173–74; education of, 174; on father's handling emergencies, 158–60; on father's speeding tickets, 175; at father's spinal surgery, 221; interest of, in aviation, 225–26; law career of, 225; maintaining Blackbird secrecy, 195;

Gilliland, Robert, Jr. (RJG's son) (*cont.*) at National Aviation Hall of Fame induction, 226–27, 228–30, 231–32; parents' expectations for, 174; photograph of, in father's boots, 122; relationship of, with father, 173–74, 225; taking care of father, 224–25; during the Vietnam War, 193–94; watching SR-71 first flight, 164–65

Gilliland, Robert Jordan "Bob" (RJG): on arbitrary rules, 18, 22–25, 38–39, 60–62, 82–83, 226; athleticism of, 20, 42, 82, 109, 172–73; awards and honors of, 222–23, 226–32; birth of, 13; business career of, 95–97, 201–2; call sign of, 164; calmness of, under pressure, 25, 63–64, 79, 104, 105–6, 130, 158–60, 179–80, 212, 227; childhood homes of, 13, 17–18; childhood of, 15–21, 220; competitiveness of, 15–17, 19–20, 25; death of, 233; divorces of, 96, 214, 225; education of, 18–27, 32–33, 36, 104; as elite pilot, 57, 59, 70–71, 74, 157–60, 167–68, 179–80, 198, 212; European liberty trips of, 45–47, 52–56; first marriage of, 96; friendliness and sincerity of, 73, 83, 208; homes of, 119; humor of, 112–13; impact of Kelly Johnson on, 156–58; independence and nonconformity of, 25–26, 38–39, 57, 60–62; injuries and illnesses of, 16, 64, 65, 220–22, 223; intelligence and curiosity of, 15, 19–20, 37, 93, 157, 213–14; legacy of, 208, 211–12, 213, 222–23, 228, 230; and love of adventure and exploration, 82, 89–90, 158, 172, 173–75; and love of flying, 18–19, 57, 79, 95–96, 97, 129; and love of nature and outdoors, 17–18, 81–82; military basic training of, 31; military flight training of, at Randolph, 52, 57–62; military flight training of, at Williams, 62–66, 103; military service of, 27–29, 48–49, 70–79, 81–83, 90–95, 103–4; military training of, at Bainbridge Naval Center, 31–32; military training of, at Naval Academy, 32–45, 50–52; military training of, during summers, 45–47; nicknames of, 35–36; parents' expectations for, 15–16, 19–20; planes owned by, 158–59; relationship of, with brothers, 17, 97, 171–72; relationship of, with children, 173, 174, 223, 225; relationship of, with father, 15–16, 20, 26, 29, 94, 96; relationship of, with mother, 16, 17–18, 171; second marriage of, 104; self-confidence of, 15–16, 91; vehicles of, 1, 62, 63–64, 174–75, 224

Gilliland, Sandra Wright (RJG's first wife), 96
Gilliland, Scott (RJG's grandson), 223
Gilliland, Tandy (RJG's sister-in-law), 17, 21, 172
Gipp, George, 104
Glasser, Gerald, 228
Glenn, John, 131
Goldwater, Barry, 135, 160
golf, 16, 49, 65
Goodlin, Chalmers "Slick," 84
Graham, Richard, 135–36, 182
Grant, Ulysses S., 9
Great Britain: and Berlin Airlift resupply mission, 55–56; bomber contract of, with Lockheed, 137; Legends of Aerospace tour in, 218–19; Mildenhall RAF base in, 190, 202–3, 205–6; postwar rationing in, 45; during World War I, 4, 6
Great Depression, 14–15
Great Lakes Naval Station, 31
Green, Andrew, 218–19
Greenamyer, Darryl: as A-12 pilot, 187; business partnership of, with RJG, 201; as F-104 instructor, 114–15; on RJG's piloting skill, 168; speed records set by, 200–201, 225; as SR-71 pilot, 151, 180
Groom Lake: commuting to, 120–21; names for, 120; secrecy of, 117, 120–21, 133, 164; selection of, 117. *See also* Skunk Works (Lockheed Advanced Development Projects)
Gross, Courtland, 97
Gross, Robert, 97, 99
ground looping, 59
G suits (pressure suits), 90–91

Hall, Harley, 193–94
Hammond, Jim, 93
handball, 172–73
Hanks, Tom, 197
Happy Bottom Riding Club, 86–87, 105
Hardin, Alexander McAlpin, 9

Hardin, Elizabeth Robinson, 9
Hardin, Joseph, 8
Hartinger, Jimmy, 65–66, 102
Hartman, David, 198–200, 216, 222–23, 230
Hayes, Anne Gilliland (RJG's daughter): childhood of, in Italy, 108; at National Aviation Hall of Fame induction, 231–32; parents' expectations for, 174; relationship of, with RJG, 173, 174, 223; at RJG's surgery, 221; watching SR-71 first flight, 164–65
Hayes, Laura (RJG's granddaughter), 223
Hayes, Nate (RJG's grandson), 223
Hayes, Richard (RJG's son-in-law), 223
Hayes, Stuart (RJG's grandson), 223
hazing (Naval Academy), 39–40
heat and temperature challenges, 143–50
Hedrick, Wayne, 13
helicopters, 112, 140, 184–85
Hibbard, Hall, 98, 100, 156
high-altitude testing, 123–24
hiking, 18, 25, 109, 173
Hillenbrand, Laura, 221
Hindenburg Line, 3, 5–7
Hitler, Adolf, 33, 137
Hoa Lo prison camp ("Hanoi Hilton"), 192–93
Hoover, Bob, 85, 87, 221
Hotel d'Angleterre (Copenhagen), 47
Hudson bomber (Lockheed), 137
Hughes, Howard, 34, 98
Hupmobile, 7–8

Imperial Hotel (Tokyo), 79
inlet system (SR-71), 143–45, 147–50, 182, 183, 186
Intrepid (aircraft carrier), 219–20
Irwin, Jim, 194–95
Italy, 108–9, 113–15
Iven C. Kincheloe Award, 131–32, 225

J35 Allison engines, 67–68
J58 turbo-ramjet engines, 147–50
Jackson, Andrew, 8
Jacobs, Jesse, 92, 157
Jacobs, Jimmy, 172–73
Japan, 26–27, 33, 34, 189
jet-powered aircraft: and commercial aviation growth, 140; impact of, on military, 74; limitations of, 143; risks associated with, 91–93; Skunk Works' development of, 99–109; of the Soviet Union, 76; sweptwing design of, 76, 92, 102; technological advances in, 140, 143; transition to, 62–63, 67–69, 74. *See also specific aircraft*
Jets (football team), 140
JN-4 biplane "Jenny" (Curtiss), 101
Joersz, Al, 207, 210
Johnson, Carroll, 22, 24, 26
Johnson, Clarence "Kelly": and A-12 Blackbird development, 125–26, 129, 143; and A-12 Blackbird proposal, 124–25; and Blackbird development, 142–52; Blackbird variations proposed by, 134–35; character and personality of, 99–100, 141–42, 156–57; death of, 209; efficiency of, 99–101, 102, 116–17, 141–42; engineering and design genius of, 98–99, 100, 136–40, 142–52, 156–57; and F-104 development, 102–3; following the Weaver-Zwayer crash, 185–86; and founding of Skunk Works, 99; honors received by, 141; interviewing RJG, 111, 113–15; on Lyndon Johnson's unmasking the SR-71, 136; and M-21 Blackbird development, 134, 170–71; managerial style of, 99–100, 126–27, 141–42, 157; and P-80 development, 100–102, 138–39; relationship of, with RJG, 129, 156–58, 171; retirement of, from Skunk Works, 200; risks taken by, 142, 156; on security measures, 185–86; and SR-71 development, 142–52, 185–86; and SR-71 postflight instrumentation tape analysis, 179–80; and SR-71 proposal, 135; and SR-71's first test flight, 152–53, 155–56, 160–71, 228; and SR-71 test flight debriefings, 177–78; starting at Lockheed, 98–99; and Tony LeVier, 101–2; and U-2 development, 116–17, 139; and YF-12A proposal, 131
Johnson, Howard C. "Scrappy," 106
Johnson, Lyndon B.: impact of, on the Blackbird program, 164, 170; reelection of, 160; on Soviet Union overflights, 131, 190; and the SR-71 acronym, 135–36; and unmasking the Blackbird program, 133–34, 135–36, 145, 206

Index 247

Jordan, Carol Gilliland (RJG's niece), 174
Jordan, Robert (RJG's maternal grandfather), 7–8, 9–10, 13, 14, 17
Jordan, Robert, Jr. (RJG's brother-in-law), 10–11
JP-7 fuel blend, 150
Justice, Charlie "Choo Choo," 32
Justice, Steve, 142, 143, 148, 202, 210

Kadena Air Base (Okinawa, Japan), 189–90, 191
KC-135 Stratotanker (Boeing), 177, 202
Kennedy, John F., 125, 128–29, 135, 160
Khrushchev, Nikita, 118
Kincheloe, Dorothy, 131–32
Kincheloe, Iven C., Jr., 91, 103, 131–32
Kirchoff's law of thermal radiation, 145
Kittinger, Joe: on career choice, 71, 124; on Cold War tensions, 66–67; as high-altitude test pilot, 123–24; at National Aviation Hall of Fame induction, 230–31; relationship of, with RJG, 123, 221, 230–31; as Vietnam prisoner of war, 193
Korean War: aerial reconnaissance during, 77; jet fighter technology during, 75–76, 102; Kelly Johnson's work during, 102; pilot deaths during, 71–72, 78; RJG serving in, 76–79, 167; RJG volunteering for, 75
Kotchian, A. Carl, 200

L-1011 airliner (Lockheed), 155
La Canada Flintridge home, 119, 174
Lacy, Clay, 100–101, 140
Ladd, Alan, 76
Landstuhl Regional Medical Center (Germany), 216
Law, Pete, 134, 139, 144, 145, 149, 157
Law, R. R., 51–52
Layton, Jack, 190
Le Bonheur Children's Hospital (Memphis TN), 10–11
Lee, Steve, 207
Lee, Tom, 197–200, 214–19
Legends of Aerospace goodwill tour, 197–200, 214–20
Lemay, Curtis, 136
LeVier, Tony: and childhood love of flying, 101; on effect of compressibility, 138; and Lockheed's F-104 program, 114; as Lockheed's greatest test pilot, 101–2, 112, 171; on RJG's signed photograph, 171; and the U-2 program, 117
Libya, 70–71, 207–8
Lindbergh, Charles, 18–19, 112
Lloyd, Nick, 3
Lockhart, Gene, 54
Lockhart, June, 54
Lockheed Aircraft Corporation: Constellation airliner, 98, 120; contract of, with RAF, 137; contracts of, with NATO countries, 106–8, 113–15; and defense contracting competition, 91, 146; Electra, 97–98, 137, 143–44, 156; F-80, 67, 76; F-117A Nighthawk, 211; founding of, 97; impact of, on aviation industry, 97–98; Kelly Johnson hired by, 98; Kelly Johnson retiring from, 200; L-1011 airliner, 155; Lou Schalk's career at, 70, 103, 111–12, 126, 128, 132, 149, 161; P-38 Lightning, 98; P-80 Shooting Star, 63, 67, 100–102, 138; Pentagon contract awards to, 99, 102, 131, 135; PV-2 Harpoon bomber, 137–38; RJG as test pilot for, 104–9, 113–15; T-33 trainer, 63, 90–91; Tony LeVier as test pilot for, 101–2, 112, 114, 171; XP-38 Lightning, 138; XP-80/P-80 Shooting Star, 100–102, 138. *See also* A-12 "Archangel" Blackbird (Lockheed); Blackbird program (Lockheed); F-104 Starfighter (Lockheed); Skunk Works (Lockheed Advanced Development Projects); SR-71 Blackbird (Lockheed); U-2 (Lockheed)
Lollobrigida, Gina, 108
Lovell, Jim, 69, 197–200, 215–19
Luftwaffe, 62, 107
Lusitania, 4

M2-F2 (Northrup), 225
M-21 Blackbird (Lockheed), 134, 170–71
Manhigh, Project (high-altitude testing), 123–24
March Field Air Museum, 227
Markowitz, Jamie, 214, 215, 219–20, 221, 224
Markowitz, Jane, 222
Mason, Roger, 214
Matheney, Jim, 34–35, 41, 42–43, 89
Matterhorn (mountain), 109

McCain, John, 51
McConnell, Joe, 76–77
McFarland, E. B., 5
McKellar, Kenneth, 28, 32–33
McVoy, Jim, 35–38, 40, 43, 50–54
ME-262 (Messerschmitt), 62, 84, 100
Mechling, Edward P., 94–95
Memorial Hall (Naval Academy), 48, 49
Memphis TN, 10–12
Mercury astronauts, 122–24, 140
Messerschmitt, 62, 84, 100
MiG-15 (Mikoyan-Gurevich), 76, 78–79, 102
MiG Alley (Korean War), 76
Mildenhall Air Force Base, 190, 202–3, 205–6
Military Air Transport System, 53–54
Miller, Dick: as SR-71 RSO, 1–2, 178–79, 226; and SR-71's maiden flight, 161; and the Weaver-Zwayer crash, 180, 181, 185
Miller, Donna, 213, 229
Millington Naval Base, 49
missiles: compared to bombers, 134–35; fired at Blackbirds, 191–92, 204; intercontinental ballistic, 134–35; Soviet capabilities for, 135, 204, 205–6; submarine-launched, 205–6; surface-to-air, 135, 191–92, 204; during the Vietnam War, 191–92
Mitchell, Albert, Jr., 184–85
moon suits (pressurized suits), 1, 122, 184
Moore, Kay Combs, 230
Morale Entertainment, 214–20
Morrow, Jim, 202–3
Muroc Army Air Base, 84–89. *See also* Edwards Air Force Base
Murphy, Bob, 152
Murphy, Pat, 59
Murray, Frank, 120–21, 127–28, 179, 190
museums, 209–11, 227

NACA (National Advisory Committee for Aeronautics), 91
Namath, Joe, 140
napalm, 77–78
Napoleon I, 3
NASA (National Aeronautics and Space Administration): and Ames Hangar One, 212; and *Apollo 8*, 69, 197; and *Apollo 11*, 198, 217, 225; and *Apollo 13*, 69, 197; and

Apollo 15, 194–95; and *Faith 7*, 123; formation of, 122; and Mercury astronauts, 122–24, 140; and Project Gemini, 124
National Advisory Committee for Aeronautics (NACA), 91
National Air and Space Museum, 209–10
National Aviation Hall of Fame, 226–27, 228–32
National Cathedral School (Washington DC), 10
Naval Academy: admissions exams for, 28; Bancroft Hall dormitory at, 35, 43–44, 48; and canon firing for visiting admirals, 49–50; celebrating ending of World War II, 34–35; graduates of, transferring to U.S. Air Force officer corps, 47–49; hazing at, 39–40; and Molded Cake Caper of 1945, 44–45; and Plebe Summer, 34; prestige associated with, 61; RJG attending, 35–45; RJG's demerits at, 38, 43–44; RJG's graduation from, 50–52; RJG's primary appointment to, 32–34; RJG's secondary appointment to, 28; and summers training on battleships, 45–47
Navy, U.S.: air strikes of, against Libya, 207–8; and aviator training path, 49; and carrier-based night flying, 69; and PV-2 Harpoon bomber, 137–38; RJG enlisting in, 28–29; and RJG's basic training, 31–32; V5 naval aviator program of, 27–28
Nellis Air Force Base, 187
Nelson, Norman, 182
Nemzek, Tom, 48–49
Neubiberg Air Base (Germany), 66–74
Nevada Test Site, 117
New York Jets (football team), 140
Nimitz, Chester, 44
9th Reconnaissance Wing, 189–90, 207
nitrogen gas, 150
Norris, Jim, 175–76
North American Aviation, 59; B-25 bomber, 60, 70, 96, 103; B-70 Valkyrie, 134, 164; F-86 Sabre, 76–77, 81, 92–93; P-51 Mustang, 59; T-6 Texan, 59; X-15 rocket plane, 103, 164; XB-70 Valkyrie, 164
North American Defense Command, 66
North Carolina (battleship), 46
Northrup Corporation, 88–89

Index 249

Oak Ridge National Laboratory, 103
Oburu, Winnie, 224
O'Donnell, Emmett "Rosie," 95
120th Infantry Regiment (U.S. Army), 5–7
Operation Black Shield, 190
Operation Thunderhead, 193
Osterheld, Curt, 207
Oxcart program (CIA): Bill Weaver's work with, 181; declassification of, 190; impact of the U-2 incident on, 190; maintaining schedule of, 147; secrecy of, 131; Skunk Works awarded contract for, 125. *See also* A-12 "Archangel" Blackbird (Lockheed); Blackbird program (Lockheed)

P-38 Lightning (Lockheed), 98
P-47 Thunderbolt (Republic), 66, 67, 70
P-51 Mustang (North American Aviation), 59
P-59 Airacomet (Bell Aircraft), 62
P-80 Shooting Star (Lockheed), 63, 67, 100–102, 138
Palm, Vera, 113
Panama Limited, 29
Pan American Airways, 34, 140
Parangosky, John, 100
Park, Bill: as A-12 test pilot, 127, 132; awards and honors of, 132; and Bill Weaver, 181; contest of, with RJG, 175–76; at Convair, 127; and JFK's assassination, 129; as M-21 test pilot, 170; as SR-71 test pilot, 149, 175–76
Parker, Woody, 192
Pawn Star, 211–12
Pentagon: and air strikes against Libya, 207–8; and cockpit size restrictions, 60; and contract awards to Lockheed, 99, 102, 131, 135; during the Korean War, 71–72; in post–Vietnam War era, 200; protocols for assignments from, 82–83; at SR-71's maiden flight, 161; transitioning to jet aircraft, 74; and U.S. Air Force officer corps training, 47–48; use of satellite technology by, 204–5. *See also* Air Force, U.S.
Perkins, Hamilton "Ham," 35–37, 40–41, 43–44, 47
Perot, Ross, Jr., 230
Pershing, John J. "Black Jack," 5
Peterson, Art, 180, 186

Peterson, Bruce, 225
pilots: of commercial aircraft, 199; competitiveness of, 72–73, 175–76; crashes of, during bad weather, 199; crashes of, during testing, 88–89, 91, 103, 138, 164, 180–86, 201; dangers faced by, 1–2, 67–70, 77–79, 84–86, 88–89, 91–93, 101–2, 127–28, 130–31, 139, 149–50, 156, 199; deaths of, 63, 69, 72, 77–78, 88, 91, 103, 138, 164, 170–71, 182–86, 199; and the Happy Bottom Riding Club, 86–87; height restrictions for, 60–62; in high-altitude testing programs, 123–24; and Iven C. Kincheloe Award, 131–32; during the Korean War, 72, 77–79; and love of adventure, 71, 89–90; and path to flying SR-71, 207; qualities needed for, 57, 68–69, 107, 157, 179–80; RJG's impact on, 208; role of, in testing and development, 182; at Skunk Works, 101–2, 111–12, 126–31; stereotypes of, 66; struggles of, with matrimony, 214; during the supersonic age, 88–89; training of, 92; during transition from propellers to jets, 63, 67–70
Ping-Pong, 76–77
Powers, Francis Gary, 118, 125, 190, 204
Presidential Succession Act, 32
pressure suits, 1, 90–91, 122, 123–24, 184
Project Excelsior (high-altitude testing), 124
Project Gemini (NASA), 124
Project Manhigh (high-altitude testing), 123–24
Project Suntan (liquid-hydrogen-powered plane), 142
propeller-driven aircraft, 34, 63, 74
PV-2 Harpoon bomber (Lockheed), 137–38

R-12/RB-12 (Lockheed), 134–35
Rall, Gunther, 106–7
Ramstein Air Base (Germany), 81–82, 216
Rancho Mirage, 224
Randolph (aircraft carrier), 46–47
Randolph Field flight school (Texas), 57–62
Ray, Walter, 190
Reagan, Ronald, 66, 202, 207
reconnaissance aircraft: F-117A Nighthawk, 211; impact of U-2 program on, 116–19, 125; Lyndon Johnson's announcement of, 133–34, 135–36; modified B-36 bomber, 116;

modified F-86 Sabre, 77; during the Vietnam War, 190–93. *See also* A-12 "Archangel" Blackbird (Lockheed); SR-71 Blackbird (Lockheed); U-2 (Lockheed)
refueling: of the A-12 Blackbird, 187; of the CL-400, 142; Paul Crickmore's ride-alongs during, 202–3; of the SR-71 Blackbird, 177, 192
Republic Aviation: F-84 Thunderjet, 66, 67–68, 70–72, 76–79, 90, 92, 167; P-47 Thunderbolt, 66, 67, 70
Reynolds, Gene, 113, 156, 160
Rice, Donald, 209
Rich, Ben, 125–26, 139, 141, 145, 148, 150, 209
Ridley, Jackie, 85, 87
Ritchie, Steve, 198–200, 215–20
Robinson, David, 9
rocket-powered aircraft: impact of, on space race, 123; limitations of, 142–43; X-1, 84–85, 87–88; X-2, 91; X-15, 103, 164
Rogers Dry Lake, 86
Roosevelt, Franklin D., 32
Rostow, Walt W., 190
Rousch, Roy, 211
Royal Air Force: contracts of, with Lockheed, 137; and Empire Test Pilots' School, 92; and Mildenhall Air Force Base, 190, 202–3, 205–6; Paul Crickmore's ride-alongs with, 202–3
RS-71 Blackbird (Lockheed). *See* SR-71 Blackbird (Lockheed)
Rutan, Burt, 213
Rutan, Dick, 131, 213, 231

satellite technology, 204–5
Saturday Evening Post, 134
Schalk, Lou: as A-12 test pilot, 126, 128, 132, 149, 161; awards and honors of, 132; background of, 111; emergencies faced by, 69–70, 126; as F-104 test pilot, 103; fishing trips of, 81; on Kelly Johnson, 141; and Kelly Johnson selecting Bill Weaver, 181; and Kelly Johnson selecting RJG, 104, 111–12, 113, 114; as P-47 pilot, 70; relationship of, with RJG, 81, 104, 111–12; at the SR-71's retirement, 209; as SR-71 test pilot, 149
Scotland, 45–46
Scott, David, 195

SETP (Society of Experimental Test Pilots), 131–32, 213
Sevier, Camp (Greenville SC), 6
Sevier, John, 8
Shelton, Jim, 176–77, 182, 192, 208
Shiloh, Battle of, 9
Si Bon (restaurant), 224, 226
Simler, George B., 75, 82
Simpson, O. J., 214
skiing, 82, 108, 173
Skliar, Bill, 130
Skunk Works (Lockheed Advanced Development Projects): and A-1 Blackbird, 143; and A-11 Blackbird, 133; and A-12 Blackbird, 124–31; creation of, 99; and debriefings following test flights, 163, 177–78; efficiency of, 100–101, 102, 116–17, 141–42; engineering challenges faced by, 137–39; Gene Reynolds's career at, 113, 160; independence of, 99; jet-powered aircraft developed by, 99–109; Kelly Johnson retiring from, 200; Lou Schalk's career at, 70, 103, 111–12, 126, 128, 132, 149, 161; and Project Suntan, 142; RJG as test pilot at, 1–2, 119–22, 124, 127–31, 136, 149–53; RJG joining, 111–15; secrecy of work at, 99, 111–12, 119–22, 131, 134, 135–36; security at, 115, 185–86; technological innovations and designs of, 102–3, 140–51; test pilots of, 101–2, 111–12, 126–31; Tony LeVier's career at, 101–2, 112, 114, 117, 171; and U-2 program, 116–18; work culture at, 99–100; and XP-80 development, 100. *See also* A-12 "Archangel" Blackbird (Lockheed); SR-71 Blackbird (Lockheed)
Smith, H. R., 183–84
Smithsonian Institution, 209–10
Smoke Hall (Bancroft Hall, Naval Academy), 48
Society of Experimental Test Pilots (SETP), 131–32, 213
Solomon, Ken, 67–68, 73
sound barrier, 76, 84–88, 201, 218
Soviet Union: aerial reconnaissance of, 115–19, 131; and arms race, 133–35; and atomic bomb testing, 66, 115; during the Berlin Airlift, 55–56; during the Cold War, 66–67,

Soviet Union (*cont.*)
75–76, 121, 205–6; and ending of U.S. reconnaissance overflights, 125, 131, 190, 204–5; during the Korean War, 78–79; missile capabilities of, 135; in the space race, 122–23; SR-71 missions near, 205–6; submarines of, 205–6, 207; and sweptwing aircraft design, 76, 92; threats posed by, 55–56, 63, 66–67, 75–76, 121; titanium from, 144–45; and U-2 incident, 118; during World War I, 3

Sputnik, 122

SR-71 Blackbird (Lockheed): acronym changes of, 135–36; air-conditioning system of, 146; and black paint innovation, 145–46; camera and sensor systems of, 152, 181–82, 205, 207; and center of gravity problem, 166, 178–80, 181, 186; chemical ignition system of, 150; cockpit design of, 151; and competition against RJG's F-104, 175–76; crashes of, 180–81, 182–86; cruise speed of, 147–48, 152; dangers and risks facing test pilots of, 1–2, 149–50, 166, 178–80; and deaths, 180–86; debriefings following test flights of, 163, 177–78; declassification of, 203; design modifications and features of, 151–52; ejection system of, 151, 162, 178–79; ending of testing program and development of, 200; enduring legacy of, 210–11, 216–17, 227–28; and engine design innovations, 147–50; engineering challenges in design of, 137, 143–51, 156, 181–82, 186; evasive capabilities of, 152, 192, 204; fictional portrayals of, 211; first test flight of, 152–53, 155–56, 160–71, 228; fuel blend of, 150; heat-related challenges of, 143–50; impact of U-2 incident on, 190, 204–5; inlet system of, 143–45, 147–50, 182, 183, 186; Kelly Johnson's legacy in, 135, 142, 151; limited operational theater of, 204–5; Lyndon Johnson unmasking of, 135–36, 145, 206; missiles fired at, 191–92, 204, 208; and mission following Libyan airstrike, 208; and missions during the Cold War, 202–7; and missions targeting Soviet submarines, 205–6, 207; museums housing, 209–11, 227; nicknames of, 191; operational rollout of, 189–90; public fascination with, 146, 202–4, 206–7, 210–11, 227–28; radar system of, 181–82; reconnaissance features of, 152, 181–82, 205–6, 207; refueling of, 177, 192; RJG as chief test pilot of, 1–2, 136, 176–80, 226; and RJG's joke on Toof Brown, 187–89; and RJG's legacy, 208, 211–12, 231; secrecy of, 135–36, 170, 171–72, 177, 187–89, 195, 202, 203–4, 206; shape of, 146; speed records in, 207, 209; stealth technology design elements of, 146, 205, 211; taxi test of, 155, 163; technological innovations of, 143–51, 181–82, 227; testing program of, 149–50, 176–86; test pilot team of, 180; titanium used in, 143–45; twenty-fifth anniversary flight of, 208–9; unstarts of, 150, 178–79; U.S. Air Force's initial order for, 135; U.S. Air Force's retirement of, 209; variations of, 189; during the Vietnam War, 190–93; and Weaver-Zwayer crash, 180–86

stainless steel, 143–44
Stanley, Roy, 152
Stapp, John Paul, 123–24
Stephens, Fox, 133, 164, 177
Sterick Building (Memphis TN), 13–14, 93–94, 95–96, 97
Sterling, Ross, 13
Steven F. Udvar-Hazy Center (Smithsonian), 210, 225
Stevenson, Coke, 44
Stewart, Jim, 90–91, 158
Stokes, Stan, 176
St. Quentin Canal (France), 3, 5–7
Strickland, Colonel, 61–62
Stump, Felix, 49–50, 51, 52–53, 71
submarines, 205–6, 207
Sulgrave Manor, 13
Sullenberger, Chesley "Sully," 199
Sullivan, Dennis, 190, 191
Suntan, Project (liquid-hydrogen-powered plane), 142
supersonic age, 76, 84–85, 88–89, 102
sweptwing design, 76, 92, 102. *See also* F-86 Sabre (North American Aviation); MiG-15 (Mikoyan-Gurevich)

T-6 Texan (North American Aviation), 59

t-33 (Lockheed), 63, 90–91
Taegu Air Base "k-2" (South Korea), 76–79
teb tanks, 150
Tennessee Air National Guard, 94, 95–96, 103–4
thermal radiation, Kirchoff's law of, 145
30th Division "Old Hickory Division" (U.S. Army), 3, 5–7
36th Fighter-Bomber Wing, 66
Thompson, Warren, 204
three-point landings, 59
Thrust supersonic car, 218
Thunderhead, Operation, 193
titanium, 144–45
Torick, Ray, 107–71
Torino (Italy), 108
Trans World Airlines, 34, 98
Trippe, Juan, 34
Truman, Harry, 41–42, 44, 47, 71, 88
Tymczyszyn, Joe, 131–32
Tyson, Mike, 173

u-2 (Lockheed): challenges flying, 116, 139; cia's program of, 116, 117–19; compared to the a-12 Blackbird, 125–26; during the Cuban Missile Crisis, 135; design challenges of, 139; development of, 116–17, 120; Kelly Johnson's design for, 116, 139; Kelly Johnson's interview regarding, 125; limitations of, 139, 142–43; and Powers incident, 118–19, 125, 190, 204–5; Tony LeVier as test pilot of, 117
Udvar-Hazy Center (Smithsonian), 210, 225
University Club (Memphis tn), 12
University of Michigan, 98
University of Tennessee, 104
unstarts, 130, 150, 183

v5 program (naval aviator training), 27–28
Vanderbilt University, 5, 32–33, 36, 50
Varney, Walter, 97
Vida, J. T., 209
Vietnam War, 161; and attempted pow rescue mission, 193; ending of, 194; and Operation Black Shield, 190; and Operation Thunderhead, 193; RJG's experience with, 192–94; use of Blackbirds during, 190–93

Vinson, Bobby, 192
Virden, Ralph, 138
Vojvodich, Mele, 77, 127–28, 190
von Grote, Roger, 173
von Richthofen, Manfred "Red Baron," 173

Walker, James, 164
Ward, Frank, 51
Washington, George, 13
Weaver, Bill, 105, 119, 157, 180, 181–86, 226
Webb, Sawny, 21
Webb, William R. "Son Will," 23, 25
Webb School (Bell Buckle tn), 5, 21–27, 50
Weber, Hal, 100, 157
Weeks, Jack, 190
Werblin, Sonny, 140
West Berlin (Germany), 55–56, 208
Whalen, Mike, 214–15
Whittle, Frank, 230
Wien, Lawrence A., 96
Williams Air Base (Chandler az), 62–66
Wilson, Woodrow, 4
Wischerd, Bob, 63–64
Wolfe, Tom, 88, 178
World's Fair (New York, 1940), 20–21, 220
World War I, 3–4, 5–7
World War II: aftermath of, 45–46, 54–56; aircraft during, 62, 92, 98, 137; Berlin Airlift missions following, 54–56; Bob Cardenas's experiences in, 84; Bob Hoover's experiences in, 85; Chuck Yeager's experiences in, 85; early years of, 22; ending of, 33, 34; Gunther Rall's experiences in, 106–7; Pacific Theater of, 33; Pearl Harbor attack during, 26–27; RJG at basic training during, 31; RJG at Webb School during, 22, 26–27, 29; role of aircraft in, 59, 60; service football teams during, 32
Wright, Frank Lloyd, 79
Wright, Sandra, 96
Wright brothers, 18

x-1 rocket plane (Bell Aircraft), 84–85, 87–88
x-2 rocket plane (Bell Aircraft), 91
x-15 rocket plane (North American), 103, 164
xb-70 Valkyrie (North American Aviation), 164

XP-38 Lightning (Lockheed), 138
XP-80/P-80 Shooting Star (Lockheed), 100–102, 138
Yalu River (MiG Alley), 76
YB-49 bomber (Northrup), 88–89
Yeager, Chuck, 85, 87–88, 105, 122, 140, 178
Yeager, Jeana, 213

Yeilding, Ed, 206–7, 208–9, 230
YF-12A Blackbird (Lockheed), 131, 133, 134, 143, 150–51. *See also* A-12 "Archangel" Blackbird (Lockheed)
Zamperini, Louis, 221–22
Zugspitze (mountain), 82
Zwayer, Jim, 181–86